THE LUFTWAFFE
1933–45

THE LUFTWAFFE
1933–45

HITLER'S EAGLES

Chris McNab

CHARTWELL
BOOKS, INC.

This edition published in 2014 by
Chartwell Books, Inc.
A division of Book Sales, Inc.
276 Fifth Avenue Suite 206
New York, New York 10001
USA

This 2014 edition published by Chartwell Books, Inc. by arrangement with
Osprey Publishing Ltd.
31 West 57th Street, 6th Floor
New York, New York 10019
USA
Email: info@ospreypublishing.com

A CIP catalogue record for this book is available from the British Library

Page layout by Ken Vail Graphic Design, Cambridge, UK
Index by Alan Thatcher
Typeset in Bembo and Conduit
Originated by PDQ Media, Bungay, UK

EDITOR'S NOTE

In the compilation of this volume we relied on the extensive Osprey library of previous military history publications. Works of particular relevance are listed in the Further Reading section.

The following will help in converting other measurements between metric and imperial:

1 mile = 1.6km
1lb = 0.45kg
1 yard = 0.9m
1ft = 0.3m
1in = 25.4mm
100fps = 30.48m/s

IMAGE CREDITS
Front cover: akg-images
Back cover: Cody Images
Unless otherwise stated, all the images in this book are courtesy of Cody Images.

ISBN: 978 0 7858 3107 5

Printed in China through World Print Ltd.

14 15 16 17 18   10 9 8 7 6 5 4 3 2 1

Ranks of the Luftwaffe, with USAAF and RAF equivalents

Luftwaffe	USAAF	RAF
Generaloberst	General	Air Chief Marshall
Generalleutnant	Major-general	Air Vice Marshall
Generalmajor	Brigadier-general	Air Commodore
Oberst	Colonel	Group Captain
Oberstleutnant	Lieutenant-colonel	Wing Commander
Major	Major	Squadron Leader
Hauptmann	Captain	Flight Lieutenant
Oberleutnant	First lieutenant	Flying Officer
Leutnant	Second lieutenant	Pilot Officer
Hauptfeldwebel	Sergeant-major	no equivalent
Stabsfeldwebel	Master sergeant	Warrant officer
Oberfeldwebel	Technical sergeant	Flight sergeant
Feldwebel	Staff sergeant	Sergeant
Unterfeldwebel	no equivalent	no equivalent
Unteroffizier	Sergeant	Corporal
Obergefreiter	Corporal	Leading aircraftsman
Gefreiter	Private first class	Aircraftsman first class
Flieger	no equivalent	Aircraftsman second class

Note on Luftwaffe units
The Luftwaffe's principal tactical units had no precise equivalents in the USAAF and RAF. For basic guidance on the structure of Luftwaffe units such as the Geschwader, Gruppe and Staffel, see Chapter 2.

CONTENTS

INTRODUCTION

A force of Heinkel He 111s near their target over England during the summer of 1940. Once deprived of their Bf 109 escorts, the German bombers were acutely vulnerable to the predations of British Spitfires and Hurricanes.

The story of the German Luftwaffe (Air Force) has been an abiding focus of military historians since the end of World War II in 1945. It is not difficult to see why. Like many aspects of the German war machine, the Luftwaffe was a crowning achievement of the German rearmament programme. During the 1920s and early 1930s, the air force was a shadowy organization, operating furtively under the tight restrictions on military development imposed by the Versailles Treaty. Yet through foreign-based aircraft design agencies, civilian air transport and nationalistic gliding clubs, the seeds of a future air force were nevertheless kept alive and growing in Hitler's new Germany, and would eventually emerge in the formation of the Luftwaffe itself in 1935.

The nascent Luftwaffe thereafter grew rapidly, its ranks of both men and aircraft swelling under the ambition of its commander-in-chief, Hermann Göring. It also gained pre-1939 combat experience during the Spanish Civil War (1936–39), which helped it to refine tactics and technology before testing them on an even larger scale over Poland and Western Europe in 1939–40.

The traumatic defeats experienced by the Allies during these first years of war are in no small measure due to the capabilities of the Luftwaffe as a tactical air force. While the superb Messerschmitt Bf 109 achieved air supremacy and inflicted attrition on Allied air fleets, Junkers Ju 87 dive-bombers acted as precision-attack flying artillery ahead of advancing ground forces and Heinkel He 111, Junkers Ju 88 and other bombers pounded broader targets. Aviators grew in confidence, and some became literal celebrities as they racked up dozens of kills and missions. Men such as 'ace' fighter pilots Helmut Wick (56 kills), Wilhelm Balthasar (47 kills) and Werner Mölders (100 kills) struck a glamorous chord with a public that was becoming acclimatized to victory, gracing the covers of magazines and newspapers and featuring in the nightly newsreels.

Warning signs were there from the start, however. Although the Polish Air Force, for example, was crushed in relatively short order, unescorted German bombers and dive-bombers still proved vulnerable to fighters, even obsolete Polish biplanes. More ominous, and of utmost significance to the eventual outcome of the war, was the Luftwaffe's costly failure to subdue the Royal Air Force (RAF) during the Battle of Britain, a battle that exposed the tactical shortcomings of the German Air Force. (The subsequent Blitz also revealed the more significant issues with the Luftwaffe's capability to act as a strategic bombing force.)

Yet the failures over Britain would soon be forgotten, and eclipsed, by the enormity of the victories over the Soviet Union in 1941, during the opening phases of Operation *Barbarossa*. Despite facing a numerically greater opponent, the Luftwaffe was utterly dominant during the first six months of *Barbarossa*, and would remain ascendant for the next three years. On the first day of operations alone, it is possible that the German Air Force destroyed more than 1,800 Soviet aircraft. The kill rates achieved by the Luftwaffe's fighter pilots in this theatre beggar belief. The young Erich Hartmann, the greatest of all the German fighter aces, destroyed 352 enemy aircraft during his astonishing combat career, mainly while flying a Bf 109 over the Eastern Front. In addition to the Fighter Arm, the Luftwaffe's bomber, ground-attack and transport forces were also playing their part. Bomber aircraft helped reduce cities like Leningrad and Stalingrad to smoking rubble, while Ju 87s – some fitted with 37mm cannon as dedicated tank-busters – continued to take a toll on Soviet troops, vehicles and positions. The transport arm did its best to keep troops resupplied across thousands of kilometres of front, although its failure to maintain the encircled 6. Armee at Stalingrad in the winter of 1942/43 showed that the Luftwaffe was still limited in its capacity for large-scale airlift.

At the same time as the Luftwaffe was carving its name over the skies of the Soviet Union, the production of aircraft also increased impressively, principally through Albert Speer's rationalizations of the war industry between 1942 and 1945. In 1939 the total output of military aircraft was 8,295 aircraft. In 1944, by contrast, the production figure was a stunning 39,807 units.

So with such figures in mind, why was it that the Luftwaffe progressively lost air superiority on all fronts between 1943 and 1945? As we shall see, there is no denying the scale of the nemesis that visited the Luftwaffe in the later years of the war. The Allied strategic bombing campaign not only brought unprecedented levels of destruction against the German homeland; it also diverted huge volumes of Luftwaffe aircraft into a fight to the death above the skies of the Reich. The losses inflicted upon the Allied aircraft were profound, and the process of countering the heavy bombers produced new radar-equipped night-fighters, such as the Bf 110G-4, and the first generations of jet aircraft such as the Me 262. Yet, ultimately, such aircraft were not enough to stem the endless tide of Allied aircraft. So it was that, in the end, the Luftwaffe's downfall was every bit as epic as its rise. The life expectancy of new pilots dropped to just a few weeks, and Hitler's once-proud air force was unable to prevent the eventual defeat of Germany.

This book is not only a history of the various elements of the Luftwaffe. It will also paint a detailed portrait of the men and machines who fought and served with the German Air Force from its origins to its defeat. As we shall see, the Luftwaffe was a broad organization. It encompassed not only combat and transport aircraft, and their related personnel, but also anti- aircraft (AA) units, field divisions, and fire service teams. It was at the cutting edge of the strategic and tactical developments of the Wehrmacht (Armed Forces), and provided the world with the first true glimpse of the power of coordinated air and land forces. This book will seek to explain, therefore, not only the Luftwaffe's central role in Germany's offensive then defensive war plans, but also how the individual aviator, ground crew and soldier played his part in these plans, both in victory and defeat.

THE RISE AND FALL OF THE LUFTWAFFE

During the late 1930s, a flight of Dornier Do 17s makes an impressive flypast at one of the Nazi Party's Nuremberg rallies. By this time, the Luftwaffe had cast off years of secrecy to openly flaunt its major rearmament programme and new aircraft technologies.

At the end of World War I, the possibility of Germany creating an effective post-war air arm seemed truly remote. At the Armistice in November 1918, the Luftstreitkräfte (Air Forces) boasted no fewer than 2,709 combat aircraft, 56 airships and 186 balloon detachments. However, it took just two clauses in the post-war Treaty of Versailles to bring to an end Germany's aviation combat capability. Article 198 expressly prohibited Germany from maintaining 'either land-based or naval air forces', and Article 202 decreed that all existing military aircraft had to be surrendered to the Allies.

Not surprisingly, the terms of the Versailles Treaty were viewed differently by the two sides involved. The victorious Allies saw them as stringent but justified. The German population, however, regarded them as harsh and repressive. This fact was seized upon by many anti-government politicians in post-war Germany, not least among them Adolf Hitler. During his rise to power he took every opportunity to criticize the authorities for 'kowtowing to the iniquities of the Versailles Diktat'. Yet long before Hitler was appointed Reichskanzler (Reich Chancellor) in January 1933, the Weimar government – the very régime he was accusing of slavish compliance with every Allied demand – was already secretly laying the foundations for the creation of a new German air force.

The Treaty of Versailles banned German military aviation, but there was much activity to circumvent the treaty's articles. Agreements between Germany and the USSR at the Treaty of Rapallo in 1922 led to the establishment of clandestine air training facilities at Lipetsk, Russia, by 1925 and throughout Germany the formation of innocuous gliding clubs enabled thousands of young men to gain experience in basic aircraft handling. In the 1930s the Deutscher Luftsportverband (German Air Sports Association, DLV) also trained future military aircrews at the deceptively misnamed Zentrale der Verkehrs Fliegerschule (Central Commercial Pilots' School). Civil aviation was not prohibited in Germany, so the pilots from this establishment could legitimately go on to employment in the Deutsche Luft Hansa Aktiengellschaft, the German airline formed in 1926 (it became simply Lufthansa in 1933). During the first half of the 1930s, Lufthansa used aircraft that would eventually become Luftwaffe types – the Junkers Ju 52, the Ju 86 and the Heinkel He 111 – making it an easy business to introduce combat training into the programme.

Through such means, Germany was able to begin rebuilding its air force. Foreign suspicions grew beyond doubt, but the British and the French, caught up in broader political and economic struggles, did little to resist the military expansion. Such lax policing was a source of encouragement to Hitler when he took the Chancellorship in 1933, and he immediately set about his goal of reconstructing the German armed forces. Nevertheless, just the process of building a new air force presented a mountain of difficulties, as Williamson Murray has noted:

Still the problems facing the Nazis in January 1933 in the creation of an air force that could serve as an effective tool of diplomatic and military policy were enormous. Only a tiny cadre of experienced officers existed within the Army and Navy; Lufthansa experience was not directly convertible into a military force; and the German aircraft industry, weakened not only by the depression but also by internecine quarrels amongst its almost bankrupt firms, was not prepared for massive expansion.

– Williamson Murray, *Strategy for Defeat: The* Luftwaffe *1933–1945*,
Eagle Editions, Royston (2000)

Five of the formative characters behind the development and command of the Luftwaffe: (from left to right) Erhard Milch, Hugo Sperrle, Adolf Hitler, Hermann Göring and Albert Kesselring.

What the Luftwaffe did have at this time, Murray goes on to point out, was the backing of Hermann Göring, a charismatic but vain ex-Great War fighter pilot. Göring, through his close relationship to Hitler, managed to secure the funding and industrial focus to create a new air force in an internally competitive atmosphere. Investment went into developing aircraft, training men and refining tactics. The Versailles Treaty meant that such development was still somewhat limited, but in February 1935 Hitler decided the days of secrecy were over, as he openly and wholeheartedly embraced rearmament and militarization. He publicly announced the formation of the new Luftwaffe. Göring was given chief command with the rank of *Reichsmarschall* – a role for which he would later prove spectacularly ill-qualified. For both operational and economic reasons, priority was given to the creation of a tactical air force suitable for close support of ground offensives during a short, aggressive war.

This strategic policy is crucial to the subsequent history of the Luftwaffe in World War II, for the death of Generalleutnant Walter Wever in June 1936 effectively sealed the fate of the Luftwaffe bomber arm. As the Chief of Staff, Wever foresaw the need for a long-range *Luftoperationsarmee* (strategic air army) capable of destroying an enemy's industrial heart. His successor, Albert Kesselring, instead evolved a vast fleet of general-purpose medium bombers, functioning primarily in the operational role. This was a kind of 'tactically strategic' force, intended only to cripple enemy communications, supply lines and industry just long enough to influence the outcome of a specific offensive.

Military personnel attend the ceremonial opening of a glider field in 1934. Gliders were a long way from powered aircraft in terms of performance, but they gave thousands of young men the basic understanding of aviation that would inform subsequent combat skills.

Hermann Göring (left), as head of the Luftwaffe, was not the commander-in-chief the German Air Force required during World War II. His vanity meant he often overcommitted or misunderstood the capabilities of both men and aircraft.

A flight of Heinkel He 59 floatplanes, serving with the Legion Condor in 1939, fly near Mallorca in the spring of 1939. The Spanish Civil War provided the Luftwaffe with a virtual laboratory for developing aerial combat tactics in the run-up to the onset of World War II.

The purely tactical operations would be covered by the *Sturzkampfflugzeug* (dive-bomber), in which the high command invested near total faith. High-altitude bombing was considered costly and imprecise, with much, if not all, of the bomb load falling wide of its intended target (as later evidenced by the comparatively messy Allied bombing patterns). Two-engined bombers such as the Heinkel He 111, Dornier Do 17 and Junkers Ju 88 provided flexible bombing platforms against both area and tactical point targets. The Junkers Ju 87 'Stuka' dive-bomber also offered greater accuracy compared to heavy bombers, in return for a modest outlay in aircraft, ordnance, fuel and personnel, and almost eliminated the risk of damaging non-military areas. Convinced of its war-winning properties by operational trials in Spain, the *Reichsluftfahrtministerium* (National Air Ministry; RLM) cancelled all long-range bomber developments in favour of the Stuka. Dive capability became a prerequisite of all future bomber designs, and was eagerly applied to anything that might be capable of withstanding such extreme manoeuvres; even existing medium bombers were modified and tested, often with predictably tragic results. Consequently, the *Kampfgeschwader* (bomber forces) were only ever equipped for rapid, but ultimately unsustainable, victory.

Such concerns were in the future, however. The outbreak of the Spanish Civil War in July 1936 provided Hitler with an early opportunity to test out his nascent air force. Germany was quick to side with the Nationalists of General Franco, sending a fleet of 20 Ju 52/3m bomber-transports to assist in the airlifting of Nationalist troops across the Straits of Gibraltar from Spanish Morocco to southern mainland Spain. In response, Joseph Stalin despatched a Soviet expeditionary force, including nearly 150 aircraft, to support the Republican Government. This in turn prompted Hitler to increase his aid to the Nationalists, and in November 1936 the Legion Condor, a standing force of some 100 first-line aircraft plus supporting troops, was established on Spanish soil.

The following month the Italian dictator Benito Mussolini created a similar, albeit smaller, force for service alongside the Nationalists. With the Republicans bolstered by the Communist-organized International Brigades, all the main protagonists were in place, the battle lines had been drawn and the fighting started to rapidly escalate.

However, operations in Spain had already provided some unwelcome surprises for the Germans. Foremost among them were the inadequacies displayed by the Legion Condor's aircraft, particularly the Ju 52/3m bombers, which were said to be 'outclassed in all respects by their Russian opponents'. It was to report on this disturbing situation that one of the Legion's leading bomber exponents, Oberleutnant Rudolf Freiherr von Moreau, was summoned back to Berlin at the end of 1936 – just as the Heinkel He 111B was beginning to enter service.

With the prestige of his still relatively fledgling Luftwaffe at stake, Hermann Göring decided to risk committing a small force composed of his three newest bomber types to the Spanish venture. He reasoned that, although the machines were almost completely untried, here was a unique opportunity to test their capabilities in battle. Early in 1937, therefore, 12 of the new generation of German bombers – four He 111Bs, four Do 17Es and four Ju 86Ds – were shipped to the Iberian war zone, arriving at Seville in mid-February. Here, they were formed into an experimental bomber squadron known as VB/88. Operational conditions in Spain soon established the combat potential, or otherwise, of the three types. With its uncertain handling and unreliable diesel engines, the Ju 86D came a very poor third. One example crashed behind enemy lines within days of the unit's activation. Although it was rapidly replaced, two more aircraft had been lost by the early summer of 1937. The surviving duo were then 'handed over' to the Spaniards for a substantial fee! The Do 17E was considered to be on a par with the He 111B in terms of handling and general performance, but was let down by its limited bomb-carrying capacity. One of the four was lost, shot down by an I-15 fighter over Bilbao on 18 April 1937. Deliveries were to continue, however, and some dozen in all had been sent to Spain before the decision was taken to standardize VB/88 on He 111s. The remaining Dorniers (a second having been lost in the interim) were subsequently transferred to the Legion's reconnaissance *Gruppe*. The Heinkel had proven itself beyond doubt to be the superior machine of the three. Not only was it to equip VB/88 in its entirety, it would go on to become the Legion's standard bomber. In all, nearly 100 He 111s were to serve in Spain.

The Spanish Civil War also had a refining effect on Germany's fighter force. The Jagdwaffe (Fighter Arm) was initially equipped with Heinkel He 51 and Arado Ar 68 biplanes. These aircraft had braced and staggered wings, fixed, spatted undercarriages and open cockpits, making them little removed from the fighters of World War I. Indeed, they were slower than civilian monoplane types such as the He 70, and only marginally faster than the He 111. Yet the combat capability of the Luftwaffe was revolutionized with the introduction of the monoplane Bf 109. (The development and performance of particular aircraft types is further described in later chapters.) The first of ten pre-production Bf 109B-0s took to the air in November 1936, and the following month three aircraft were sent to war-torn Spain for an evaluation under operational conditions with the Legion Condor. The trials were beset with problems, but they did give both Messerschmitt and the Luftwaffe experience of what to expect when production Bf 109B 'Berthas' entered service in Germany in February 1937.

The dominance of the Republican forces' I-15s and I-16 *Ratas* (rats) in Spanish skies resulted in 16 Berthas being shipped to Spain just weeks after their delivery to the Luftwaffe. Accompanying them were II. Gruppe, Jagdgeschwader 132 (II./JG 132) personnel, who formed 2. Staffel (a Staffel roughly equates to an RAF squadron), Jagdgruppe 88 (2./J 88). Operational by April, the unit ultimately did not see its first combat until the battle for Brunete in July, when it was discovered that the Bf 109B and the nimble Soviet-built Polikarpov fighters were evenly matched below 3,000m (10,000ft). At higher altitudes, the Bertha was untouchable, and German pilots soon worked out that Republican aircraft could be easily picked off if attacked from above and behind using high-speed dives – this would be the Bf 109 pilot's stock tactic throughout World War II as well. Improved versions of the Bf 109 soon emerged, and amongst the leading aces from this campaign were Werner Mölders (14 kills), Wolfgang Schellmann (12 kills) and Harro Harder (11 kills), all of whom would enjoy more success with the Bf 109E in the first 18 months of World War II.

The Spanish Civil War was the proving ground of Hitler's new Luftwaffe. It had demonstrated that with the right aircraft and good training, plus cooperation with ground forces in terms of ground-attack strikes, using the new aerial terror machine, the Ju 87, it could dominate less well-equipped or trained opponents. It would soon be able to prove that reality on a far wider stage.

RIGHT: Ostensibly destroyed by the Treaty of Versailles, the German Air Force nevertheless kept itself alive during the 1920s through secret aircraft development abroad, plus extensive pilot training on gliders at home, as seen here.

COMBAT LEADER

The main limitation to the growth of the Luftwaffe prior to World War II was industrial in nature. With all Germany's armed forces undergoing rapid development, there was much competition over resources amongst German services and production facilities. There were particular problems in manufacturing aero engines, which was one of the factors that limited the development of four-engined strategic bombers in favour of two-engined medium bombers. Nevertheless, the Luftwaffe had built itself to a potent size by the eve of war in September 1939 – it fielded 2,916 frontline combat aircraft, as opposed to 1,660 belonging to the RAF – plus it had the advantages of good training and recent combat experience.

The Luftwaffe, alongside the German Army, launched itself against Poland on 1 September 1939, Luftflotten (Air Fleets) 1 and 4 being the main formations deployed. While the German ground forces made good progress across terrain baked hard by the long, hot summer of 1939, they were aided by the overwhelming air superiority established within the opening three days by the vastly more impressive Luftwaffe. The dominance of the Luftwaffe over the Polish Air Force can be overemphasized, and there were some individual actions that resulted in significant German losses, particularly when Polish fighters jumped unescorted bombers. Indeed, the Polish campaign cost the Luftwaffe some 230 aircraft, despite the Germans' three-fold superiority in numbers. Yet with a modern air force pitted against just 400 mostly obsolescent operational aircraft, the result was never in doubt. In a pattern that would become dreadfully familiar over the ensuing years, German aircraft strafed and bombed much of the Polish Air Force to destruction on the ground, effectively removing it from the equation. German aircraft also flew hundreds of sorties in support of troops on the ground, operating essentially as an aerial artillery to the German Army. The Ju 87 in particular came to the fore, illustrating an exceptional ability to deliver accurate strikes against pinpoint targets. Air liaison groups operated alongside the ground forces, typically in SdKfz 251 halftrack comms vehicles, relaying targets to the air assets as threats and opportunities emerged.

Poland finally surrendered to the German forces on 27 September, and the Luftwaffe basked in its glory as Hitler already made plans for a Western-looking conquest. In between the invasion of Poland and the launching of the *Blitzkrieg* (lit. 'lightning war') in the West on 10 May 1940, the Luftwaffe endured the *Sitzkrieg* (lit. 'sitting down war'), or the 'Phoney War', as it was dubbed by the Allies. Aircraft from both sides would periodically venture across their respective defensive borders (the Maginot line in France and the *Westwall* or Siegfried line in Germany) on tentative reconnaissance flights. Most action during this period took place over the *Dreiländereck* (three nations corner) on the northernmost corner of the Franco-German border, as this was the shortest route for Allied reconnaissance aircraft heading for the Ruhr.

Many of the leading Bf 109E aces claimed their first victories during this period, including Oberleutnant Rolf Pingel and Oberleutnant Hans von Hahn. Aside from engaging French fighters, the *Jagdflieger* (fighter pilots) also took on RAF Hurricanes that were based in France in support of the British Expeditionary Force (BEF), as well as Blenheim and Wellington bombers sent to attack German ports along the North Sea coast. The only Spitfires – an aircraft that would become the Luftwaffe's arch rival – encountered were unarmed Photographic Development Unit (PDU) aircraft, two of which were brought down in March and April 1940. By the time the 'Phoney War' ended, the *Jagdgruppen* had claimed no fewer than 160 victories, and numerous Bf 109 pilots had received their first taste of aerial combat.

The Luftwaffe was back in major action again in April 1940, for the invasion of Denmark and Norway. A distinctive element of this operation, explored in more detail in Chapter 6, was the Luftwaffe's deployment of airborne forces, either by parachute drop from transport aircraft such as the Ju 52, or by direct airlanding. Bombers also worked in an anti-ship capacity, targeting Norwegian, British and French vessels along the coastline.

Yet these operations were dwarfed by the scale of what was to follow. In a forerunner of the Battle of Britain, practically the whole of the Luftwaffe's single-engined fighter

Director of the Luftwaffe's T-Amt (Technical Office) General Ernst Udet (in Luftwaffe uniform, right) and State Secretary of the RLM Erhard Milch (similarly dressed, left) visit a French airfield in 1937, no doubt mentally making notes on their future opponents.

A Henschel Hs 126 light aircraft flies over a column of Rommel's 7. Panzer Division in France, 1940. Short-range reconnaissance aircraft such as this worked in close radio-link with armoured columns, and helped in matters such as artillery spotting.

strength was brought together for the invasion of France and the Low Countries, which began on 10 May 1940. More than 1,016 Bf 109Es and over 1,000 pilots prepared themselves to wrest control of the skies over western Europe. In addition, 350 Bf 110 twin-engined fighters, 1,100 medium bombers and 400 Stukas provided a potent tactical bombing capability.

The German campaign itself was divided into two parts, code-named *Gelb* (Yellow) and *Rot* (Red). Operation *Gelb* would commence with an all-out attack on Holland and Belgium, which, it was calculated, would cause the BEF and French northern armies to rush to the aid of the Low Countries. With the Allies out of their prepared defensive positions along the Maginot line, the Wehrmacht would launch its primary offensive against the vulnerable rear of the Allied forces, with Panzers sweeping around behind them and racing for the Channel. The Low Countries and Anglo-French divisions would be cut off from supplies and reinforcements in the process, and thus quickly defeated. Operation *Rot* would then swing into action, with German troops advancing west across the Somme into central France.

Luftflotten 2 and 3 would now take centre stage in the air war. From Luftflotte 2, the pilots of JG 2, JG 26, JG 27 and JG 51 cut swathes through the obsolescent Allied fighters that attempted to blunt the German onslaught. On 12 May, with the launching of the armoured thrust at the rear of the stretched Allied forces, Luftflotte 3's units at last joined in the action too. Two days later, during a series of actions over Sedan that saw Allied bombers attempt to destroy the strategically crucial River Meuse bridge crossings, Bf 109 units downed no fewer than 89 aircraft in an action that effectively sealed the German victory in France. Yet despite successes such as this, the campaign in the West was very much a calculated risk for the Jagdwaffe, as it possessed insufficient reserves of fighters, fuel and ammunition in order to support a sustained campaign. Fortunately, the rapidity with which Allied forces capitulated in the face of the *Blitzkrieg* meant that resources never reached breaking point. Indeed, just 147 Bf 109s were lost in May (including aircraft destroyed in the Norwegian campaign), followed by 88 in June.

Supply lines became stretched as the fighting in northern France reached Dunkirk, however, with serviceability amongst Luftwaffe units reaching an all-time low due to a lack of fuel, poor parts supply, austere operating bases (often little more than farmers' fields) and sheer pilot exhaustion. Ironically, it was at this point that Bf 109 units began at last to encounter Spitfire squadrons flying from bases in southern England in support of the sea evacuation of troops from Dunkirk. RAF Fighter Command succeeded in preventing German bombers from sinking many of the vessels that transported troops back to England primarily because the *Jagdstaffeln*, lacking serviceable aircraft and suitable bases, could not adequately protect the vulnerable *Kampfgeschwader* and *Stukageschwader* – a portent of things to come later that summer.

Although the evacuation of Dunkirk had ended on the morning of 3 June, fighting in France continued as part of Operation *Rot* until a ceasefire was agreed some 22 days later. The Luftwaffe pilots then engaged in some rest and recuperation in preparation for an all-out attack on the United Kingdom.

THE BATTLE OF BRITAIN

A famous precondition of *Unternehmen Seelöwe* (Operation *Sealion*) – the planned German invasion of Britain – was that the Luftwaffe subjugate the RAF prior to invasion forces setting out to cross the Channel. Göring was famously ebullient about this prospect, and indeed relished the prospect of effectively defeating a nation state through air power alone.

Opposing the growing ranks of German aircraft across the Channel were 29 squadrons of Hurricanes (462 aircraft) and 19 squadrons of Spitfires (292 aircraft). Fighter cover would therefore be critical. The Jagdwaffe slowly began to return to the Channel coast in strength during July and early August 1940, some 809 Bf 109Es being in France by 20 July, and this number increased to 934 by 10 August. Once again, these aircraft would be charged with achieving aerial supremacy as the German *Kampfgeschwader* and *Stukageschwader* strived to knock out RAF Fighter Command in preparation for the seaborne invasion of southern England.

The Battle of Britain has been split into four phases by historians, commencing in early July with *Kanalkampf* (Channel Battle), executed primarily by the Ju 87 (the only aircraft really capable of precision maritime strikes) with fighter support. During this period, German aircraft probed British defences primarily through attacks on coastal convoys, as well as port facilities on the south coast. *Kanalkampf* would last until 12 August, and although Fighter Command succeeded in matching the Luftwaffe in trying circumstances, it had suffered significant losses – including 27 Spitfires destroyed and 51 damaged. Many of these had been claimed by Bf 109E pilots conducting *Freie Jagd* (free chase) sweeps independently of the bombers, seeking out RAF fighters.

The date 13 August was dubbed *Adlertag* (Eagle Day) by the Luftwaffe, and it signalled the start of the sustained campaign against RAF airfields, radar stations and other key

A Dornier Do 215 light bomber, a development of the Do 17, seen during operations against British coastal facilities in July 1940. Only just over 100 of these aircraft were produced during the entire war.

military targets such as aircraft and aero engine factories. The Dornier, Junkers and Heinkel bombers sent to strike at these targets were well-escorted by Bf 109Es from eight *Jagdgeschwader*, as the single-seat fighter force reached its peak strength. During 11 days of sustained attacks, which saw both sides suffer heavy losses, the Luftwaffe hoped to assert its dominance through sheer weight of numbers. Certainly, the German aviators enjoyed some success on *Adlertag* and immediately afterwards, when a number of the more inexperienced RAF pilots were lost. However, all three of the major raids that day were picked up by radar and then intercepted. Although runways were damaged, they were quickly made operational again, as the craters were filled in and key radar stations were always back up-and-running in a matter of hours. Eagle Day was designed to be

Somewhere in France in the summer of 1940, a *Kampfgeschwader* ground crew readies bombs in preparation for a raid over the UK. Although the Luftwaffe imposed serious damage on the British infrastructure, and killed tens of thousands of civilians, it was unable to stop Britain's war production efforts or to subdue its resistance.

the beginning of the end of Fighter Command. In this respect, the Luftwaffe did not even come close to success.

Between 24 August and 6 September, the Germans continued to target Fighter Command airfields and aircraft factories, with growing success. The RAF would later call this 'the critical period' of the Battle of Britain, as it found losses ever harder to replace, stretching the pilots and their aircraft to the limits of their endurance. Yet despite suffering serious casualties (136 Spitfires were lost in August alone), Fighter Command was in turn inflicting heavier losses on German forces. Indeed, Bf 110 and Ju 87 Stuka *Gruppen* had been so badly affected that they would play little part in the rest of the campaign. Critically, Reichsmarschall Hermann Göring questioned the tactics of continuing to attack radar stations when the British had so many, and he was also explicit in his order that airfields which 'had been successfully attacked one day should not be attacked the following day', presumably because he regarded it as a waste of effort. With this Göring virtually guaranteed the continued operational capabilities of the frontline Spitfire and Hurricane squadrons. German Bf 109 pilots' chances of winning the battle were therefore scuppered by the amateurish interference of their commander-in-chief.

In contrast, British fighter pilots fell under the command of Air Chief Marshal Hugh Dowding. He had been responsible for introducing the 'Dowding system' whereby radar, raid plotting and radio control of aircraft were integrated. In the hands of this dedicated professional, ably assisted by Air Vice-Marshal Keith Park, commander of No. 11 Fighter Group, the British enjoyed a distinct advantage despite the scores of German bombers and fighters increasingly darkening the skies over south-east England.

On 7 September, believing that Fighter Command was on its knees, Göring ordered his forces to target London instead, in an effort to bring more RAF fighters into the air. Eventually, the capital would be attacked by both day and night, culminating in two massive daylight raids (involving more than 250 bombers and 300+ Bf 109Es) on 15 September – immortalized thereafter by the British as Battle of Britain Day.

By now the *Jagdflieger* were forbidden to fly their favoured *Freie Jagd* sorties, ranging far and wide in front of the bombers. Instead, Göring ordered them to provide close formation escort for the bombers, which had suffered growing losses to the seemingly indestructible RAF. As if to prove that Fighter Command did indeed still have plenty of fight left in it, both waves of bombers were met by close to 300 Hurricanes and Spitfires. In what would prove to be one of the final large-scale raids made by the Luftwaffe during the campaign, 19 Bf 109Es were shot down. These aircraft were the last of nearly 400 Bf 109Es that had been lost or badly damaged in the four weeks from 13 August. Fighter Command lost seven Spitfires and 20 Hurricanes on the same day.

On 30 September, the last massed daylight raids on London and the south-west were flown. Some 300 bombers attacked the capital in two waves, and the escorting

RIGHT: The pilot of a Bf 109, crashed in England during the Battle of Britain, climbs out to face captivity. Note the Bf 109's cannon muzzle in the centre of the propeller cone, and the two 7.92mm machine guns mounted atop the engine.

200 Bf 109Es suffered their worst losses of the Battle of Britain – 28 'Emils' (the Bf 109E phonetic name) were shot down, whilst the RAF lost 13 Hurricanes and four Spitfires. Luftwaffe bomber units had lost more than 40 per cent of their operational effectiveness.

It was clear by now that Fighter Command was far from beaten, and *Unternehmen Seelöwe* was shelved on 12 October. By then Göring had ordered that a third of all his Channel-based *Jagdgeschwader* strength had to be converted into fighter-bombers for 'tip-and-run' *Jabo* (short for *Jagdbomber* – ground-attack aircraft) sorties due to the vulnerability of the medium bomber force in daylight raids. These missions were flown at high altitudes of between 7,900m and 10,000m, and Spitfire units struggled to intercept the Bf 109E *Jabos*. Conversely, little damage was done by the attacks, which were flown for nuisance value as much as anything else.

In this dramatic image, an RAF Spitfire dives past a Dornier Do 17 as it makes a firing run. Although manoeuvrable and fast compared to the He 111, the Do 17 was still seriously outperformed by the new generation of monoplane fighters.

The Battle of Britain officially ended on 31 October, by which time 1,792 German aircraft had been lost in combat, a staggering blow to Göring's prestige. The battle had exploded many myths. The Ju 87 was shown to be hideously vulnerable when flying unescorted against an enemy with excellent fighter resources. The He 111 and Ju 88 were similarly exposed if not properly escorted, and limitations of fuel meant that German fighters could only loiter for about 15 minutes over England before being forced to turn for home.

The success of Fighter Command in staving off the imminent threat of German invasion did not, however, end the German bombing campaign against British cities. In fact the Blitz, as it came to be known, had only just begun. The Germans hit the Midlands city of Coventry on 14 November and followed this up with raids on Birmingham, Bristol, Manchester and Liverpool. London, too, was obviously a massive target for the Luftwaffe as a symbol of British defiance as well as the heart of the governmental system. German bombing continued into 1941, with the last raids of the Blitz coming in May that year.

In the early years of the war, the Luftwaffe provided Hitler with a first-rate propaganda tool, as up until the Battle of Britain it appeared to outclass most of its opponents. Here we see a Luftwaffe news cameraman, filming an operation from the nose of a Heinkel He 111.

NEW HORIZONS

In 1941, the successes of the Western *Blitzkrieg* were replicated on a smaller scale in the Balkans, Mediterranean and North Africa, mainly against the RAF and Royal Navy. The Luftwaffe's involvement in the air war in the Mediterranean came about as a direct result of Italy declaring war on France and Great Britain on 10 June 1940. With the *Blitzkrieg* in the West by then at its height and France already on the point of collapse, the Italian Duce, Benito Mussolini, saw this as a golden opportunity to share in the spoils of victory with German co-dictator Adolf Hitler. Instead, Italian forces soon found themselves in dire trouble. At sea, the Royal Navy engaged Italian vessels, inflicting a succession of defeats and giving the lie to Mussolini's proud boast that the Mediterranean was *mare nostrum* – 'our sea'. In North Africa, the Italian Army invaded Egypt, only to be driven back halfway across Libya and all but destroyed by British and Commonwealth troops.

Unable to ignore the growing instability on his southern flank, Hitler ordered that Luftwaffe units be sent to the area to restore the situation. The command selected to make the transfer was General der Flieger Hans Geisler's X. Fliegerkorps, then stationed in Norway. And to provide the *Korps* with the necessary striking power, two *Gruppen* each of Ju 87s and Ju 88s were added to its order of battle. For the Stukas, the move south would give them the chance to regain something of the fearsome reputation they had lost after being trounced by the RAF in the Battle of Britain. The Ju 88 had no need to prove anything. By late 1940 it had already firmly established itself as the best bomber in the Luftwaffe's armoury.

The German aerial commitment to the Mediterranean theatre grew alongside the escalating land campaign. Initially, the Germans' aerial strength was confined to Stuka and bomber units, with Bf 110s in support, but in February 1941 14 Messerschmitt Bf 109Es from 7./JG 26 flew to Sicily to open a new phase of the air war in the Mediterranean. Beginning escort sorties over the island almost immediately, the JG 26 detachment began an unparalleled run of good fortune. Sweeping aside the weak RAF defences, the German pilots strafed Maltese airfields at will, shot down defending Hurricanes almost with impunity, and generally made life very unpleasant for the defenders, who were already having to put up with a constant pounding from Italian and German bombs.

Although the RAF put up numerous interception sorties and succeeded in ensuring that the bombing was rarely achieved without some cost to the attackers, it was singly unable to counter the Bf 109s effectively. Many of the Allied pilots had had relatively little combat time, and their Hurricanes were in the main well used. Claims were filed by a number of pilots who swore that they had most definitely shot down a Bf 109, but subsequent scrutiny of Luftwaffe records showed that the *Jagdflieger's* survival rate over Malta at this stage of the war was nothing short of miraculous. Few Bf 109s were

An Me 110 twin-engine fighter, here seen flying over the North African desert with two Ju 52 transporters in the background. Like the struggle on the Eastern Front, the campaign in North Africa was as much one of logistics as tactics.

damaged, let alone shot down, and the Luftwaffe fighters dictated the progress of local air combat on more or less their own terms.

Fortunately for the defenders of Malta, Hitler decided to invade the Balkans on 6 April, thus drawing off most of the fighter strength in Sicily, including the modest 7./JG 26 force, which moved to bases in Italy to put it within range of targets in Yugoslavia. With the Luftwaffe also committed in Greece, Malta enjoyed a brief respite, but the island would become the focus of far more intense Luftwaffe attacks over the next two years. The expanding war in the Mediterranean also obliged Hitler to secure Crete before moving the bulk of his forces, redeployed to what was soon to become the Eastern Front. The attack on Crete began on 14 May 1941, with VIII. and IX. Fliegerkorps delivering an airborne assault of unprecedented scale and efficiency, involving 520 Ju 52s, 119 Bf 109s, 114 Bf 110s, 205 Ju 87s, 72 gliders and 228 medium bombers. Once the RAF fighters were either destroyed or evacuated, the Bf 109s set about making the landing areas as safe as possible for the *Fallschirmjäger* (parachute troops), who were ordered to secure the island. Albeit at terrible cost for the parachute troops, Crete was totally in German hands by early June.

The widening aerial war in the Mediterranean was aided by the deployment of the entire Luftflotte 2 into the theatre in November 1941, which gave Hitler far greater ground-attack, bombing, fighter, anti-ship and supply capabilities. In 1942, consequently, Malta became one of the most bombed places on earth, although the Luftwaffe was never quite able to finish off either the island's capability of handling naval traffic, nor its at times perilously stretched fighter defence. Furthermore, having driven the British capital fleets from the Mediterranean in early 1941, the Luftwaffe Ju 87s and Ju 88s were then able to prey on British supply vessels running towards the North African ports along the coastline of Egypt and Libya, costing the Allies thousands of tons of shipping.

At the same time, the Luftwaffe was increasingly committed to a ground-support role in relation to Erwin Rommel's land campaign in North Africa. The battle for North Africa swung to and fro over a period of two years, and the Luftwaffe Stukas, medium bombers and fighters played a vital ground-attack role. Yet the war in the German theatre was a losing one for the German Air Force in terms of both logistics and numbers. When Rommel pushed his land forces further east, supply lines stretched accordingly, resulting in fuel and parts shortages for the Luftwaffe squadrons. At the same time, the Allied air strength gradually intensified, not least when the United States opened a second front in the North African campaign when its forces invaded Morocco and Algeria in November 1942, by which time Rommel's forces were also collapsing in the east following Montgomery's victory at the second battle of El Alamein the previous October. Luftflotte 2 steadily dwindled in size under combat losses and the relentless drain of resources to the voracious Eastern Front.

As part of a generally gloomy picture of the progress of the war in other theatres, the spring of 1943 soon recorded the last Allied push to defeat the remnants of the Afrika Korps, now squeezed back into Tunisia. On 22 April this final offensive began, and it soon proved all but unstoppable. JG 77, operating from the Cape Bon peninsula, and JG 27, from Sicily, could offer only meagre resistance to enemy airpower that was stronger now than ever before. By 7 May Bizerte and Tunis were in Allied hands, and remaining Luftwaffe units were ordered to evacuate to Sicilian or Italian airfields.

Less than a week later, on 13 May 1943, North Africa was totally under Allied control. Mussolini, even with substantial help from Hitler, had failed in his bid to create a new empire in the region. The cost for the Luftwaffe in air and ground personnel alone was huge, with too many pilots and aircraft having bled out for no gain whatsoever in a theatre which was never anywhere near as important to the Germans as Europe.

Yet the Luftwaffe's trials in the Mediterranean theatre continued in Sicily and then mainland Italy. In Sicily, Operation *Husky*, the invasion of Sicily, began on 10 July 1943, with overwhelming Allied air superiority. German pilots could not complain about a lack of targets, for Allied aircraft swarmed all over the island looking for the Luftwaffe. Against such hordes the *Jagdflieger* were virtually committing mass suicide even in attempting to take off, and on the opening day of *Husky*, claims of six bombers had to be offset by the

The business of war. A German airfield in the Mediterranean theatre in August 1942. The Luftwaffe campaign in North Africa and then Italy suffered from the diversion of resources to the Western and Eastern Fronts.

loss of four Bf 109s. Gerbini airfield became a nightmare of overlapping bomb craters as the Jagdwaffe strove to carry out the dual task of both blunting enemy bombing and covering the Straits of Messina, the strip of water which represented an escape route to Italy. Makeshift sites away from the bomb-blasted airfields enabled sorties to continue, but by 13 July all units except II./JG 51 had moved back to north-eastern Sicily. The withdrawal to Italy, which saw survivors head for the complex of bases on the Foggia plain, now began for the handful of aircraft that had been left intact by Allied bombers.

The odds were also entirely stacked against Luftflotte 2 during the Allies' Italian campaign, launched with the landings at Salerno on 9 September 1943. No fewer than 321 Luftwaffe aircraft were downed just during the preparatory air battles in the run-up to the landings. Yet we should never underestimate the dogged resilience, or the combat efficiency, of the Luftwaffe, even when it was facing sure defeat. The Salerno landings suffered heavily from attacks by Fw 190 fighter-bombers and medium bombers; Dornier Do 217s even sank the Italian battleship *Roma* with Fx 1400 'Fritz' X radio-controlled bombs, the first combat use of guided air-to-surface weapons in history.

However, the struggle, particularly once the Italians signed their armistice on 8 September, was against impossible odds. By early 1944 a German force of some 270 aircraft was facing an Allied juggernaut of 2,600 aircraft. Air defence of Italy became

In this dramatic image, an Me 109 zeroes its guns at a base camp in North Africa. Fighter wing guns were not arranged parallel to each other, but converged their fire a few hundred metres in front of the aircraft.

ABOVE: Ju 87D 'S7+AA' of the Geschwaderstab StG 3, Siwa Oasis, October 1942, after Karl Christ relinquished command of StG 3 to Walter Sigel, and the *Geschwader* officially incorporated the hitherto semi-autonomous I./StG 1 and II./StG 2 as its II. and III. Gruppen respectively. Pictured here at the time of El Alamein, Kommodore Sigel's 'Dora' displays a standard finish, definitive markings and the *Stab*'s blue trim. (John Weal © Osprey Publishing)

pointless, and the few surviving aircraft were pulled back to defend the Reich in late 1943 and 1944, leaving the Italian skies under Allied control. By this time, furthermore, Germany was facing its greatest threat from the east.

EASTERN FRONT

The German invasion of the Soviet Union, code-named Operation *Barbarossa*, was a campaign unparalleled in both its scale and ferocity. Within weeks of its launch early on the morning of 22 June 1941, the front line stretched a staggering 4,480km, linking the Arctic wastes of the Barents Sea in the north to the sub-tropical shores of the Black Sea in the south.

At first glance, the opposing armies appeared to be almost evenly matched. The Germans committed 120 divisions to the initial assault, holding a further 26 in immediate reserve, making a total of 146 divisions – some three million men in all. Facing them, the Soviet Army had 149 divisions stationed in its westernmost military districts. However, the German and Russian divisions differed greatly in composition and strengths. Take the all-important tank, for example, which played such a crucial role throughout the campaign in the east. At the outset the Germans deployed 17 armoured divisions (plus a further two in reserve) against the Soviet's 36 – a seeming majority of two-to-one in favour of the Red Army. In reality, a Russian armoured division of 1941 numbered some 400 tanks, whereas its German counterpart varied between 150 and 200 ... a fourfold advantage to the Soviets.

On paper, the Red Air Force enjoyed a simple numerical superiority. It is a little remarked fact that the Luftwaffe embarked upon Operation *Barbarossa*, the Wehrmacht's most ambitious undertaking, with far fewer frontline aircraft (2,598) than it had deployed either at the start of the *Blitzkrieg* in the west in May 1940 (3,826) or at the height of the Battle of Britain some three months later (3,705). In terms of single-engined fighters, for example, the Jagdwaffe had exactly 619 serviceable machines (predominantly Bf 109Fs) ranged along the Eastern Front on the eve of the invasion. This was just over two-thirds (68 per cent) of the Fighter Arm's total available strength, the remaining third being deployed in the West, the homeland and the Mediterranean. Yet the qualitative difference between the Luftwaffe and the Red Air Force, afflicted by poor training, obsolete aircraft and political purges, was immense. In every meaningful way, the Luftwaffe was the superior air force.

The Eastern Front, September 1941. A Russian bridge takes a pounding from bombs delivered with pinpoint precision by Junkers Ju 87 dive-bombers. The accuracy of the Ju 87 led to its use as a form of 'flying artillery' in support of ground troops.

The opening days of *Barbarossa* brought unimagined victories for the Luftwaffe, as it launched itself against a large but utterly unprepared Soviet Air Force. The German air assets were split among Luftflotten 1, 2 and 4, supporting the Army Groups North, Centre and South respectively. One of the first (arguably *the* first) German 'kills' on the Eastern Front was claimed by the *Staffelkapitän* of 1./JG 3, Oberleutnant Robert Olejnik, who described the historic action in the following report:

Arguably the finest all-round fighter aircraft of World War II, the Messerschmitt Bf 109 went through numerous variants to keep its capabilities up to those of the best Allied fighters. Nearly 34,000 of the aircraft were built between 1937 and 1945.

Everybody knew that I was an early riser and liked to fly the dawn missions. So, shortly before 0330hrs, I took off with my wingman to reconnoitre the Russian airfields along our stretch of the border.

Everything seemed quiet in the semi-darkness below. It was not until we were returning to base, and flying back over the first airfield we had visited some 20 minutes earlier, that I spotted signs of activity. Two Russian fighters were preparing to scramble. As we circled 700–800 metres (2,300–2,600ft) overhead, I saw the Russians start their engines and begin to taxi out. They took off immediately and climbed towards us, obviously looking for a fight.

OVERLEAF: Between April and November 1943 in Italy, II./JG 77 uniquely employed the Italian Macchi C205v, while awaiting delivery of replacement Bf 109s, in its war against the US bombers. Here one executes an inverted beam-attack against a flight of Mitchell B-25 medium bombers. This kind of attack was favoured for its fast exit; a sharp pull back on the stick threw the aircraft into a vertical nosedive. (Karl Kopinski © Osprey Publishing)

K. Kopinski

They were still some 300–400 metres (980–1,300ft) below us when we dived to the attack. I caught the leader with a short burst on my first pass and he went down in flames. His wingman disappeared.

Arriving back over our own airfield I waggled my wings to indicate a victory. My comrades, most of whom had only just woken up, peered sleepily from their tent flaps shaking their heads in disbelief.

Although there were other claimants to first kill status, one fact not in dispute was that the Luftwaffe's pre-emptive strikes had caught the Soviet Air Force completely off guard. All along the front the scene was the same as that described by Robert Olejnik's *Gruppenkommandeur*, veteran Channel front *Experte* (ace) Hauptmann Hans von Hahn: 'We could hardly believe our eyes. Every airfield was chock full of reconnaissance aircraft, bombers and fighters, all lined up in long straight rows as if on a parade. The number of landing strips and aircraft the Russians had concentrated along our borders was staggering.'

Staggering, too, was the price the Soviets paid for their unpreparedness. The Luftwaffe fighter pilots had a field day. In the northern sector, Major Hannes Trautloft's JG 54 had claimed 45 Russian aircraft shot down by the close of the first day's fighting, and the attached II./JG 53 had added a dozen more. JG 53's other two *Gruppen*, deployed in the central sector – the scene of the invasion's main thrust – accounted for no fewer than 62 Soviet aircraft. Hauptmann Wolf-Dietrich Wilcke, *Gruppenkommandeur* of III./JG 53, was perhaps the Eastern Front's first ace, for he downed five Soviet fighters in the course of three separate sorties on 22 June.

While the fighters accounted for the bulk of the day's aerial kills, Luftwaffe bombers and ground-attack aircraft were also hard at work. Seven *Gruppen* of Stukas delivered ground support to the armoured divisions of Panzergruppen 3 and 2 respectively, as they drove eastwards in a series of giant pincer movements towards their ultimate goal – Moscow. A number of Stukas also flew missions on this day armed with the 10kg SD 10 anti-personnel bomb. These were carried in underwing containers and dropped indiscriminately on enemy airfields and known troop concentrations. But such scattergun tactics were a waste of the Ju 87's unique capabilities, and during the early morning hours of 22 June most Stukas were employed in their more traditional role delivering precise attacks on pinpoint targets. Unlike the mauling the Ju 87s had received over Britain, during the opening day of *Barbarossa* only two Ju 87s were lost to enemy action (and a third damaged from other causes) along the entire 270km stretch of the central sector from the River Memel down to the Pripyet. In addition to Stukas, Ju 88s, He 111s and Do 117s were hitting Soviet troops concentrations and strongpoints along the length of the newly formed Eastern Front.

RIGHT: Wolfram Freiherr von Richthofen, here seen on the left with the German Army commander Erich von Manstein, held numerous major commands within the Luftwaffe during World War II. He was particularly enthusiastic about the development of dive-bombing and ground-attack tactics.

The 22nd of June was a truly disastrous day for the Russians. By the close of the day's operations it was estimated that the Red Air Force had lost 322 aircraft to fighters and flak, but that some 1,500 had been destroyed on the ground. Such was the magnitude of the enemy's losses that Hermann Göring at first refused to believe the reports of his pilots' successes. He ordered an enquiry. Within days the advancing German Army had overrun all 31 of the airfields which had been the targets of the Luftwaffe's pre-emptive opening strikes. This allowed examination of the wreckage, and showed that the initial reports submitted to the *Reichsmarschall* had, if anything, erred on the conservative side. Even the official Soviet history of the Great Patriotic War – not a work noted for its objectivity – conceded that, 'By midday of 22 June our losses totalled approximately 1,200 aircraft, including more than 800 machines destroyed on the ground'. Against this the Luftwaffe recorded the loss of just 35 aircraft of all types.

Yet although the Luftwaffe's initial strikes had inflicted enormous damage, the Red Air Force was by no means neutralized. As early as midday on 22 June, penny-packet formations of Soviet medium bombers were beginning to hit back at the German invaders. Throughout the last week of June these attacks grew in strength and frequency, but they were ill-planned

The hard reality of winter on the Eastern Front. The Russian winters had a profound effect on Luftwaffe operational capabilities, not only restricting flying hours through adverse weather, but also increasing the number of mechanical breakdowns and stretching out maintenance times.

and lacked both cohesion and adequate fighter cover. Nevertheless, as experienced by the German ground forces, the Luftwaffe faced seemingly inexhaustible numbers of Soviet aircraft, and although the air battle remained one-sided until late in the war the German casualties began to mount. For example, up until 31 October 1941, I. Fliegerkorps reported the loss of no fewer than 162 of its Ju 88s. KG 1 had suffered the lowest casualty rate with 39 of its machines destroyed. KG 76 had lost 53, but KG 77 had been hit hardest of all with 70 aircraft shot down or written off to other causes. Furthermore, the Luftwaffe's lengthening supply chain meant that the logistics of maintaining frontline air squadrons became ever harder, while the cruel winter of 1941–42 often kept squadrons grounded, and increased the wear and tear on airframes and engines. (Note also that by January 1942 only 15 per cent of 100,000 vehicles used by the Luftwaffe were in a working condition.)

As history now knows, *Barbarossa* was stopped in front of the gates of Moscow. Although German forces would resume their advance in 1942 in an offensive that would take them all the way to the city of Stalingrad, essentially the Eastern Front was becoming a war of attrition. Such was not the type of battle the Wehrmacht was suited to, and although the Luftwaffe's fighter pilots notched up astonishing rates of kill, steady

The Focke-Wulf Fw 190 was one of the most effective aircraft designs of the entire war. Not only did the Fw 190 form a superb day-fighter, it also found itself in use as a night-fighter, interceptor and ground-attack aircraft, serving on the Eastern, Western and Italian fronts.

German bombers on the production line. Ultimately, the Luftwaffe's war production failed to keep pace with losses, and from 1943 bomber output began to fall at the expense of fighter manufacture, as the air defence of the Reich took priority.

depletion would wear down the German frontline forces over the next three years. Soviet aircraft production grew to levels against which German industry simply could not compete, and included new types of Yakolev fighter and fighter-bomber that could compete, aerodynamically at least, with the German Bf 109s and Fw 190s. Germany produced some 56,000 fighters during World War II, these being distributed across multiple fronts. The Soviets manufactured 37,000 Yak fighters alone, these being concentrated on just one front. A truly unequal struggle was emerging.

The Luftwaffe was also revealing itself as an air force with acute strategic limitations. Transport aircraft and pilots were available in unrealistic numbers, and nowhere was this better demonstrated than at Stalingrad in the winter of 1942–43, when the German 6. Armee and part of its 4. Armee had found itself surrounded by a pincer-like Soviet counter-offensive. On 22 November Hitler ordered 6. Armee commander, Generaloberst Friedrich von Paulus, to move his headquarters into Stalingrad and prepare to defend it. Paulus complied, but that day notified Army Group B's commander, Weichs, that he had very little ammunition and fuel, and only six days' rations. If supplied by air, he would try to hold out, but unless he could fill the gap left by the Romanians, he wanted permission to break out south-westwards. Weichs considered an immediate breakout imperative, and so did Paulus' five corps commanders. On 23 November, Paulus, with Weichs' support, radioed Hitler, seeking permission to abandon Stalingrad. Hitler refused, bolstered by Göring's assertion on 24 November that the Luftwaffe could supply Stalingrad by air.

This was totally unrealistic. The minimum supply required to sustain the force was 750 tonnes a day, but the Luftwaffe's standard Junkers Ju 52 transport could carry at most 2.5 tonnes, so at least 300 flights would be needed daily. Winter daylight was short, and of the seven Stalingrad-area airfields, only Pitomnik could operate at night. Aircraft rapidly became unserviceable in the cold, and the transport fleet was heavily engaged ferrying reinforcements to Tunisia. These factors, and the certainty of Soviet attacks on the airlift, made Göring's promise nonsensical. On the day he made it, Wolfram von Richthofen, commanding Luftflotte 4, notified Weichs, the *Oberkommando des Heeres* (Army High Command; OKH) and Göring of his dissent. Hitler chose to believe Göring, but Richthofen proved to be right: the best day's delivery was only 289 tonnes, the average less than 100. The Soviets packed the airlift corridor with AA guns and

Generalfeldmarschall Hugo Sperrle, here shown delivering an imperious handshake to a young Luftwaffe crewman, headed Luftflotte 3 in the 1940 campaigns in the West, as well as the meagre air forces that faced the D-Day invasion in June 1944.

constant fighter patrols; between them they shot down 325 of the lumbering transports and 165 of the bombers used to supplement them.

Stalingrad was the high water mark of German operations on the Eastern Front. Thereafter, and particularly following the German strategic defeat at Kursk in July–August 1943, the German forces began an agonizing, destructive retreat back to their homeland. More German fighter units were pulled back from the Eastern Front to defend the Reich itself, suffering under the hammer blows of the Allies' strategic bomber campaign. Then, on 6 June 1944, the Allies opened the Second Front with the invasion of Normandy, bringing with them vast aerial resources. Now the Luftwaffe was handing over air superiority to the Soviets. The Bf 109 fighter unit JG 52, for example, would from June 1944 regularly face aerial odds of 40-to-1. Furthermore, well-trained pilots were in short supply. Fighter pilot output increased from the training schools, but actually could not keep pace with the cumulative losses from all the fronts. At the end of June 1944, of a total of 1,375 German fighters deployed on frontline service, only 475 were actually on the Eastern Front. Although the Luftwaffe was still exacting a heavy price on the Soviets, it was a price the Soviets could afford to pay.

WESTERN FRONT AND THE REICH

On 22 February 1942, Arthur Travers Harris was appointed to the post of Chief of Royal Air Force Bomber Command. He believed that area bombing or strategic bombing could win the war, and that by pounding Germany's industrial capability and destroying German cities, the will of the Germans, in tandem with the buildings around them, would collapse. This bomber offensive was no simple payback for the German raids on British cities. RAF Bomber Command pounded Germany for three years, culminating in the obliteration of Dresden in February 1945. The British bombers were joined in the summer of 1942 by the United States Army Air Force, whose more heavily armed B-17 'Flying Fortresses' bombed by day, and then the Allies struck around the clock in a campaign that the Germans called 'terror bombing'.

The tactics of the bombing offensive changed dramatically as the war progressed. Initial sorties were conducted by comparatively small, twin-engined aircraft such as the Vickers Wellington. The amount of ordnance that these aircraft could carry was small compared to the new, four-engined bombers that were coming into service by the time Harris took over. The introduction of the Short Stirling and later the Avro Lancaster revolutionized the distance that the bomber raids could fly, and thus the range of targets that could be hit, as well as increasing exponentially the bomb tonnage that could be carried.

A confidential report, prepared in 1941, highlighted some of the worrying problems associated with the bombing campaign and undermined the claims by the bomber

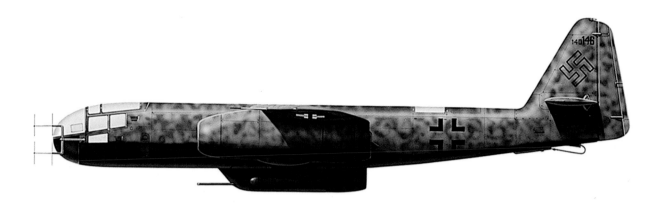

ABOVE: Ar 234B-2 (Wk-Nr 140146) of Hauptmann Kurt Bonow, KdoFührer of the Kommando Bonow, Oranienburg, March 1945. Based upon a post-war German illustration, this profile offers some indication of the overall finish of the Ar 234 night-fighter. Other points of interest include the nose-mounted radar antennae, the ventral gun pack housing two 20mm MG 151/20 cannon, and the glazed panel in the roof of the rear fuselage indicating the cramped compartment occupied by Kurt Bonow's rearward-facing radar-operator, Oberfeldwebel Beppo Marchetti. (John Weal © Osprey Publishing)

advocates that they were capable of winning the war on their own. The report, gleaned from aerial photographs of bomb targets, concluded that only one aircraft in three was able to get within 8km of its allocated target and that their accuracy was often even less impressive. The overall percentage of aircraft that managed to arrive within 194km² of the target was as low as 20 per cent.

The net result of these inaccuracies was the creation and adoption of a new tactic, that of 'area bombing'. This eschewed the attempted precision raids of the past in favour of the destruction not only of factories but also of their hinterland: the surrounding towns, complete with the workers who lived there. This policy, unfairly attributed to Harris himself, was the product of a decision not to adopt terror tactics, but rather to ameliorate the shortcomings inherent in bombing so inaccurately. It was also hoped that the net effect of this type of destruction would result in the gradual erosion of morale amongst the civilian population. Potentially, it might either bring about the collapse of the will to resist or, more ambitiously, and more unlikely, induce a war-weary population to overthrow Adolf Hitler's administration.

The German response to the Allied bombing offensive was an impressive defensive arrangement that also grew in sophistication, in tandem with the bomber formations that it was conceived to thwart, as technological advances combined with tactical reappraisals. Luftwaffe General Josef Kammhuber was appointed to lead the air defence provision for the Reich and initially achieved some startling successes. He devised a grid system, with each square in the grid being 52km², and located a fighter in each square – held there by air traffic control and guided by radar to its target whenever a bomber or bomber formation entered its airspace.

British bomber tactics had initially focused on sending aircraft into occupied Europe singly, at intervals, and Kammhuber's approach was ideally suited to dealing with them. Later, however, with larger numbers of aircraft available, the British simply swamped the German defensive arrangements. In fact, much of the strategic value of the bombing campaign lay in the extent to which it diverted valuable resources of men and equipment away from vital frontline areas. The intensity of the bombing obliged the Germans to relocate artillery pieces such as flak guns in Germany, rather than deploying them against the Soviets on the Eastern Front.

While concentrations of bombers, bringing all their firepower together, had improved their survivability in the skies over Germany, a second Allied initiative would help turn the course of the bomber offensive in a decisive fashion. This development was the introduction of fighter escorts for the whole duration of the bombing mission. It was made possible by the adoption of long-range fuel tanks, a practice that was very common

Germany's haphazard ambitions to produce a decent heavy bomber resulted in a multiplicity of designs. One of them was the Dornier Do 317, which was ultimately meant to carry up to 9,000kg of ordnance, but it did not get beyond prototype stage.

A striking image of an Me 163 rocket fighter, caught by a camera aboard a US Boeing B-17 on a raid over Germany in the last months of the war. Such aircraft were technologically impressive, but were an unnecessary diversion as Germany slid towards defeat.

when deploying fighters over long distances, but which had failed to be considered practical for combat purposes. The introduction of the Anglo-American P51 Mustang brought immediate results, forcing the fighter aircraft of Luftflotte Reich to spend as much time defending themselves as shooting down the heavy bombers.

The strategic bombing campaign against Germany never, of itself, brought Hitler's Germany decisively to its knees. Furthermore, the air defence of the Reich inflicted truly appalling losses on the attackers, testimony to both the Luftwaffe's tactical skill and first-rate interception technologies. The US Eighth Air Force, for example, lost 4,145 aircraft during operations over the European Theatre of Operations (ETO), and the loss rate of Bomber Command was about one in 20 aircraft. Yet this defensive effort highlighted to an even greater extent the lack of strategic capability in the German Air Force. Germany was never able to mount a bombing campaign of parity to that of the British or Americans, and as fighter defence took an even greater priority the production of bombers decreased even further. In 1943, German industry produced 10,898 fighters,

OVERLEAF: What might have been. A production line of He 162 *Volksjäger* jet fighters sits incomplete in a saltmine near Schönebeck, Germany, in 1945. The He 162 was another failed attempt by the Luftwaffe to level the playing field against vast numbers of Allied fighters over the Reich in the last two years of the war.

The lumbering Heinkel He 177, here seen in RAF markings following its capture, was another abortive Luftwaffe attempt to create a heavy bomber. Its mechanical deficiencies were so profound that it was nicknamed the 'flaming coffin' by its aircrews.

then 26,326 in 1944. In the same years combined, just 6,771 bombers rolled off the assembly lines. In essence, by the end of 1943 the Luftwaffe was essentially a defensive air force, of limited reach. When the Allied fighter escorts eventually matched the German fighter defences, then Hitler's air battle for the Reich was effectively lost.

Matters became far worse for the Germans with the Allied invasion of Normandy on 6 June 1944. Luftflotte 3 numbered 815 aircraft on the eve of the invasion, although only 600 were actually operational. It received a further 300 aircraft within four days of the Allied landings. However, in total the combined Allied forces utilized more than 5,000 aircraft flying more than 14,000 sorties on D-Day alone. The result was total loss of air superiority on the Western Front, and nearly 600 German aircraft destroyed over France in the first two weeks of the battle for Normandy.

With Allied forces advancing from both East and West, there was nothing the Luftwaffe could do to prevent the final defeat of the Third Reich. It made some spirited interventions, such as a massive 800-aircraft fighter-bomber sweep against Allied airbases in Belgium and the Netherlands on 1 January 1945, known as Operation *Bodenplatte*. Two hundred Allied aircraft were destroyed in the action, but the Germans in turn lost 300. Within a couple of months, the Luftwaffe was a frail shadow of its former self. Experienced pilots were in short supply, as was aviation fuel, and around the German capital fighter aircraft were literally being rolled out of the factories for destruction within hours of taking off. The late-war introduction of jet and rocket fighters, such as the Me 262, Me 163 and Me 263, were little more than a technologically costly distraction from the inevitable defeat that was looming.

ABOVE: Me 163B-0 V41 'PK+QL' of Major Wolfgang Spate, *KdoFührer* of Erprobungskommando 16, Bad Zwischenahn, May 1944. This is the aircraft in which Wolfgang Spate flew the world's first operational rocket-fighter sortie on 14 May 1944. Celebrating the culmination of two years' hard work, the ground crew had given it a special tomato-red paint job overall. Spate was not best pleased when he first caught sight of it, commenting somewhat grumpily that von Richthofen had at least achieved some victories before having his famous triplane painted bright red! (John Weal © Osprey Publishing)

BELOW: Me 262A-1a (Wk-Nr 170063) 'White 9' of Feldwebel Helmut Lennartz, Erprobungskommando 262, RechlinLarz, September 1944. Like most early production Me 262s, 'White 9' wears a two-tone grey underside. Lennartz himself, who on 15 August 1944 had claimed the first B-17 to be downed by an Me 262 jet, subsequently went on to serve with both Kdo Nowotny and JG 7. He survived the war, having added eight jet kills to the five he had previously scored while flying Bf 109s with II./JG 11. (John Weal © Osprey Publishing)

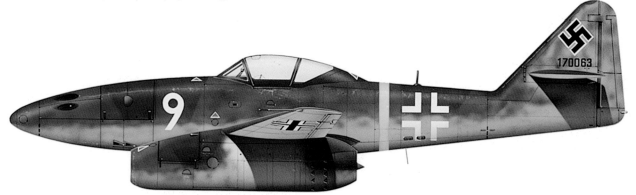

The vapour trail of a V2 ballistic missile snakes up into the sky following a launch. The advent of the V1 and V2 'vengeance weapons' could not compensate for the lack of a convincing strategic bomber force in the Luftwaffe's arsenal.

The final surrender of Germany in May 1945 rendered the surviving combat aircraft of the Luftwaffe silent on their airfields. Of course, the causes of the ultimate defeat lay more at ground level than up in the air, but fundamental mistakes had been made amongst the highest authorities of the German Air Force, and these contributed to the collapse. The lack of a major strategic bomber force limited the Luftwaffe's long-range reach, while investment in fighter pilot training was not sufficient to produce the quantity and quality of pilots needed for a long war of attrition. There were consistent over-estimations by Göring of what the Luftwaffe could achieve, resulting in unnecessary losses and lowered aircrew morale. Transport and maritime aircraft also did not get the production priority they should have had, despite their respective importance to logistics and control of the sea lanes.

None of these criticisms take away from the sheer bravery and talent of the Luftwaffe's aircrew, nor the tenacity and skill of the ground crew who kept the aircraft flying. Ultimately, however, the overall strategic constraints of the German Air Force meant that by 1945 the memories of its glory days of 1939 and 1941 seemed distant indeed.

LUFTWAFFE —
ORGANIZATION
AND
MANPOWER

The pilot of a Heinkel He 111 takes the controls. It took around a year of basic flight training before an aircrewman specialized in either single- or twin-engine aircraft.

The Luftwaffe was a truly prodigious organization. Headed by the vain and temperamental Reichsmarschall Hermann Göring, it grew from a diminutive and secretive force during the early 1930s, to a battle-tested formation of 1.7 million men by 1941. Structuring, leading and training such as organization was no mean feat, and one not always successfully accomplished. In this chapter, therefore, we will take an overview of the Luftwaffe from its highest command elements down to its lowliest ground crew, noting the air force's core strengths and underlying weaknesses.

COMMAND AND PERSONNEL

Hermann Göring (centre), here seen flanked by two of the heroes of the Luftwaffe: Werner Mölders (left) and Adolf Galland. Mölders achieved more than 100 kills as a fighter pilot before he was killed in a flying accident in 1941.

The operational branch of the Reichsluftfahrt Ministerium (National Air Ministry; RLM, accounting for 25,000 personnel in 1939) was the Oberkommando der Luftwaffe (Air Force High Command; OKL). Under OKL the Luftwaffe was initially divided into four consecutively numbered regional *Luftflotten* (air fleets), later augmented by three more. Each *Luftflotte* commander was responsible for all air and supporting operations

LUFTFLOTTEN (HQ), AREAS OF OPERATION: PRINCIPAL CAMPAIGNS

Luftflotte 1 (Berlin), Germany: Poland 1939, North Russia.

Luftflotte 2 (Brunswick), Germany: Western Front 1939, Battle of Britain, Central Russia, Italy, Africa, Mediterranean.

Luftflotte 3 (Munich), Germany: Western Front 1939, Battle of Britain, invasion of Europe.

Luftflotte 4 (Vienna), Germany: Poland 1939, Balkans, South Russia, Hungary, Slovakia.

Luftflotte 5 (Oslo), Norway, Finland & northern Russia: Arctic Front, North Russia.

Luftflotte 6 (Poland; moved to Brussels, Smolensk & Crimea late 1941), Central Russia: Poland, Slovakia, Bohemia-Moravia, Croatia.

Luftwaffe Zentral (Berlin), renamed Luftflotte Reich on 5 February 1944. Home air defence, Denmark, East Prussia, Channel Islands, Norway, Hungary.

within his particular territory, although a subordinate *Jagdführer* (fighter leader – *Jafü*) supervised fighter operations. In turn, each self-contained fleet was divided into several *Luftgaue* (air districts) and *Fliegerkorps* (flying corps). The *Luftgau*, staffed by a *Generalmajor* and 50–150 officers and men, provided permanent administrative and logistical structures and resources for each airfield. The *Fliegerkorps* was responsible for all operational matters, including deployment, air traffic, ordnance and maintenance. This flexible system was a root cause of the Luftwaffe's combat success – it enabled rapid preparedness for any attached 'visiting' flight unit from the moment of its arrival, unencumbered by a separate administrative element. The entire airfield staff would thereupon become subordinate to the commanding officer of that unit.

Flight personnel actually constituted one of the smaller branches of the Luftwaffe, numbering only some 50,000 out of more than a million men in late 1939. The largest autonomous flying unit was the *Geschwader* (wing), named and equipped for its mission (i.e. fighter, dive-bomber, bomber, etc.) and identified by Arabic numerals (e.g. Jagdgeschwader 1 or JG 1, Stukageschwader 2 or StG 2, Kampfgeschwader 3 or KG 3, etc.). Some *Geschwader* bore additional 'honour titles', e.g. Jagdgeschwader 2 'Richthofen'.

The *Stab* (staff) flight of four aircraft under the *Geschwaderkommodore* – usually an *Oberst*, *Oberstleutnant* or *Major* – commanded three or occasionally four *Gruppen*, each with about 30 aircraft including a *Stab* element of three, and identified by Roman numerals (e.g. II Gruppe of JG 1, abbreviated to II./JG 1). Each was led by a *Major* or *Hauptmann* designated as *Gruppenkommandeur*. Each *Gruppe* comprised three Arabic-numbered *Staffeln*, each *Staffel* of nine aircraft being led by a 'Staffelkapitän', who might be a *Hauptmann*, an *Oberleutnant* or, after heavy casualties, even a *Leutnant*. The *Gruppe* number was omitted in abbreviation, as this could be deduced from the *Staffel* number (e.g. 5. *Staffel*, II. *Gruppe*, JG 1 was designated 5./JG 1). *Ergänzungsgruppen* (replacement training groups) were later added to each bomber *Geschwader*, and sometimes a temporary V *Gruppe*, giving an average strength of *c.* 90–120 aircraft. *Gruppen* were quite often transferred from one *Geschwader* to another and renumbered.

On the Galician front in 1939, Hermann Göring is briefed by his officers. Göring was head of the Luftwaffe until virtually the end of the war, although his authority was seriously weakened following his failure to provide adequate airlift to troops in Stalingrad in 1942–43.

AIRCREW – RECRUITMENT AND ENLISTMENT

Having been completely dissolved after World War I, the Luftwaffe had nothing to inherit from the old Reichswehr, and so this branch of the armed forces naturally had to be regenerated under government sponsorship. In that respect, it was indeed a National Socialist

FLIGHT UNIT DESIGNATIONS

Jagdgeschwader (JG): 'hunting' (single-engined fighter)

Kampfgeschwader (KG): 'battle' (level bomber)

Kampfgeschwader zur besonderen Verwendung (KG zbV): 'battle wing for special purposes',
until May 1943 when redesignated *Transportgeschwader* (TG) *Kampfschulgeschwader*
(KSG): 'battle school' (bomber training)

Lehrgeschwader (LG): Advanced training, demonstration & tactical development

Luftlandegeschwader (LLG): air-landing (glider)

Nachtjagdgeschwader (NJG): night-fighter

Sturzkampf(Stuka)geschwader (StG): dive-bomber; later redesignated *Schlachtgeschwader*
(SchG): 'slaughter' (ground attack), abbreviation changed to SG in October 1943

Schnellkampfgeschwader (SKG): 'fast bomber' (single-engined ground attack)

Zerstörergeschwader (ZG): 'destroyer' (twin-engined heavy fighter)

Various types of smaller autonomous units were similarly designated, e.g.: *Bordfliegergruppe*
(BdFlGr): shipborne floatplanes*

Ergänzungsgruppe (ErgGr): 'completion' (advanced training & replacement) *Erprobungsgruppe*
(ErpGr): trials (development & evaluation of own and enemy equipment)

Fernaufklärungsgruppe (F): long-range reconnaissance

Küstfliegergruppe (KüFlGr): coastal aviation

Minensuchgruppe (MSGr): mine detection

Nachtschlachtgruppe (NSGr): night ground attack

Nahaufklärungsgruppe (H): short-range reconnaissance, formerly: *Heeresaufklärungs* (Army
reconnaissance), hence 'H'

Seeaufklärungsgruppe (SAGr): maritime reconnaissance

Jagdbomberstaffel (Jabo): fighter-bomber squadron within a JG *Luftbeobachtungstaffel*
(LBeob): air observation

Seenotstaffel (See): maritime search & rescue

Wetterkundungsstaffel (Weku or Wekusta): meteorology

(* Luftwaffe and Kriegsmarine (Navy) personnel worked together in mixed air and maintenance crews
within these units.)

air force, but few men joined for political reasons. Whether they condoned, despised or
were ambivalent towards Nazi policies, most believed that the Nationalsozialistische
Deutsche Arbeiterpartei, (National Socialist German workers' party; NSDAP) offered
Germany its best hope of economic recovery. On a personal level, it would grant them
their only realistic chance of fulfilling their desire to fly. A degree of National Socialist
affiliation, therefore, seemed a small price to pay for this privilege.

A young member of a Luftwaffe youth group receives instruction in aircraft model building. The Wehrmacht was highly skilled at inculcating militaristic values in the young, and the Luftwaffe was no exception.

The miseries of depression, hyperinflation and Allied repression throughout the 1920s drove many to seek an escape. They found it in the skies. Initially, model aeroplane clubs were formed by small groups of enthusiasts, and this soon grew into a popular and cheap hobby, with countless meetings and distance-flying competitions later organized throughout the Reich. Design, experimentation and construction of these models provided a sound understanding of basic flight principles, and several innovative ideas were thus born. Many future aircraft engineers shared this background. The progression to gliding schools (*Segelschulen*) quickly followed and flying became almost a national pursuit, indeed, an obsession, with some 4,000 gliding clubs and fields blossoming across Germany and Austria. Instructors were generally World War I *Fliegerkorps* veterans. Flying provided German people with the physical and spiritual means to leave their troubles on the ground, and there was never a shortage of applicants. The government enthusiastically encouraged membership, and soon formed the Deutscher Luftsportverband (German Air

Sports Association), an overtly paramilitary gliding and powered flight organization that would nurture the nucleus of the Luftwaffe.

The covering organization for the fledgling air force was the Lufthansa *Verkehrsfliegerschule* (Commercial Flying School) founded in Berlin. The examiners could afford to be extremely selective and failure rates were often above 90 per cent. During 1932, for example, more than 4,000 had applied for pilot training. Following the ten-day course of entrance exams, just 18 were accepted (one of whom was the 20-year-old Adolf Galland, later one of the finest aces of World War II). This deliberate and far-sighted policy ensured that the future Luftwaffe would be built around a truly elite core; only the very best were available to form the pre-war and early wartime *Geschwader*.

Publicly announced 16 March 1935, the conscription of all German males between the ages of 18 and 26 for compulsory military service was ratified by the official Wehrgesetz (Military Service Act) that followed on 21 March. Conscripts were initially required to serve for one year, but this was extended to two years from 24 August 1936. Older men, aged between 27 and 35, were evaluated for training in the Ersatzreserve I (Primary Replacement Reserve). This training, broken into several five to eight week

Young Luftwaffe pilot recruits listen intently during a training class. Those men who joined the Luftwaffe at the beginning of World War II received superb standards of training, standards that had declined significantly by 1944.

periods, usually totalled 28 weeks. Upon completion, these men could be advanced to *Unteroffizierschule* as NCO candidates.

The arrival of the *Kriegsbeorderung* (call-up paper) did not, however, mean immediate enlistment. Prior to his commencement of military service, from the age of 17 years, every man was obliged to fulfil *Reichsarbeitsdienst* (National Labour Service; RAD) duty, the purpose of which was two-fold. During the six-month compulsory service, he would be actively involved in the construction of public facilities, monuments and *Autobahn* (motorways). In later years, Allied air raids diverted efforts away from building a model European nation, to rebuilding the existing one. RAD service typically involved the reconstruction of bomb-damaged factories and constant improvements to *Festungs Europa* (Fortress Europe) coastal defences. In addition to preserving and protecting the Reich, RAD duty greatly enhanced fitness and stamina among the military-aged male population, preparing them both physically and mentally for service life. Essentially, this was basic training, during which the future recruit took part in regular route marches and sporting competitions. He mastered the rudiments of foot drill and even the manual of arms, through the slightly peculiar *Spatenexerzieren* (spade drill), which was often considered more difficult

Hermann Göring presents decorations to members of the Legion Condor, for their service in the Spanish Civil War. Amongst the Legion Condor's operations was the bombing of Guernica on 26 April 1937, one of history's first examples of terror bombing.

than rifle drill proper. Herr Walter Glomp recalls that the soldier had to remember to rotate the shovel sufficiently 'to avoid striking his own head and shins with the blade'.

The conscript had no choice in the path his military service would take, but was posted in accordance with prevailing Wehrmacht requirements. With the start of war, the two-year time limitation was suspended and conscripts (along with everybody else) were obliged to serve for the duration of hostilities. The wartime conscript could still volunteer for extended duty (from four-and-a-half years to 'lifetime' service), beyond the cessation of war, although such a desire could only be voiced during his first two years of service. Those electing for a post-war career greatly improved their prospects for promotion.

Men who voluntarily enlisted prior to National Service age, or for a longer period than required by law, enjoyed the privilege of the choice of arm in which they could serve, and could even specify a specialist unit (such as tanks, submarines, aircrew, for example). Specific service could not be guaranteed, however, and those fortunate enough to reach their desired posting were still subject to appropriate medical and aptitude tests. The very act of volunteering revealed an acceptance of military discipline, and these men were generally rewarded with a significantly reduced RAD service requirement of as little as two months.

Mannschaften (other ranks) who had already signed up for an agreed duration of at least four-and-a-half years (prior to the introduction of conscription) were only classed as career soldiers after two years' service. Service with the old Reichswehr, Fliegerschaft (Flying Service) or the police forces prior to 1 March 1935 was counted towards this obligation.

Those who wished to serve as *Unteroffiziere* (NCOs) had, since the time of the Reichswehr, been required to sign up for at least 12 years' service. This could originally be extended, in two-year increments, up to 18 years, but this option was suspended in October 1939. NCOs who were technically eligible for discharge due to pre-war service could not be released during wartime unless considered unfit.

Career officers were required to sign up for an unspecified period of service, with each officer rank carrying its own obligatory retirement age. An officer could be discharged, in peacetime only, if he was considered unsuitable for promotion to the next grade. The maximum retirement age was 65 years.

TRAINING

From 1935 the main priority of the Luftwaffe was to supply itself with pilots, a priority very much reflected in its recruiting system. The raw conscript would first be assigned to a *Flieger-Ersatzabteilung* (airman replacement battalion; Fl.Ers.Abt.), where after an introductory tour of the camp, uniform issue and a *Vereidigt* (swearing-in) ceremony, he endured tetanus, smallpox, typhus, paratyphoid, dysentery and cholera inoculations,

A photograph of a pilot at the controls of a medium bomber. Pilots provided a visible elite for the Nazi propaganda machine, an elite often regarded as somewhat unsullied by the horrors of the war at ground level.

usually all within a week or two. In addition to the time-honoured regime of foot drill, rifle drill, PT and military discipline, he learned basic map reading and elementary wireless operation and procedure.

After their six-month induction period was complete, all recruits were reviewed for possible advancement as pilots. Any likely candidates were sent to a *Flug-Anwärterkompanie* (aircrew candidate company), where they would be evaluated during several tests in basic aviation theory. Those who were deemed unsuitable for pilot training, yet still showed promise as aircrew members, were then sent on to a *Flieger-Ausbildungsregiment* (aircrew development regiment) or Fl.AR. Here, they received a further two months of instruction in preliminary navigation, wireless operation, mechanical aviation and gunnery, prior to selection for specialist aircrew training in accordance with suitability and Luftwaffe needs.

By the close of 1940, however, it was clear that the early identification and training of these vital aircrew members was just as important as that of pilots. Sixteen months of intensive experience had given Luftwaffe recruiting and training staff the ability to rapidly identify those men most suited to pilot and aircrew training. The system was thus rationalized and compressed (during a broad restructuring of Luftwaffe commands undertaken that December), to enable recruits to embark upon the most appropriate training regime more quickly, and thus enable the Luftwaffe to meet its aircrew personnel demands sooner.

The *Flieger-Ersatzabteilung* was now bypassed, with all new recruits instead being assigned directly to a *Flieger-Ausbildungsregiment*, where they would receive some of their basic military training, in conjunction with the preliminary aviation instruction previously detailed. Any potential pilots among them were sent on to undergo the regular selection process within a *Flug-Anwärterkompanie*, where the remainder of their basic training was completed simultaneously alongside the aircrew evaluation tests. Upon successful completion of the Fl.AR stage (extended to three to four months by 1943), potential aircrew would progress to the appropriate specialist schools. The remaining personnel not chosen for further flight training would be redirected to a Fl.Ers.Btn. in order to complete their basic training, and thence to an alternative school for a branch most suited to their particular skills and aptitude. Those still determined to fly could request consideration for training as another, equally vital member of an aircrew.

Upon assignment to a *Flug-Anwärterkompanie*, the *Flugzeugführer-Anwärter* (pilot candidates) received instruction in basic flight theory and rudimentary aeronautics while being assessed for advancement. Those candidates displaying the required aptitude were then put forward to *Flugzeugführerschule*-A/B as soon as a place became available (usually after about two months), to commence flight training proper.

At such schools, officially abbreviated to F.Z.S–A/B, but more frequently referred to as 'A/B-*Schulen*', the cadet underwent four principal levels of instruction, each requiring qualification for its own licence, before advancement to the next stage. It was these licences, earned over a period of six to nine months, that gave the schools their name. The A-*Schein* introduced the students to basic practical flying in dual-controlled light aircraft, covering take-off and landing, stall recovery, etc., and eventually leading to solo flight. The A2-*Schein* demanded the absorption of a great deal of theory, including aerodynamics, meteorology, flying procedures and aviation law, in addition to the practical application of aeronautical engineering, elementary navigation, wireless procedure and Morse code. On top of all this, the cadets gained more flying experience on larger single-engined aircraft. The next level, the B-*Schein*, required progression to high-performance single- and twin-engined machines, usually with retractable undercarriage, including some older types of combat aircraft.

Acquisition of the final B2-*Schein* depended upon the cadet's satisfactory accumulation of between 100 and 150 hours of flight time, some 14–17 months after his induction. In late 1940, however, the A/B-*Schule* training programme was updated to take account of wartime demands for more pilots. The schools maintained the high initial selection standards, simply because of the vastly increased number of enthusiastic volunteers from which to choose, but a far greater emphasis was now placed on practical flying skills from the outset. The A2 licence was dropped, and that particular phase of the training was amalgamated into the remaining licence grades, with the A-licence generally taking three months to complete. The B1 brought the students into contact with advanced single-engined planes, while the B2 consisted of advanced navigation and the introduction to twin-engined aircraft. An elementary K1 *Kunstflug* (stunt-flying) aerobatics course was included, to provide all new pilots with a good understanding of rudimentary evasive manoeuvres (such as barrel rolls, loops and splits). This also enabled instructors to readily identify any potential fighter pilots among their students, who thereafter received more flying time than their fellow cadets. Upon completion of the B2 phase the cadet would at last be granted his *Luftwaffenflugzeugführerschein* (Air Force pilot's licence), accompanied by the highly prized *Flugzeugführerabzeichen* (pilot's badge) – his 'wings'. After an average of 10–13 months at A/B-*Schule* he was now, finally, a fully qualified pilot.

Note that the large number of ex-pilot cadets who had 'washed-out' from A/B schooling could still hold out hopes of being aircrew. While they had failed to meet the requirements to qualify as pilots, they were not simply discarded from the flight branch, but were instead re-routed with the other volunteers to a *Flieger-Ausbildungsregiment*. Here, they went through the standard two months of preliminary aviation training, while being evaluated for advanced training in one specific discipline, and were then posted to the specialist school most appropriate to their abilities. As aircrew shortages began to present serious problems around the mid-war period, personnel already serving in other

branches of the Luftwaffe could be offered an aircrew evaluation test, even though they might never have previously considered such a vocation. Men with above average signalling skills were often drawn from the *Luftnachrichtenregimenten* (air signals regiments) to retrain as *Bordfunker* (flight signalmen). A large number of serving ground crewmen had previously failed aircrew selection and longed for such duties.

Three German pilots, here showing a variety of flight and service dress. The airman on the left is wearing a one-piece leather flying suit with zip-fastened pockets, a particularly expensive variety of operational clothing.

PILOT SPECIALIZATION

Once qualified as pilots, the new airmen were categorized for service on single- or multi-engined aircraft, and here the training paths divided. Each was assigned to a specialist flying school, where he would undergo intensive training for his allotted aircraft type and duty, with potential fighter and ground-attack pilots being sent directly to *Jagdflieger-* and *Schlachtflug-Schulen* respectively.

Those selected for dive-bomber training proceeded immediately to *Sturzkampffliegerschule*. Potential *Stuka* crewmen had to endure around 15 physically demanding and nerve-wracking test dives (as passengers), to confirm their suitability for continued training. Those for whom the stresses proved too great were generally transferred to *Transportfliegerschulen*, eventually

The famous German fighter pilot Franz von Werra, seen here in Russia in 1941. Von Werra rose to prominence after he escaped from a Canadian POW camp, and made his way back to Germany.

serving with *Kampfgeschwader zur besonderen Verwendungs* (battle wings for special purposes, i.e. transport). The *Stuka-Schulen* differed tremendously in their methods. Some commenced dive-training almost immediately, while others waited until around 100 hours of additional formation flying and aerobatics had been accrued. The four-month training period (or sometimes, up to a year) mainly concentrated on accuracy in various dive approaches, but also included extra navigation and flight theory, with approximately 50 hours of flying time.

Pilots destined to operate twin-engined aircraft did not immediately advance to their own specialist schools, however, but were instead sent on to *Flugzeugführerschule*-C or 'C-Schule', often sharing location and airfield with a regular flight school. Here they received advanced instruction in instrument and astronomical navigation and the use of electrical and radio direction-finding equipment. They studied the complexities and handling characteristics of multi-engined aircraft, including 50–60 hours of flight time (rising to 70 hours by 1941), for which they were taken up in small groups and rotated; as one took his turn in the pilot's seat, a fellow student operated throttle levers under instruction. During the course, which lasted anything between two and six months, pilots spent several hours on 'link' simulation trainers (allowing them to get hopelessly 'lost' and recalculate complex headings, without wasting valuable fuel).

Following C-*Schule*, the men were assigned to a separate *Blindfliegerschule* (blind flying school), for a four- to six-week advanced course in instrument navigation and dead reckoning, with some 35–60 hours' flight time. When they eventually graduated around 20 months later, these pilots were among the most highly trained specialists within the Luftwaffe. With an average 300 flying hours behind them, they were ready to proceed to their final schools for advanced training in one particular discipline (bomber, transport, reconnaissance or heavy-fighter).

Details of every flight, including aircraft type, duration and purpose, were recorded in the personal *Flugbuch* (log book), maintained throughout (and occasionally beyond) the pilot's military service.

CONDITIONS OF SERVICE

Those men who passed through aircrew training successfully entered an elite military society. Therefore, general living conditions within a home *Kaserne* (barracks) were usually very good. The six-man *Stuben* (rooms) were adequately furnished with a table, chairs and iron-framed beds, with sheets and blankets, spaced a regulation 80cm apart (the width of each man's locker). A *Stubenälteste* (senior man), appointed from each *Stubenbelegschaft* (room complement), was directly responsible to the *Staffelkapitän* for his comrades' adherence to daily orders, duties and room cleanliness. Communal ablutions rooms (with hot water) boasted several large wash fountains, showers and sometimes baths.

The Junkers Jumo 211 engine was a key powerplant type amongst Luftwaffe aircraft, used in the Ju 87 and Ju 88, and some He 111 variants, amongst many others. Maintaining such engines was a daily duty for ground crew.

Meals were generally of a good standard, although portions were reduced under wartime restrictions, freeing supplies for fighting troops. For breakfast one could expect bread rolls, coffee and preserves, while main meals tended towards soups and casseroles, usually with a high potato content. Sausages naturally featured in the weekly diet, which included the traditional *Sonntagsbraten* (Sunday roast) of beef with vegetables. Flieger Gerhard Adam found his rations sufficient, 'but the young are always hungry, we could have eaten more'.

The limited leisure time was usually filled by writing letters home, or playing billiards and the ever popular card game *Skat*. Some continued their model-making hobby, the more accomplished craftsmen often producing recognition models. Several bases provided facilities for photography, reading and various artistic pursuits, and perhaps a gymnasium. Men of a musical or thespian bent naturally gave impromptu performances for roommates and were frequently cajoled into organizing concert parties (painfully familiar to most servicemen). Frontline bases were regularly visited by travelling libraries and bookshops, music or theatre companies and occasionally even mobile cinemas. In 1939 Göring barred all servicemen from smoking in public and, although available in the *Kasino* (mess), alcohol was strictly rationed, with excessive drunkenness resulting in up to 48 hours' incarceration. Even when relaxing at an off-base bar, the need for sobriety in the morning meant things rarely got out of hand.

For those who did transgress, typical punishments included extra duties, confinement to barracks and, during flight training, push-ups and airfield laps with parachutes strapped to their backs. Untidiness, lateness or dereliction of duty drew similar punishment, with more serious offences invoking temporary pay deductions or leave cancellation. Discipline was firm but essentially fair, and most men came to respect and value their NCOs for their even-handedness.

Luftwaffe personnel were paid on or about the 10th, 20th and 30th of each month. The airman's *Besoldung* (salary) comprised many elements and varied greatly, depending on allowances and conditions. Besides his *Grundgehalt* (basic salary), during peacetime or non-active service, he might receive *Wohnungsgeld-Zuschutz* (lodgings allowance), to

Luftwaffe personnel pictured in front of the train taking them out to the Eastern Front. Logistically, the German campaign in the Soviet Union stretched the Luftwaffe beyond its limits, increasing rates of attrition and reducing serviceability.

cover accommodation where billeting was unavailable. Personnel stationed in Berlin, Hamburg and Vienna received an additional *Örtliche Sonderzuschlage* (regional special surcharge), at 3 per cent of the basic wage, because of the higher cost of living in those cities. Specialist qualifications might entitle him to *Gehalt-Zuschutz* (pay contributions), whereas disciplinary fines or service loan repayments were covered by *Gehaltskürzung* (pay deductions). *Berufssoldaten* (professional soldiers) were subject to a 1 per cent *Lohnsteuer* (income tax), calculated on a *Tagessatz* (daily rate) and deducted on payment days (50 *Pfennig* (pf) *per diem* for *Flieger*, 75 pf for *Gefreite*, etc.), but this did not apply to wartime conscripts.

Based on mid-war scales, the average *Flieger* started on 65 Reichsmarke (RM) per month, while a *Gefreiter* made 77 RM and an *Obergefreiter* 98–105 RM. By the time he made *Hauptgefreiter*, his income had almost doubled to 118.70 RM.

NCOs of *Unteroffizier* and *Unterfeldwebel* rank made around 128–160 RM and 170–180 RM respectively. *Feldwebel* received a modest increase to 195 RM, whereas *Oberfeldwebeln* took just 5 RM more. A *Hauptfeldwebel* was originally paid the same as an *Oberfeldwebel*, plus a 5 RM monthly bonus (totalling 205 RM), but in May 1942, his basic pay was raised to 250 RM and the bonus system scrapped. The *Stabsfeldwebel* earned between 212.50 and 244.50 RM per month after 13 to 18 years' service.

Officers' pay scales featured a notable stepped system, producing a degree of overlap with wages of some higher or lower ranks. The lowest-grade *Leutnant* curiously received the same pay and allowances as an *Oberfeldwebel*, while the remaining six grades rose in increments, of around 25 RM each, to 300 RM. The lowest of four *Oberleutnant* grades started on 283.34 RM, again rising in 25 RM steps to 350 RM. Three *Hauptmann* grades rose neatly from 400, to 500 and 575 RM, while a *Major* enjoyed a respectable 641.67 to 700 RM per month. The highest-paid 'frontline' officers were *Oberstleutnant* on 808.34 RM, and *Oberst* with 1,050 RM.

A man's precise grade was chiefly dictated by the number of children he had. In military service he was fed, clothed and housed by the Wehrmacht, and the state family allowance was therefore reduced by 10 per cent. Child benefits were also reduced according to the size of his family; by 6 per cent for one or two children, or 3 per cent for three or four, but these deductions were amply compensated for by military *Kinderzuschlage* (child allowance), based on a percentage of his lodgings allowance. As a reward and incentive to procreation (supplying more Aryans for the Reich), families of five or more incurred no reduction to state benefits. If a man was wounded and hospitalized, a 10–20 per cent contribution was deducted, towards the cost of treatment, medical supplies, food and laundry. A wounded general officer could expect fees of up to 35 per cent. In the event of death, the airman's family would still be well cared for, with a pension, and child and housing benefits being paid directly to the widow.

WOMEN

Besides *Luftwaffenhelferinnen* (female auxiliaries), opportunities to meet women were limited to brief off-duty periods in local villages. It was seldom difficult for aircrewmen to attract attention, and predatory girls soon learned to recognize the distinctive qualification badges, unsurprisingly gravitating towards pilots. (Many new pilots were disappointed to learn they were not officially aircraft commanders, but quickly realized that most others made the same assumption.) Where leave restrictions prevented travel home, wives or girlfriends could sometimes journey to nearby towns for a few days together, although none were permitted on base for security reasons. Men who had already found their sweethearts often felt it prudent to await peace before making serious commitments. For those who chose to marry immediately, group weddings were often arranged. After the usual investigations into the future brides' racial purity, several airmen would be granted a short pass (of a few hours) to wed before returning to duty. For those overseas, this was simply not possible and so many had to make do with a *Ferntrauung* (long-distance wedding service), conducted over the telephone. Enforced separation tested any relationship, and some airmen inevitably discovered that a girlfriend, fiancée or even wife had taken a new beau. Incidentally, from 30 November 1935, non-membership of the NSDAP was legally recognized as grounds for divorce.

Wehrsold (active service pay), nicknamed '*Kopfgeld*' (head money) since World War I, supplemented basic wages, along with *Kriegsbesoldung* (war pay) for frontline duties. On top of all this would be the *Fliegerzulage* (flight pay); as pilot Peter Spoden recalls, crews received 'I think about 50 Marks or so per month, but we fellows were not interested in money in those days'. He does add, however, that 'for every take-off we got a '*Start-Ei*' ('egg') until the end of the war. That was more important.' Limited opportunities to spend this pay meant the greater part was usually sent home. When Herr Spoden returned to post-war Munich from POW camp, he was able to withdraw 'several hundred devalued *Reichsmark*, worth a few cigarettes on the black market'.

Aircrew were generally entitled to at least 14 days' annual leave, though depending on operational demands and personal circumstances, more could sometimes be arranged. Before the invasion of Russia, *Urlaubsschein* (leave permits) for up to two weeks' Christmas leave were occasionally still possible. Seriously wounded men automatically received *Genesungsurlaub* (convalescence leave) following hospital treatment, and by 1943 emotionally exhausted airmen could be granted *Erholungsurlaub* (recuperation leave) of up to one month. Families left behind often faced equal dangers to frontline soldiers and *Sonderurlaub* (special leave) was only granted to men stationed within a reasonable distance of home, and only upon the death of a parent; it was not deducted from normal leave allowance.

PROMOTION

The Luftwaffe was highly selective, and for the average recruit the likelihood of achieving a commission from the ranks was particularly slim. Although a comparatively new service, the Luftwaffe suffered from a privileged hierarchical system more akin to that of the Kaiser's army a generation before. The majority of original staff and flying officers were drawn from army and navy professionals, who brought many of their traditions with them. Regular officers were 'elected' to their ranks by fellow candidates in a passing-out ceremony. They were contemptuous even of reserve officers, so the sight of enlisted airmen achieving success frequently provoked much resentment and envy.

An ambitious junior aircrewman would first have to court the appropriate social circles if he were serious about promotion. That said, many more egalitarian officers withstood opposition and ridicule from their peers to help a *protégé*. Yet once promoted, acceptance was generally swift and complete. This lamentable air of snobbery persisted well into 1941, but was steadily eroded by field promotions, necessary to replace high officer casualties. To address these losses, from 1940 only one officer was permitted per crew. A gradual levelling of rank disparity between pilot and observer took place, *Oberfeldwebel* becoming more prevalent among both. In practice, a man's rank was almost irrelevant. Position was based entirely upon ability, and *Leutnante* were frequently appointed *Staffelkapitän* over higher-ranking officers. This policy ran throughout the operational structure, creating the peculiar situation in which an *Unteroffizier* observer would have 'command' over an *Oberleutnant* wireless-operator in flight, but reverted to normal subordination on the ground.

Details of pay, leave and promotions were recorded in the *Soldbuch* (pay book), along with enlistment, training, inoculations, uniform, awards, optical and dental examinations. Reflecting heightened security demands, the holder's photograph was fixed inside the cover from 1943. A red pencil strike across the front of the *Soldbuch* indicated cancellation, the soldier either a POW or deceased.

SERVICE OVERSEAS

Although all personnel had already received a full course of immunization during their recruitment and training programmes, the movement of a unit overseas entailed a further round of booster shots for everyone. Contrary to the normal practice of injecting the upper arm, throughout the Wehrmacht vaccinations were administered to the chest: into a man's right breast if he were left-handed, or his left breast if right-handed. Thus any temporary, localized paralysis caused by the more virulent cholera and paratyphoid strains would not seriously impede his daily duties.

Werner Mölders was not only one of Germany's foremost fighter aces, with more than 100 kills to his credit, but he also helped develop the Luftwaffe's core fighter tactics, such as the 'finger four' formation.

ABOVE: Ju 88A-4 'L1+HW' of 12./LG 1, Western Desert, *c.* August 1942. Ju 88s like this one had to cope with some of the worst environmental conditions of the war, with engines, air filters and other parts continually abraded or clogged by fine dust or sand. (John Weal © Osprey Publishing)

Men based in Western Europe enjoyed a reasonably comfortable and civilized existence, little removed from their home stations, with the local civilian population of some countries often surprisingly well disposed towards their new neighbours. While most resented the occupation of their homeland, many citizens of Belgium and Holland in particular could not help but be impressed by German military achievements and displayed a curious admiration for aircrewmen. Although not overtly collaborationist, they occasionally insisted on buying drinks and questioning the airmen about their daring exploits. The locals, with whom acquaintanceships grew, appreciated respectful behaviour, and many were genuinely saddened when their resident *Geschwader* transferred to another base.

If a short leave period prevented travel home to Germany, the airman could spend the available time exploring his immediate surroundings. Even with wartime restrictions, public transport systems were such that travel further afield was not impossible. Many indulged in cultural and historic tours around ancient capitals and landmarks, visiting museums and galleries. Enormous numbers of Wehrmacht personnel undertook pilgrimages to the Ossuary of Verdun and the many German and Allied cemeteries tracing the length of the previous Western Front, often to visit the last resting place of a father or uncle.

Those in need of a more relaxing atmosphere could repair to the Fliegerheim (Flyers' Home), established in Paris early 1941. This former baroque palace in the Parc Monceau had been converted by German construction firms, under guidance of the Sonderhaustab (Special Buildings Commission), to provide peaceful sanctuary for mentally and physically drained aircrews. Staffed by Deutsches Rotes-Kreuz (German Red Cross) workers, the hostel was well equipped with a very popular table tennis and games room, a writing room, library and reading room, several lounges and a refectory serving tea, coffee and light meals. The wine cellar was appropriately transformed into the *Bierstüberl* (beer lounge). Overlooking the main entrance hall, a giant bronze bust of the Führer was installed at the foot of the marble staircase with its huge ornamental wrought iron banister; this no doubt had its own effect upon the men's flagging morale.

For the crews posted to France, Paris was, of course, also a Mecca for those young airmen seeking a rather more uplifting experience, and the nightclubs of Montmartre and the Folies Bergère were ever popular destinations. Naturally, the local *femmes de la nuit* were also kept busy. To German servicemen, prostitutes were known either as *Dirnen* (girls), the easily translated *Huren* or more poetic *Bordsteinschwalben* (curbside swallows). The most common term, however, was the rather unpleasant *Nutten* (slits).

Other men were able to establish more meaningful relationships with local girls, but, tragically, many of these women were later subjected to acts of humiliation and recrimination, meted out by their own countrymen against perceived collaborators.

A Heinkel bomber stands guarded under camouflage netting near the West Wall, February 1940. As the war progressed and the Luftwaffe lost air superiority in many theatres, bombers became exposed to destruction on the ground by Allied fighter strafing attacks.

KG 26 pilot Horst Juventus was so distressed by the disappearance of his French sweetheart, following threats from the local Resistance, that he requested transfer from operational duties: 'a pilot pining for lost love was no use at all … I could prove a real danger.' His girlfriend was never seen again.

For those stationed in Africa, scorching days, freezing nights and viciously abrasive Ghibli sand storms made the Western Desert one of the harshest environments in which Luftwaffe men had to serve. Aircraft were not the only things to suffer from the constant ingress of sand. The sharp granules, which always got into any food (and everywhere else), caused cumulative damage to tooth enamel, and dental complaints became commonplace. Combined with a limited fluid intake, the passing of sand through the digestive system could produce a painful irritation all of its own. However, the human body is a remarkably adaptable machine, and, in time, subtle physical changes took place. Servicemen noticed a general deceleration in hair growth, reducing the need for frequent shaving and thus conveniently saving water rations. Another (less appealing) biological effect was the passing of particularly dry stools. On the infrequent occasions that a man needed to evacuate his bowels in the latrine, or take a *Spatengang* (spade walk), his intestinal tract had already absorbed much of the moisture from the faeces. There was always a little more to be extracted, however, and within moments the deposit was neatly chopped up and carried away by '*Sheisskäfer*' (identically known to the British as 'shite beetles'), that seemed to appear from nowhere and disappeared just as smartly.

Personnel serving in North Africa were paid in Italian lire, although the opportunities to spend any of it were somewhat limited. Leave was infrequent and, in the more remote locations, quite pointless. Nevertheless local Arab merchants soon learned to supply as many demands as they could possibly identify, by way of services and bazaar souvenirs.

The Heinkel He 177 'Greif' (Griffon) was Germany's most convincing realization of a true strategic bomber type. It had a range of 5,500km and a 6,000kg bomb-load, but technical problems and competing air production demands meant it was built in limited numbers.

Just like their British opponents, many Germans picked up a few words of Arabic or Swahili during their dealings with traders, and daily conversation among themselves became liberally sprinkled with these phrases.

Contact with women was virtually non-existent, and only likely at major ports and cities. Where they could be found, very few German servicemen would dare employ the indigenous 'working girls' as this was in direct violation of the German Race Acts of September 1935 (designed to protect Aryan blood and German honour), a law aggressively enforced by the *Feldgendarmerie* (field police). Instead, such needs were admirably fulfilled by the only officially sanctioned military brothel in North Africa, at No. 4, Via Tassoni in Tripoli, entirely staffed by Italian women. The use of no other establishment was permitted for enlisted men and NCOs, including those licensed for Italian military use.

The demanding climate, ever diminishing supplies, and the seemingly unending nature of the entire campaign, contrived to make the Mediterranean one of the toughest theatres of World War II. This aside, postings north of Africa had their compensations. The personnel stationed in Italy, Sicily, Salonika or the Greek Isles were almost overwhelmed by the great range of local '*Delikatessen*' that supplemented their diet. Meals regularly featured fresh or sun-dried tomatoes and fish, oranges, mandarins, cheeses, olives and, of course, plenty of pasta. Given the chance, the airman could enjoy a tremendous selection of wines, too. Steeped in history and culture, the Mediterranean region presented excellent leave potential, and thousands explored the Acropolis, ancient Roman villas and the comparatively modern architectural splendour of Rome.

Until 1943, an ostensibly Fascist Italy imposed none of the restrictions found elsewhere and the German serviceman was able to consort freely with local women. Alternatively, he could turn to one of countless civil or military bordellos, such as that hosted by La Tenutaria del Casino or 'La Signora' Luccia Cecotti, at No. 10, Via Ludovico Cavitelli, Cremona. This facility was just one of several founded within range of the Caserna Manfredini, an Italian Army barracks 80km south-east of Milan. Although the girls at these establishments were regularly checked, as in most armies, contraction of any serious social disease was considered a self-inflicted wound. If it was determined that the soldier had failed to exercise proper precautions, he would be duly charged with such an offence. Several brands of condom, such as 'Odilei' in *Troppenfest* (tropical) packaging, were readily available to Wehrmacht personnel.

There were also many hazards of service in Russia. The infamously bitter winters jammed control surfaces with ice and made tyres brittle. Slick runways caused countless take-off and landing accidents, accounting for as many losses as enemy action. Temperatures dropped to -34°C, causing engine oil, grease and lubricants to freeze solid, and rendering up to 75 per cent of all aircraft inoperative throughout the winter of 1942. Petrol-driven Kärch heaters were employed in attempts to pre-warm (or rather,

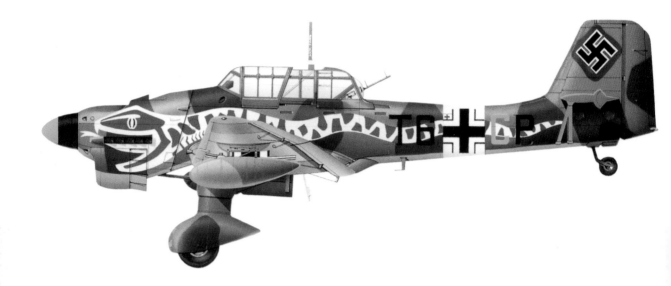

ABOVE: Ju 87R-2 trop 'T6+CP' of 6./StG 2, Tmimi/Libya, July 1941. Camouflage was obviously of secondary importance when this extraordinary paint job – producing undoubtedly the most colourful of all desert Stukas – was undertaken. Such a snake motif adorned at least two different aircraft, but whether they were both flown by the same pilot – Leutnant Hubert Pölz – or were a short-lived *Staffel* (or even *Kette*) decoration is unknown. If the former, Pölz's individualism certainly stood him in good stead, for he later won the Knight's Cross and Oak Leaves on the Eastern Front, ending the war as *Kommandeur* of I./SG 151. (John Weal © Osprey Publishing)

thaw) the engines, which would be cloaked in thermal jackets and fed through 'umbilical' hoses, although the process had to be commenced many hours ahead of start-time. Typically, it was the ground crews who suffered the cold more than most. Working both day and night with intricate electrical, mechanical and engine components, which prohibited the use of gloves and with the constant danger of exposed skin bonding to frozen metal, they incurred a high incidence of frostbite and hypothermia.

Units lucky enough to have concrete billets or abandoned factories at their disposal were forced to burn furniture, doors and window frames in the absence of any other solid fuels. The majority of airfields were bereft of such accommodation, and, since tents were completely inadequate, underground quarters had to be constructed. This troglodyte existence did, at least, provide respite from the savage ice winds and afforded some protection from incessant Red Air Force raids. A Russian winter does not last forever, but the spring thaw merely created alternative problems with which to bind a Luftwaffe unit. The *Rasputitsa* (lit. 'time of no roads'), as the Russians themselves called it, instantly reduced all unmetalled surfaces and airstrips to a sucking morass. Baking hot and dusty summers brought dangers of their own, with many ground crewmen succumbing to heat stroke.

Vast crop fields concealed another altogether unexpected problem. Personnel of KG 51, living in tented encampments at Balti in Bessarabia during 1941, spent much of their time battling a plague of mice. Such infestation carried high risks of disease, with droppings left in nibbled food stocks, the undetected gnawing of aircraft components and equipment, and the startling discovery of unwelcome company in personal kit. The heat also had detrimental effects upon food preservation, with the resulting generally poor diet and unsanitary conditions inevitably producing gastroenteritis and dysentery. Autumn was but a short, muddy transition to another bitter winter with frequent heavy downpours that flooded airfields and accommodation. Although bitter, none of the subsequent winters equalled that of 1941–42.

A Ju 88 in flight over a winter landscape. The Ju 88's high speed – the Ju 88A-4 variant could fly at 450km/h – made this aircraft one of the more challenging for Allied fighters to destroy.

The demands heaped upon the aircrew stretched them to, and often beyond, their limits. Crews made three to four sorties per day, each (in the case of bomber crews) between four and five hours long, and most units remained operational for at least six months (some up to nine months) without a single day off since the start of the campaign. Unsurprisingly, medical officers of several units reported that extreme nervous exhaustion was widespread among aircrews. Relentless long-range flights, constant mortal fear and the physiological stresses of bomb runs through heavy flak severely degraded bodily and mental constitution. Men became fractious, a typical symptom of sleep deprivation, sometimes breaking into unprovoked weeping spasms. Air and ground crews alike were on the verge of a collective nervous breakdown. Some *Geschwaderkommodore* were forced to implement timetables that at last made rest periods possible in rotation. Men seized the opportunity to sleep, sometimes for days at a time. Others resolved to get as far away as possible, as quickly as possible. Although rare and fleeting, a little peace had great restorative power upon a man's spirit. Returning mentally refreshed, he nevertheless began to sink back into the general state of nervousness within a few hours.

While leave shortages severely undermined morale, perhaps the most distressing and all-pervading of miseries was the lack of contact with home. Although every effort was made to convey mail to and from Germany, the demands for ammunition, fuel and medical

The Dornier Do 217E entered service in 1941, and offered greater bomb-load and performance compared to its parent, the Do 17. As well as a medium bomber, the Do 217 acted as an anti-shipping and reconnaissance aircraft and a night-fighter.

supplies across the 1,600km front simply had to take priority. The desperately over-worked *Transportflieger* did all they could to alleviate the situation, shoehorning mail sacks into their Ju 52s wherever possible, but untold tons of letters were never delivered. Some units detailed men to undertake epic road journeys, lasting several days, to deliver and collect mail from rear depots themselves. A simple and effective expedient was finally devised in 1943 to establish occasional radio links with Berlin. A bomber flying at high altitude, trailing its 70m-long cable aerial, enabled *Luftnachrichten* signallers to relay short (often coded) messages between squadron personnel and their families. The meteorological officer of KG 51, Doktor Rumbaum, learned of the birth of his daughter in this humorous message: 'New tail-less aircraft type fit for take-off. Production plant ready to accept further work.'

In the remote agricultural regions of Russia, Byelorussia and Ukraine, most villagers (never enamoured of their Soviet overlords) greeted the invading German Army as liberators and proffered friendly assistance. A mutually beneficial trading system was established with peasant farmers who sold geese, eggs, pigs and cattle to the airmen to supplement meagre rations. (This was in contrast to Red Army soldiers, who, with little to exchange, simply commandeered supplies.) Acts of fraternization carried enormous risk for the villagers, if discovered by a *Politruk* or military *Kommissar*, yet they frequently

A formation of He 111s conduct a bombing mission, 1941. The bomb run was one of the most dangerous phases of any flight, as it involved the aircraft staying straight and level until bomb release, regardless of anti-aircraft fire or enemy fighters.

courted still greater danger by assisting shot-down Luftwaffe airmen to return to their own lines. The slaughter of these docile villagers, principally by *SS-Einsatzgruppen* under the edicts of Nazi racial policy, soon squandered the potential of these helpful allies and ensured total and brutal defeat for the Third Reich.

Thus were the basic conditions of the Luftwaffe aircrew. Of course, such conditions were transformed utterly by the experience of war, as we will discuss in subsequent chapters. Yet for now we turn to something that was close to the heart of many aircrew, who saw themselves as one of the more dashing facets of the German war machine – how they looked.

UNIFORMS – SERVICE AND WORK DRESS
HEADGEAR

Luftwaffe uniforms were striking and confident. The *Schirmmütze* (peaked cap) had a grey-blue wool crown, black cotton band and black leather or '*Vulcanfiber*' peak. The enlisted ranks' model had a patent leather chinstrap, and crown and band piping in the wearer's *Waffenfarbe* (arm of service colour). Officers' caps carried plaited chin cords and piping in silver-coloured (or gold-coloured for generals) wire thread, irrespective of branch. Insignia consisted of the *Hoheitsabzeichen der Luftwaffe* (air force national insignia), a flying eagle clutching the swastika; this surmounted the *Mützenabzeichen* (cap badge), a *Reichskokarde* (cockade) in national colours supported by *Eichenlaubkranz und Schwingen* (oakleaf garland and stylized wings). Both insignia were of stamped white alloy for enlisted ranks, woven silver-coloured wire for officers up to *Oberst*, and gold-coloured wire for generals. The *Fliegermütze* (flyer's cap) was a simple grey-blue wool sidecap with a deep 'curtain' and rounded front and rear corners. A *Hoheitsabzeichen*, in white cotton thread for enlisted ranks and wire for officers, surmounted a slightly padded *Reichskokarde* woven onto grey-blue wool. Officers' *Fliegermützen* were further distinguished by wire or '*Celleon*' (cellophane) piping to the edge of the curtain and the circumference of the cockade.

From 19 December 1938, Luftwaffe *Gebirgsdienst* (mountain service) units received a grey-blue *Bergmütze* (mountain cap) with a short peak, emulating the Austrian-style cap of *Gebirgsjäger* (mountain riflemen) alongside whom they served. Its deep folded curtain could be lowered to protect the neck and ears in cold weather, with the single-button flap closure fastened beneath the chin.

On 11 June 1943, the Wehrmacht as a whole adopted the *Einheitsfeldmütze* 43 (M1943 universal field cap), itself inspired by the *Bergmütze* but with a longer peak and two-button flap closure. Also issued to Luftwaffe personnel, the *Einheitsfliegermütze 43*, was of grey-blue wool with blue-painted alloy buttons. Officers' *Bergmützen* and *Einheitsfliegermützen* bore wire piping to the crown seam only.

ABOVE: Ju 88A-4 JK-260/'4' of PLeLv 44, Onttola, Finland, June 1944. Another country to use the Ju 88 bomber against the Soviet Union was Finland, which purchased 24 A-4s from Germany in the spring of 1943. Unlike many of the Hungarian and Romanian units (above), Finnish squadrons were not integrated into the Luftwaffe's command structure, but remained separate entities under the direct control of their own air force. (John Weal © Osprey Publishing)

TUNICS

A grey-blue *Rock* or *Tuchrock* (cloth tunic) with four pleated pockets, turn-back cuffs, exposed four-button front and open collar, was adopted for everyday wear early in 1935. The enlisted ranks' tunic had straight-edged pocket flaps, with patch breast pockets and expanding 'bellows' skirt pockets. It was lined in grey-blue cotton drill, incorporating an interior left breast pocket, *Verbandstoff* (wound dressing) pocket to the right front skirt, and short straps at the waist to accommodate belt-support hooks.

Officers were obliged to purchase a fine quality equivalent for everyday wear, usually tailored in wool tricot cloth with sateen or cotton lining. All pockets were of patch type, with straight or gently scalloped flaps. Generous turn-back cuffs routinely served as document pockets. A lightweight white cotton version, prescribed as *Sommeranzug* (summer dress), comprised *Sommerrock*, straight *Sommer* or *Weisse Hose* (white trousers) and white-topped *Sommermütze* with removable crown for ease of cleaning. Although officially suspended at the outbreak of war, its continued purchase was in fact permitted.

The most distinctive item of Luftwaffe dress, the *Fliegerbluse* (flyer's blouse), was developed concurrently for exclusive use as flying uniform. This short, close-fitting garment was simple and inexpensive to produce and quickly became the favoured tunic of all branches and on all occasions. The enlisted ranks' *Fliegerbluse* 35 was without external pockets and bore no national badge (a breast eagle). Five large ceramic or fibre buttons were concealed by a fly front, and a convertible collar with a small hook-&-eye enabled it to be fully fastened at the neck when necessary. It was partially lined with grey-brown cotton cloth, incorporating buttoned interior breast pockets, belt-hook support straps, and buttoned field dressing pocket. The cuffs could be tightened; a small woollen tab stitched to the inside of the cuff could be passed through a slit in the rear seam to an external button, or alternatively it could remain secured to an internal button. Officers' *Fliegerblusen* were essentially similar but of finer quality cloth and fully lined with sateen or cotton; as with most items of officers' kit, these privately purchased garments show many subtle variations in detail. The upper part of the collars of both tunics bore edge-piping *Kragenlitze* – in the appropriate *Waffenfarbe* for NCOs and enlisted ranks, silver for officers up to *Oberst*, and gold for generals. An order of 20 March 1940 discontinued the *Waffenfarbe* piping, but officers' bullion piping was retained.

From 6 May 1940 pockets were added to the skirts of the *Fliegerbluse*. These were internally hung but, for NCOs and enlisted men, had large external flaps with rounded corners, fastened with exposed alloy buttons; for officers they were gently curved and flapless.

An order dated 1 October 1940 stated that the national eagle badge was to be fitted to the right breast of the *Fliegerbluse*, reflecting the garment's elevation from work clothing to part of the *Dienstanzug*. Grey-blue 'Kunstseide' (rayon, synthetic silk) superseded cotton drill lining at the end of 1942, though the cut remained unaltered.

A Luftwaffe unit on the Eastern Front in September 1942 sits and has lunch outside on its airfield. Luftwaffe aircrew were treated as something of an elite until the very end of the war.

On 11 November 1938 a new dual-purpose tunic, the *Waffenrock*, had been approved as a replacement for both 1935 garments; this was identical to the *Rock*, except for a five-button front closure and convertible collar with concealed cloth tab and button ensuring a neat fit. The idea stood little chance against the popularity of the *Fliegerbluse*, however, and production ceased *c*.1940. A few *Waffenrock*, usually privately tailored officers' examples, remained in use until 1945.

INSIGNIA

Model 1935 *Schulterklappen* (shoulder straps) displaying the appropriate *Waffenfarbe* were sewn into the shoulder seams of other ranks' *Rock* and *Fliegerblusen* 35. They were routinely manufactured from scrap cloth generated during tunic production. This fixed design, a feature common to most Wehrmacht uniforms, soon caused supply problems and so, on 20 March 1940, removable versions were adopted by all services. Often produced by home-workers, *Schulterklappen* 40 were supplied directly to issuing stores in the desired *Waffenfarbe*. Tunics were consequently manufactured with a cloth stirrup and button to each shoulder, also simplifying production. The use of fixed *Schulterstücke* (shoulder boards) continued on officers' *Fliegerblusen* and *Rock* for smartness, although removable versions were available.

The status (i.e. officer, NCO or enlisted man), exact rank, and branch of service were identified on the collars of both tunics, with additional upper sleeve insignia for senior enlisted ranks. A special sequence of simplified upper sleeve rank patches were worn on flying clothing. Specialist qualifications for non-officer ranks were identified by badges on the lower (usually left) sleeve. Aircrew qualifications and accumulated mission awards were indicated by pin-on metal badges worn on the left breast.

SHIRTS AND TIES

NCOs and other enlisted ranks were to have no undershirt visible with either tunic or blouse, and a white V-necked pullover *Trikothemd* (tricot shirt) was supplied. For parade dress and special occasions, including their own weddings, a *Weiss Hemd* (white shirt) and *Schwarze Halsbinde* (black necktie) were permitted. Officers wore the cotton *Blaumeliertes Hemd* (mixed blue, i.e. blue mixed with unbleached thread) with separate button-on collar for everyday wear. They were to provide themselves with white shirts for best dress. Officially, a black tie was to be worn at all times.

On 27 September 1943 a grey-blue *Stoffhemd* (cloth shirt) was approved for wear without a tunic in hot weather by all ranks. These were provided with shoulder strap fittings, a machine-woven breast eagle on a triangular backing of matching cloth, and

A heavily decorated Luftwaffe officer. His decorations include the Knight's Cross on his left breast pocket, and the German Cross in gold on the opposite pocket, the latter beneath a Luftwaffe eagle and swastika emblem.

A Luftwaffe *Stabsfeldwebel*, here seen wearing a lightweight canvas flying cap with inbuilt communications headset. The yellow colouration of the shoulder boards indicates that this man belongs to aircrew.

large, pleated breast pockets with buttoned flaps. A grey-green version, originally adopted from 17 December 1943 for field units, became standard issue to all ranks and branches on 19 September 1944, and the grey-blue type was discontinued.

TROUSERS

The straight grey-blue *Tuchhose* 35 issued to enlisted ranks incorporated slightly angled hip pockets, a buttoned slash pocket at the right rear, and a patch-type watch pocket to the right front; a rear V-notch and half-belt provided adjustment for the waistband. Some senior NCOs elected to wear *Stiefelhose* (breeches), with identical waist details. Officers' *Tuchhose* and *Stiefelhose* were of superior cloth and tailoring; pocket openings tended to be vertically set, buckled waist adjustment tabs were provided at each hip, and the watch pocket was internal. The popular *Reithose* (riding breeches) were identical to *Stiefelhose* but with the addition of inner thigh reinforcement panels in matching cloth or, more often, contrasting stone-grey suede or moleskin.

FOOTWEAR

The traditional high *Schaftstiefel* (shafted boot), and the *Schnürschuh* (laced shoe) adopted from 13 March 1941 for economic reasons, were worn by enlisted ranks. Officers wore soft black leather riding boots with breeches, and low-quarter black shoes with straight trousers.

OVERCOAT

A mid-calf length grey-blue wool *Übermantel* 35 completed the main uniform issue. The double-breasted coat had two rows of six standard *Gekörnte-Knöpfe* (pebbled-finish buttons) to the front, slanted hip pockets with buttoned flaps, and turned-back cuffs. A rear half-belt provided adjustment and, when unfastened, allowed the deep-pleated coat to double as a blanket. Small metal hooks and thread loops permitted the skirts to be folded back to the hips, easing marching, but this was dropped during 1940, when the alloy buttons were also painted grey-blue. Shoulder straps and collar patches were worn on the overcoat, but the latter were officially abolished on 29 May 1942. Fine quality officers' overcoats were usually lined with sateen cloth and, while details varied according to taste and budget, all were required to incorporate supports and an access slit under the left pocket flap to attach the sword or dress dagger when appropriate.

The blanket-lined *Einheitlicher-Tuchmantel* (universal cloth overcoat) with enlarged collar, detachable hood and vertical hand-warmer torso pockets was approved on 17 October 1942.

WORK CLOTHING

The *Drillichmütze* (drill cap) was simply a black cotton drill version of the wool *Fliegermütze*, lined with black linen. It bore a dull white cotton national badge on black wool backing, but not the cockade. The two-piece *Drillichanzug* 35 (drill cloth suit) – styled the '*Drilchanzug*' until 1940 – was originally issued in unbleached cotton, officially termed *Rohgrau* (raw grey); but from 16 July 1937 mechanics were supplied with a more practical black-dyed version. The unlined blouse was a fly-fronted, loose-fitting jacket fastening with four large ceramic or fibre buttons and one small dished alloy button at the neck; a hook-&-eye enabled the collar to be fully closed, and a cloth tab and button secured it when up-turned. The cuffs were split, adjustable to one of two dished alloy buttons. An internal left breast pocket replaced the original external patch type from 19 August 1936. The straight-cut drill trousers had buttoned flaps to the hip pockets, and a buttoned slash pocket was added to the right rear from 19 August 1936. Alloy friction buckles with cloth straps were provided at each side for adjustment, and small slits below the waistband could be secured over *Taillenhaken* (belt support hooks) fitted to the blouse. Economy dictated a return to *Rohgrau* drill cloth from 4 June 1940, although the *Drillichmütze* remained black. The blouse was often tucked into the

Flight uniform on the Eastern Front could be extremely varied, based on what was available and on personal preferences. Note the two individuals here with belts of signal cartridges attached around their calves, these being fired from a 2.6cm Walther flare pistol.

trousers, giving the impression of a one-piece overall, and black and undyed items were frequently worn in combination.

In addition to the more popular *Drillichanzug*, one-piece overalls were also available in both lined and unlined versions. The *Arbeitsschutzanzug 36* (working protective suit), approved 4 April 1936, was again originally issued in *Rohgrau* cotton drill, but from July 1937 these too were supplied in dark blue or black. A front fly closure was fastened with eight buttons, the upper five being of the large type found on the *Drillichbluse*, and the lower three of smaller size; there were also a hook-&-eye and a buttoning cloth tab to the collar. Hip pockets let into the side seams were coupled with access slits to clothing worn under the suit. Adjustment to cuffs was by cloth straps and buttons, and to ankles by tie-tapes. A matching cloth waist belt with an alloy friction buckle passed through narrow loops at each hip, and an open-topped, centrally divided patch pocket was fitted to the left breast. In 1937 a second type appeared, with the breast pocket enlarged and moved to the right side, the dividing stitch-line deleted, and a large buttoned flap added. The waist belt, prone to snagging on parts of the aircraft, was replaced by internal cloth tunnels containing fixed cotton tie-tapes.

The *Arbeitsschutzanzug, gefüttert* (lined) matched the unlined suit in style, colours and modifications, but was produced in heavier denim of tight herringbone weave; body and legs were lined with blanket cloth, and the sleeves, crotch and seat had cotton reinforcements – this suit weighed approximately 3kg.

These suits remained largely unaltered throughout the war, although from late 1942 the cotton parts of the lined overalls were being replaced with rayon. Large stocks of military overalls and work clothing were appropriated from occupied countries, and supplies of these frequently augmented the German models. Occasionally a *Schwarze* ('Blackie', a reference to the colour of ground crew overalls) was able to acquire worn-out items of flight clothing from aircrew to make his life a little more comfortable. Particular favourites were flight boots for warmth on cold, wet airfields, and the trousers of the two-piece flight suit, with all their useful pockets for tools and spares.

Insignia were sparse, but junior ranks could wear the *Winkel* (chevrons) appropriate to their grade on the left sleeve. NCOs were distinguished by a full-length (or from 4 September 1942, partial) *Kragentresse* (lace insignia) to the collar. A system of *Ärmelstreifen* (sleeve stripes, worn around the cuffs) was adopted from 27 May 1935 for senior NCOs: *Feldwebel* was denoted by a single stripe, *Oberfeldwebel* by two, and *Stabsfeldwebel* by three and a stylized star. The breast eagle was seldom worn on work clothing.

The wearing of steel-studded boots when working around fuel- and ammunition-laden aircraft carried the risks of sparks, slipping, and damage to the thin alloy skin of the aircraft; nevertheless, the majority of maintenance personnel routinely wore them. Some removed the studs, while others – at their own or unit expense – had replacement rubber soles fitted. Large *Gummiüberschuhe* (rubber overshoes), fastened with four (or, from 1938, two) steel clips, were a limited issue until materiel shortages cancelled them in *c.* 1941. Many elected to wear rubber-soled canvas sports shoes. In the main, thin rubber or padded canvas mats were draped across wing roots to provide safe purchase and protect the aircraft.

FLIGHT CLOTHING
FLIGHT HELMETS

Flieger-Kopfhauben were produced in both summer and winter weights, either with or without integral *Funk-Telegraphie/Telephonie* or FT-*Gerät* (radio-telegraphy/telephony equipment). Throat microphones were fixed to a leather neck strap attached to the nape

Airmen training to fly on the Junkers Ju 88 inspect each other's gear before boarding their aircraft. Recruits would go through a six-month induction before even being considered for air crew.

of the helmet, with press-stud fastening at the front. The internal communications loom emerged just above this in a 1.3m-long cable with a black plastic quick-release jack plug. Oxygen mask fittings comprised flat metal hooks at the sides, and an adjustable wire stirrup mounted inside a tunnel at the crown. A pair of press-stud-fastened leather straps to the rear sides secured the headband of the goggles. The helmets incorporated an awkwardly over-complex system of twin chinstraps, one having to be passed through a slit in the other.

Principal summer-weight helmets were the *Flieger-Kopfhaube für Sommer mit FT-Gerät – Baumuster* S 100 (flight helmet for summer with RT equipment, Model S 100), and the LKp S 101, both made of *Braunmeliert* (mixed brown) thread *Schilfleinen* (reed linen), lined with tan or grey '*Kettatlas*' sateen. Winter-weight versions, of dark brown leather with lambswool lining, were designated LKp W 100 and LKp W 101. The 100-series were identifiable by domed black-lacquered aluminium earphone covers. The WI-series, adopted *c.*1938, featured improved communications equipment and leather-covered plastic earphone covers, incorporating a small ridge which held the goggle headband in place.

A German airman thoughtfully inspects the battle damage to his Fw 189, a twin-boom tactical reconnaissance aircraft produced between 1940 and 1944.

ABOVE: Bf 109G-6 'Yellow 1' of Leutnant Alfred Hammer, Staffelkapitän 6./JG 53 'Pik-As', Vienna-Seyring, February 1944. Note the score depicted on the rudder of Hammer's Bf 109. The last of 11 victories here was a B-24 downed on 30 January 1944. (John Weal © Osprey Publishing)

A lightweight version, the *Flieger-Netzkopfhaube* or LKp N 101, with fine-mesh crown for improved ventilation in summer or the tropics, was approved on 16 June 1941 for use by fighter and destroyer pilots, but soon found favour among other aircrews. The earphones were set within large rigid leather side panels, connected by leather bands across forehead and nape. Oxygen mask fixing hooks were augmented or replaced by hexagonal-based aluminium posts fitted to the leading edges of these side panels, creating two distinct models. The first could take all two- or three-strap mask types, while the other (without adjustable crown stirrup) could only accept two-strap masks.

The communications cable had always been something of an encumbrance and was frequently shortened by base technicians, sometimes drastically so, with the balance transposed to the aircraft interior fittings.

ONE-PIECE FLIGHT SUITS

Most of the world's air force flying suits were simple developments of conventional overalls, with little consideration given to their potential as an aid to survival; their wearers continued to rely upon the chance of recovering survival packs stowed in the aircraft itself. Although the *Fliegerschutzanzug* (flight protective suit) was officially designated simply as a *Kombination* (overall), successive models incorporated innovative features that later became standard in flight clothing design the world over.

Fliegerschutzanzüge were available in summer and winter weights, further sub-designated for flight over land or sea, the latter constructed of materials affording greater insulation. Most aircrews followed this system of matching suit to environment, although availability or personal preferences often dictated what was worn.

Summer: The *Kombination, Sommer*, 1934 (K So/34) was made of the same lightweight, durable *Braunmeliert* cloth as the LKp S helmets. The most notable feature was a long, concealed zip-fastener running diagonally from left hip to right shoulder, where it was covered by a buttoned wind-flap. A zipped patch pocket for maps, etc. was set high on the left breast. A vertically mounted 13.5cm × 3cm brown leather strap, stitched to lower mid-chest and forming two separate loops, provided anchorage for the oxygen mask hose clamp. The sleeves were of three-piece 'raglan' style, incorporating elasticated inner cuff bands with zip closures to the cuff proper. Zip-fastened openings were provided at each hip for access to trouser pockets beneath, and horizontally zipped internal pockets to each knee accommodated survival equipment. Inner calf seams also closed with zips, and the crotch was fitted with a horizontal fly (for easier opening when seated). The K So/34 underwent a series of minor changes, creating seven principal variations. On 17 December 1935 the addition of a short press-stud strap to each sleeve cuff was ordered, to prevent the zip fastener creeping open.

The adoption of an inflatable *Schwimmweste* (life jacket) in 1937 triggered the most significant development. It was intended that the suit be worn *over* the vest to protect it from snagging in the aircraft and chafing by parachute harness; it was therefore necessary to provide quick access to the vest's inflation canister. The most immediate solution was the insertion of a short zip at the midriff, just below and parallel to the main zip. When the vest required oral topping-up, however, the collar and main zip would have to be unfastened in order to reach its inflation tube.

The Berlin company of Karl Heisler developed a quick-opening '*Reissverschluss*' (rip-fastener) device, comprising a series of 35 leather loops passed through 36 steel eyelets and secured by a cord. Tied to the centre of the cord, and concealed beneath a triangular safety flap with press-stud fastening, was a large steel *Griffring* (grasp ring); a continuous pull on this drew the cord from its tunnel and opened the fastener.

This design gave complete and rapid access to both the vest's inflation canister and the mouth tube. The large opening also provided for the expansion of the vest and alleviated chest restriction. Its presence dictated the omission of the chest pocket. Heisler exclusively supplied the device to contracted flight suit manufacturers, hence the appearance of Karl Heisler labels (stitched directly to the fastener) inside suits made by Cunsel & Schroedter of Berlin, Bekleidungsfabrik Habett of Württemberg, and Striegel & Wagner ('*Striwa*') of Bavaria. To speed production, Friedrich Emmerich of Berlin and Tschache & Co. of Dresden later made the device under licence. The rip-fasteners were delivered with cord ends knotted to prevent accidental deployment, and many appear to have remained that way throughout their service life.

From 20 May 1937, manufacturers were instructed to fit zipped pockets into the outer thigh seams for two wound dressing packets (at left), and the *Flieger-Kappmesser 37*

RIGHT: Josef Priller (seated, left) was a German fighter ace with 101 aerial kills to his credit. Standing by his side is Erich Hartmann, who ended his combat career with an astonishing 352 kills, mostly achieved on the Eastern Front.

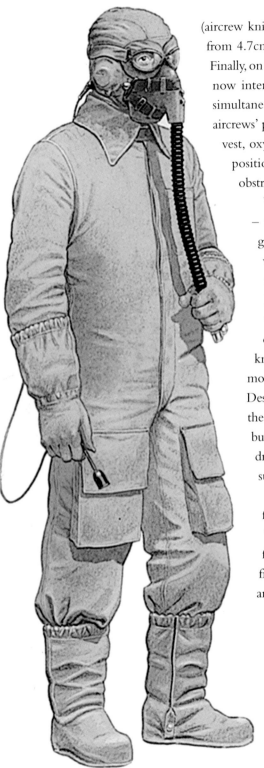

(aircrew knife) was secured within a small inner pocket; a width increase from 4.7cm to 5cm to this inner pocket was ordered on 10 November. Finally, on 7 June 1940, a slightly reduced left breast pocket was reinstated, now internally mounted with zipless external access. The fly zip was simultaneously lengthened and set vertically. As if in recognition of aircrews' persistence in wearing the suit under rather than over the life vest, oxygen hose chest loop-straps were reduced to 2cm wide and positioned slightly higher – encroaching on the pocket – to avoid obstruction by the vest.

Winter, Land: The *Kombination, Winter, Land,* 1933 (KW 1/33) – nicknamed the '*Bayerisch*' (Bavarian) – was of fine quality grey-blue or brown '*Velveton*' moleskin cloth, lined throughout with sheepskin. A conventional vertical front closure was retained, in keeping with its contemporary K So/33 and KW s/33, but fastened with eight large ceramic buttons rather than a zip. Large patch pockets with deeply scalloped flaps and ceramic buttons were provided at the hips and just above the knees. These suits generally lacked the chest loop-straps of other models, the oxygen hose being clipped to the front placket instead. Despite its designation, possible use for flights over water prompted the addition of a vertical *Schwimmweste* access zip to the right of the button closure, or the *Heisler-Reissverschluss*. Outer thigh knife and dressing pockets also appeared concurrently with those of the summer model.

This layout remained unaltered until 7 June 1940, when all future production was ordered standardized with other types. The button front was replaced by a diagonal main zip, a vertical fly was added, and an internal pocket with external access was fitted to the left breast – existing stocks could be modified with an external patch pocket.

LEFT: Major Wolfgang Späte, *Geschwaderkommodore* of JG 400 at Brandis in April 1945, models the special one-piece suit designed to protect pilots flying the Me 163. Note the elasticated cuffs to the gloves and boot tops. The goggles and oxygen mask were essential extras to guard against toxic vapour fumes in the cockpit. Although it was claimed to be acid-proof by the manufacturers, many pilots complained that the material of the suit 'leaked like a sieve'. Späte failed to score in the Me 163, but subsequently achieved last-minute jet 'acedom' on the Me 262. (John Weal © Osprey Publishing)

Winter, Sea: Evolved from the leather KW s/33, the KW s/34 was made of dark brown '*Kalbin*' (calfskin), with diagonal main zip, heavy fleece lining, and large black or brown mouton collar. Principal details and modifications followed those of the K So/34 although, during 1940, the bulky hide was rejected in favour of supple '*Nacktpelz*' (lit. 'naked pelt', or sheepskin); the suede outer surface was left undyed. The KW s/34 was fitted with midriff zip or *Heisler-Reissverschluss* from 1937, sometimes concurrently. Although the zip could be resealed, thereby preserving some warmth and comfort when immersed, it was difficult to operate with cold, wet or gloved hands.

The KW s/34 was costly and slow to produce, and a pre-war Austrian type, distinguished by two full-length zips running from collar to ankle cuff, was frequently issued instead.

Electrically heated: When necessary, winter suits could be worn over the dark grey cotton *Kombination mit electrischer Beheizung* (K 20/24), an electrically heated undersuit adopted from 25 June 1936. This was worn in conjunction with *Flieger-Füsslinge mit electrischer Beheizung* (F 20/24) heated socks, and *Flieger-Handschuhe mit electrischer Beheizung* (Ha 14/24) heated gloves, worn over fine *Unterziehwollhandschuhe* (lit. 'under heated wool gloves'). The power cable of the heated clothing left the suit at the small of the back, and could be passed through a hip pocket vent of the outer suit for connection to the aircraft's circuit. This suit fell from use by 1939.

For single-seaters: The winter suits, awkward enough in the confines of a bomber, were quite unsuitable for the tiny cockpit of the fighters, although many saw such use. On 16 February 1940 a new *Kombination, Winter, für Flugzeuge mit beschränkten Raumverhältnissen, 1940* (KW Fl bR/40) was approved for use in 'aircraft with limited space'. These comparatively lightweight suits, of tightly woven grey-blue '*Schappe*' synthetic silk twill, were lined throughout with 4mm *Schappe* velveteen of deep blue or purple, which also faced the large fall collar. Although not heated, the suit bore an electrical circuit with external connectors at wrist and calf, to convey power from the aircraft's rheostat supply to heated gloves and boots. Of standard diagonal-zipped style with *Heisler-Reissverschluss*, this suit was also subject to the modifications of 7 June 1940.

TWO-PIECE FLIGHT SUITS

Production of one-piece suits was officially halted on 24 April 1941, although some existing contracts were not completed until 1942. Each type was henceforth to be produced as a *Flieger-Schutzanzug, Kombination (zweiteilig) 1941*, and these two-piece suits began to see service by the middle of that year.

The jacket was a relatively simple affair with single left breast pocket, and a double loop-strap of leather or matching cloth to one side of the vertical main zip. The real

OVERLEAF: Technical ground crew set to work repairing the engine of a Bf 109 fighter. As the war progressed, the pressures upon groundcrew to keep aircraft operational mounted, especially as losses began to keep pace with production.

advance lay in the design of the trousers, with their voluminous pockets for rescue and survival equipment. The selection of items carried was to individual choice, but routinely included emergency rations and medical kit. Frequently worn with jackets other than that intended, the trousers not only offered versatility and greater ease of movement, but had obvious practical advantages during latrine visits. The use of insignia on the two-piece suits was limited; breast eagles and sleeve rank badges or epaulettes were often fitted to the cloth versions, while sheepskin types were usually left unadorned.

Summer: The jacket of the K So/41 had a small fall collar with press-stud tab, and plain split cuffs with two-button adjustment. The bulk of production was in grey-blue (sometimes grey-green) cloth with wool-knit waistband, but an alternative version was produced in the same tan *Braunmeliert* cloth as its parent K So/34. This type had a matching cloth waistband, adjustable at each side by internally mounted alloy friction buckles and cloth straps, and closed with two 'Prym' press-studs. Stocks of the tan cloth were exhausted during 1943. The trouser waistband was adjustable by friction buckles at each hip front, and fitted with buttons or web loop attachments for cloth braces. An internal flannel apron was often fitted to prevent heavy equipment from chafing the wearers' thighs.

Winter, Land: The KW 1/41, equivalent of the '*Bayerisch*' KW 1/33, was primarily manufactured in soft blue cloth (occasionally olive-green), with sheepskin lining and large fleece collar. The canvas waistband had friction buckle adjusters. In addition to an internal chest pocket with external opening, two diagonal slash pockets were set at lower front and usually fastened with press-stud tabs. Trouser cloth tended to be more tightly woven than that used for the jacket and of a deeper grey-blue colour.

Winter, Sea: Original production of the KW s/41 was of high quality natural sheepskin with dark brown or black inner fleece and collar. The single patch chest pocket and loop-strap were of either matching suede or contrasting leather, and the canvas waistband fastened with two press-studs. Diagonal slash pockets with press-stud fasteners were later added. The sheepskin trousers were considered too weak to support fully laden survival equipment pockets and so lacked this feature. Canvas reinforcement panels extending from the waistband were incorporated to distribute the load and resolve this weakness, these versions being produced in brown and grey-blue dyed sheepskin with similarly coloured pockets and reinforcements.

Electrically heated: The KW Fl bR/4I was of the same heavy duty grey-blue canvas as the one-piece KW FI bR/40, with *Schappe* lining and connectors for heated boots and gloves; similar contacts were necessarily added to the waistbands of jacket and trousers to complete the circuit. An all-leather version of this suit was produced in late 1943, of substantial black, brown or grey hide, to provide limited protection from the highly corrosive synthetic fuels then in use.

GLOVES

Four types of brown leather *Flieger-Lederhandschuhe* were adopted in 1933. Summer types were designated '*mit*' or '*ohne*' *Stulpe, ungefüttert* ('with' or 'without gauntlet, unlined'), HS 5 m/33 and 0/33. Winter equivalents were designated '*gefüttert*' (lined), FW 5 m/33 and FW 5 0/33. Press-stud or buckle-fastened straps were provided at wrist and cuff for a wind-resistant fit. Electrically heated FW m/40 gloves developed for the wired KW Fl bR/40 and /41 suits were of soft grey-blue or brown suede, with 8w/24v element, fine *Schappe* lining, and connectors at the gauntlet cuff. Black, brown and grey-blue coloured heated and unheated gloves were produced in conjunction with the all-leather KW/41 suit.

FOOTWEAR

The *Flieger-Pelzstiefel* (flyer's fur-lined boots) had a stout leather foot with rubber heel and sole. The black or charcoal-grey sheepskin shafts had full-length steel zips at inner and outer calf, to ease fitting over several layers of clothing; the outer calf zip was discontinued for economy during 1940. Leather tightening straps, buckled around the top of the shafts and across the front of the ankles, were intended to prevent boots being torn off by parachute opening shock. Material quality deteriorated from the mid-war period, with shafts assembled from joined off-cuts rather than single panels, and fugitive dyes resulted in some discoloration; but construction standards remained high. *Heizbare Flieger-Pelzstiefel* (heated flyers' boots) for the KW Fl bR/40 and /41 suits differed only in the inclusion of an llw/24v electric element inside the lining and leather connector tabs at the outer top.

RIGHT Major Georg-Peter Eder, Staffelkapitän of 9./JG 7 at Parchim in February 1945, is seen wearing typical late-war garb of a two-piece black leather zippered flying suit with large patch pockets on each thigh, plus officer's pattern belt and the Luftwaffe version of the M1943 'standard model' soft cap issued to all services. Note also the sun-goggles, rank tabs, and the Knight's Cross with Oak Leaves at his throat. Scoring his first two kills on 22 June 1941 (the opening day of the attack on the Soviet Union), Eder's incident-packed career included being shot down on 17 occasions and wounded a dozen times in the process. (John Weal © Osprey Publishing)

NON-ISSUE FLIGHT JACKETS

Jagdflieger were quick to adopt practical items suited to the close confines of the cockpit, a short leather jacket being the preference. Such garments were not issued but generally purchased at individual expense from various sources, and some sub-units or just small groups of friends would acquire matching jackets. Among the most coveted of the home-produced versions was an expensive black leather suit with distinctive zip-fastened slash pockets. With the occupation of conquered nations countless alternatives were readily available from civilian outlets wherever the pilot was stationed. Differences in cut, fastenings and pockets soon proliferated, with a particular French style among the most popular. The occasionally encountered cloth versions tended to be blue, grey-blue or cream, with wool-knit waistband, collar and (sometimes) cuffs. When fitted with insignia the flight jackets were extremely handsome in appearance – which naturally appealed to the inherent panache of fighter pilots. Although collar patches were rarely added, a few NCOs applied *Metallschwingen* directly to the collar.

Additional sources were the British Air Ministry, US Army Quartermaster Department and Soviet *Voiyeno-Vozdushnui Syl* – many items being 'souvenired' from downed Allied aircrews. The USAAF A2 flyers' jacket was a particular favourite, and was routinely worn by the legendary Heinz Bar; while Adolf Galland was famously pictured in RAF Irvin sheepskin jacket and trousers. Whatever their origin, all were for operational wear only and were not permitted to be worn off-base, where a more 'military' form of attire was demanded.

High-quality brown leather and suede boots with inner calf zips, commercially available from Paul Hoffmann & Co., Berlin, were particularly popular during the early years. Black all-leather *Flieger-Überziehpelzstiefel* (lit. 'over heated fur boots') with fine white lambswool-lining, designed for wear over the electrically heated F 20/24 socks, were officially discontinued in June 1939 but remained in (vigorously polished) service throughout the war.

TROPICAL UNIFORM

By comparison with colonial powers, Germany had had only limited experience of such uniform before the war. In 1940 well-established foreign designs provided the starting point for the Hanover Institute's Tropical Studies Department, and the resulting uniforms were among the best in the Wehrmacht's inventory – practical, comfortable, versatile and dashingly modern in appearance.

While those of the Army tended towards an olive green hue, the Luftwaffe *Tropenanzug* was of more traditional orange-sand colour – at least when new. The combined ravages of African sun, dust storms, heavy sweating and frequent washing (often in petrol, marginally less scarce than water) all took their toll, and some items became bleached almost white. Resupply problems kept heavily worn and repaired items in use longer than was normally acceptable. Shirts and footwear suffered most, although these could occasionally be supplemented from captured Allied stocks. Apart from insignia, the items constituting *Tropenanzug* 41, issued to all ranks and branches, were identical from *Flieger* to *General*.

HEADGEAR

The cloth-covered *Tropenhelm* (sun helmet) had a noticeably deep curve to the wide brim, providing efficient protection, and a tan leather chinstrap. It was usually lined with light green, a combination of tan and green, or occasionally orange cotton cloth; these colours, like the red of the Army version, were believed to provide the best defence from solar radiation while allowing body heat to dissipate. Stamped metal insignia, following those worn on the steel helmet, were fixed to each side of the *Tropenhelm* in the form of a *Wappen* (shield) of national colours to the right, and the Luftwaffe's flying eagle *Hoheitsabzeichen* to the left.

Far more popular was the *Tropenfliegermütze* (tropical flyer's cap), a lightweight cotton version of the wool *Fliegermütze*, usually lined with fine tan linen. The cap bore a dull white eagle woven onto tan cotton backing, but retained the continental *Reichskokarde*. Period photographs and surviving examples regularly show a vertical crease to the centre of the body, where it was folded and carried in a pocket when not required.

All ranks were also entitled to the *Tropenschirmmütze mit Nackenschutz* (tropical peaked cap with neck protector). These heavy tan cotton caps had a broad crown, a distinctly large peak and a button-on neck curtain which gave good protection, but were costly to produce and difficult to store and carry. They were supplied with BeVO[2] woven versions of standard *Schirmmütze* insignia; but some officers chose to embellish them with wire or metal equivalents, added crown-seam piping, or bullion wire chin cords substituted for the original 1.2cm brown leather chinstrap.

Strangely, the Luftwaffe did not issue its own official version of the famous 'Afrikamütze', although some factory-made examples were available, and some personnel had approximations made up by unit or local tailors. These caps were often slightly less shapely than the official Army pattern (e.g. without the small bulge to the crown front), and generally lacked ventilation eyelets to the sides. Another expedient was simply to add Luftwaffe insignia to a traded or 'liberated' Army issue cap.

ABOVE: Ju 87B-2 trop 'A5+MK' of 2./StG 1, Derna/Libya, October 1941. After their brief stint in the Balkans, I./StG 1 returned to North Africa, where they would remain until the end of the campaign (latterly as II./StG 3). The overall RLM 79 tan finish worn by 'MK' is outward evidence of the *Gruppe's* adaptation to desert warfare. Note that the white theatre band has been relocated behind the fuselage cross. (John Weal © Osprey Publishing)

TUNIC

The *Tropenrock* (tropical tunic) was a four-pocket design with convertible collar, echoing the failed *Waffenrock* 38, but with six-button closure and made of hard-wearing cotton canvas. The collar fastened with a single hook-&-eye and a concealed tab and button, although this was rarely used. A tropical *Hoheitsabzeichen*, heavily woven in dull white on a tan backing, was machined above the right breast with tight zigzag stitching during manufacture. Only the breast pockets were pleated, while skirt pockets were of 'bellows' construction; some of the more frugal manufacturers cut the main panel in two sections and joined them with a central vertical seam. The shallow cuffs had buttoned vents allowing some adjustment. Only the armpits and pockets were lined, with a combination of heavy canvas and absorbent open-weave hessian, although belt hook support straps and field dressing pocket were retained.

SHIRTS AND TIES

Both the *Tropenhemd* '*mit lang*' and '*mit kurz*' Armel (tropical shirts with long and short sleeves) were of robust cotton and featured fashionably long, pointed collars which could accept plastic stiffeners. Large pleated breast pockets had deeply scalloped flaps. A special version of the breast eagle, woven in white onto a triangular cotton backing ranging in hue from tan to light chocolate, was provided, as were cloth stirrups and brown-painted pebbled alloy buttons for the *Schulterklappen* 40. The front and pocket buttons were of either brown or grey ceramic, composition fibre or dished steel, and most were removable by means of a smaller plastic button sewn to the rear. Both types of shirt featured very long tails enabling them to double as nightwear, and spare cloth was often cut from these to repair worn collar and cuffs. For walking-out and parade dress the broad cotton *khakibraun Tropenbinder* (tropical necktie) was worn.

TROUSERS

The long *Tropenhose* were of conventional straight cut. They featured a matching cloth waist belt with an alloy friction buckle, contained within a tunnel, two rear pockets with gently scalloped concealed-button flaps, and two angled slash hip pockets. They saw only limited service, production being halted during 1942 in favour of the more comfortable and practical *Tropenüberfallhose* (lit. 'assault trousers'). These had very loosely cut legs, with a large map pocket to the front of the left thigh, and were gathered and bloused at the ankle by means of a strap and buckle arrangement like that of the waist belt. This could be fastened in two ways: either through the buckle, or (more quickly) drawn across the front of the ankle and engaged with a small button at the outer seam. One manufacturing variant used narrow square-ended straps fastening to machine-stamped, open-frame steel buckles like those found on *Gebirgsjäger Rucksacke* and *Gelkenbinden* (puttees).

Kurze Tropenhose (tropical shorts) followed exactly the line of the trousers, terminating just above the knee. In the Wehrmacht the wearing of shorts was officially restricted to off-duty periods, other than walking-out, in rear areas only. In North Africa their use on frontline bases was permitted, and shorts were even occasionally worn as flight clothing.

RIGHT: Hauptmann Franz Schall, *Staffelkapitän* of 10./JG 7 at Parchim in March 1945, wears breeches similar to those worn by Kurt Welter, but paired with knee boots and a lightweight flying blouse. Prominent are the Luftwaffe eagle on the right breast, *Hauptmann*'s rank tabs on the shoulders, and the Knight's Cross, which was awarded on 10 October 1944 for 177 victories. After transferring to jets, first with the Kommando Nowotny and then JG 7, Schall scored 14 kills before he lost his own life on 10 April 1945 during an emergency landing at Parchim when his Me 262 ran into a bomb crater and exploded. (John Weal © Osprey Publishing)

Hermann Göring salutes with his marshal's baton during a march past by German troops. During World War I, Göring had himself risen to the rank of fighter ace, with 22 confirmed kills.

Some officers and senior NCOs chose to wear tropical versions of the riding breeches produced in tan whipcord fabric (also occasionally used in the manufacture of the *Tropenrock*, *Tropenhose* and *Überfallhose*), but these were unpopular due to the discomfort of tightly fitted calves.

FOOTWEAR

Throughout the first half of the desert campaign most personnel had to wear the standard issue long or ankle boots; unless regularly oiled the leather was prone to severe cracking from the harsh, dry heat, particularly at the toe-bend and ankle. During 1942 the specially developed ankle-high *Tropen-Schnürschuhe* and higher *Tropen-Schnürstiefel mit Segeltuchschaft khakibraun* (with khaki-brown canvas shaft) began to arrive in quantity.

OVERCOAT

Unlike the Army, the Luftwaffe did not adopt a tropical version of the overcoat, and the grey-blue *Übermantel* remained standard despite the extreme cold of the desert nights.

WINTER UNIFORM
HEADGEAR

Apart from the issue sheepskin *Pelzmütze* with short peak and curtain, a wide variety of headgear from various sources was employed. Some were fashioned by the men themselves, who occasionally inflicted unofficial modifications upon the standard *Fliegermütze* in the form of rabbitskin or sheepskin curtains to the sides. Some acquired the high-topped Romanian lambswool *caciula,* or the Red Army *ushanka* with folding earflaps.

UNDERGARMENTS

Supplementary *Angorawäsche* (angora wool underwear) was issued, and some were lucky enough to receive a 37–42cm by 120–150cm flannel *Leibbinde* (waistband), a traditional item which helped maintain body core temperature. Two types of grey-white ribbed-knit sweater, with 15mm grey-blue collar stripe, were available. The six-button cardigan-style *Unterjacke* had a V-neck designed to be unseen when worn with the *Rock* or *Fliegerbluse*. The round-necked pullover *Schlupfjacke* 36 had a three-button placket that could be turned back out of sight when necessary. The collar stripe was omitted on the replacement *Schlupfjacke* 42. Quilted rayon *Zwischenweste u. Zwischenhose* (lit. 'between-vest & between-trousers'), fastening with cotton tapes, were produced from 1941, the trousers with external waistband loops through which braces were passed before buttoning to *Tuchhose*. Although intended as additional inner layers these items were occasionally worn as outer garments. Sheepskin waistcoats and rabbitskin jackets, *Pelzjacken*, with large axial vents for ease of movement, were also produced as undergarments but frequently worn as topcoats. The grey knit *Halschal* (neck scarf) and *Kopfschützer* (head protector) – a tubular toque – provided additional insulation.

OVERGARMENTS

Full length sheepskin coats with cloth collar and tape-reinforced seams were issued to personnel in exposed positions, such as vehicle drivers and gunners. Thigh-length versions with a large fleece collar were also produced. Late in 1941 uniquely styled cotton canvas oversuits were developed, reversible from olive-grey to white and with distinctive squared or diagonally stitched quilting, but these were mainly issued to *Fallschirmjäger*. This extravagance was dropped during mid-1942 in favour of the Army's *schwere Winteranzug* (heavy winter suit), comprising *Überziehjacke*, *Überziehose*, *Kopfhaube* or *Kappe* (hood) and *Fausthandschuhe* (mittens). The mouse-grey, and later *Buntfarbendruck*

BELOW: Fw 190A-3 'White 11' of Hauptmann Herbert Wehnelt, *Staffelkapitän* 7./JG 51, Orel, c. January 1943. Its coat of winter white already showing distinct signs of wear and tear, Wehnelt's 'White 11' has also had the upper part of its aft fuselage yellow theatre band painted over to reduce visibility from above. (John Weal © Osprey Publishing)

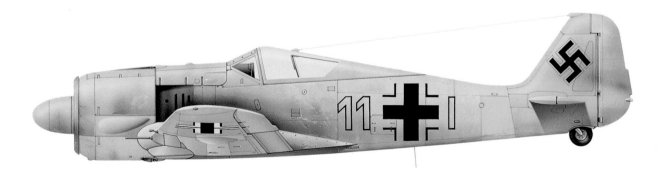

A German radar antenna sits in Europe somewhere during World War II. The Luftwaffe developed one of the world's most sophisticated interception systems, giving warning of approaching bombers as soon as they entered mainland European airspace.

(mixed-colour print) and *Sumpfmuster* (marsh pattern) camouflaged sides were either fully reversible to *Altweiss* (off-white), or non-reversible with grey-blue rayon lining. Huge stocks of captured or salvaged Soviet quilted jackets and trousers were washed, repaired and re-issued.

FOOTWEAR

The enormous *Filzschuhe* (felt shoes) adopted from 5 March 1940, and often wrongly described as unpaired, were designed to fit over standard boots during prolonged static duties – particularly sentry duty. Coarse hair felt uppers, buckled at front or rear with two leather straps, were stitched to rigid leather toe and heel sections, which in turn were nailed to thick wooden soles to distance and insulate the feet from snow and ice. An alternative type was available to those engaged in more active tasks, such as vehicle and artillery crews. Stout grey hair-felt uppers with brown leather front and rear seam reinforcement were stitched to a leather foot, or often separate heel and toe sections, with moulded rubber soles. A similar third type, *Schneestiefel* (snow boots), chiefly used by motorcyclists and drivers, had proofed and lined white canvas uppers and shafts, incorporating lace-up collars that could be drawn to form a wind- and snow-tight seal below the knee. Whitened leather reinforcing strips overlapped the noticeably peaked toe section. Soviet *valenkii* felt over-boots also saw widespread use.

SAFETY EQUIPMENT AND SURVIVAL AIDS
HEADGEAR

Aircrew seeking increased head protection initially had to improvise with the standard issue *Stahlhelm* 35 or 40 steel helmet, some of which had the sides forced or hammered outwards in base workshops so as to accommodate the earphones of flight helmets worn underneath. Several experimental models followed from 1940 – e.g. the *Flieger-Sturzhelm* (crash helmet), and Siemens SSK 90 constructed from leather-covered steel plates – but trials proved unsuccessful. A *Flieger-Stahlhelm* proper, similar in design to the *Fallschirmjäger* style but with large cut-outs for the earphones, was finally adopted in late 1944, but was produced in very limited numbers and saw little use.

OXYGEN MASKS

Numerous models of *Höhenatemmaske* were employed. Most comprised a green rubber facepiece, sometimes with a soft leather skirt for warmth and wind protection, and were secured to the helmet by two or three elastic or sprung straps. The hose was ribbed to prevent twisting or icing. The most common models were the HM 5 or HM 15 (large) and 10-67, with three-strap fittings; the two-strap 10-6701, occasionally converted to three straps; the three-strap 10-6702, and the two-strap 10-69. These were variously produced by Auer-Gessellschaft of Berlin, and Drägerwerke of Lübeck.

GOGGLES

Late 1930s developments culminated in the M295 and M295a *Windschutzbrille* (wind protective glasses) with one-piece grey-brown rubber frame; and the M306 *Fliegerschutzbrille* with separate rubber eyepads connected by a screw-adjusted bridge. The curved lenses permitted optimum vision, while offering good protection from flying debris. Most were supplied by Auer or Lietz, in a metal or cardboard container complete with cleaning leather or cloth and a selection of 'Neophan' or 'Umbral' tinted lenses against solar, searchlight or snow glare. *Splitterschutzbrille* (splinter protective glasses), with non-refractive lenses developed by Nitsche & Gunther, consolidated all these attributes.

CLOTHING & EQUIPMENT

Fliegerschutzbrillen, with flip-down red filters, helped reduce searchlight flare by night, desert sun and snow glare (1). The 1936 K20/24v suit (2) was worn beneath unwired flight suits for use with heated gloves and boots. A contact at shoulder-blade level was provided for heated goggles.

The modern 1941 *Fliegerhose (4)* incorporated special stowage pockets for the 27mm flare-pistol and telescopic signal-flag (3), ten flare-cartridges and *Kappmesser 37* gravity-activated knife and two wound-dressings (5) alongside numerous other survival items. An internal 'apron' was sometimes incorporated, providing some comfort and chafe protection (6). Noteworthy details include steel or cloth lanyard-securing loops, canvas pocket-supports, seat-reinforcing panels, electric cable exit position and leather bandage securing-loops. Security buttons or pull-tags were occasionally added by '*Fallschirmwarte*' (parachute/safety equipment fitters) upon request (4). Early clothing manufacturers' labels provided vital, industrial targeting information to enemy intelligence, so in late 1942, a *Reichsbetriebsnummer* (Imperial works number) system was adopted for secrecy (7). Some producers missed the point, however, and briefly used the Rb.Nr., alongside their factory address! The three principal oxygen-mask types were the 2-strap *Dräger* 10-69 (8), 3-strap *Auer* 10-67 with chamois face protector (9) and double-strap *Dräger* 10-6701 (10). Illustrated beside the 1-man lifeboat-pack (11), the contents of the 3-man survival-accessories pack, as detailed on its label (12), included medical kit, sun-shades and frostbite creams, with booklets detailing cold and sea survival techniques. Additional flare-cartridges were carried in commercially produced *Patronengurt* belts of varying design (13), and *Patronenreimen* cartridge-straps (14), typically secured to upper calves. The 1.5 volt, 0.5 amp *Seenotleuchte* air-sea rescue signal light (15), with a battery duration of 8 hours, could be clipped to a lanyard (and left to float), or directly to the *Schwimmweste*, here an SWp 734 B1 (16). (Karl Kopinski © Osprey Publishing)

LIFE VESTS

Aircrew serving in single-seat and multi-seat aircraft could wear either of two main life vest types according to preference or availability. The first was the Heisler-designed kapok-filled *Schwimmweste* 10-76A, of dull yellow cotton canvas and distinctive semi-rigid 'sausage' construction, with cord loop and wooden toggle fastenings, and a large lifting collar designed to hold the wearer's head above water. The design quickly proved a danger to unconscious or wounded airmen: as the back panel was larger than the front, and therefore more buoyant, it could easily flip a man face-down in rough water. Introduced by the end of 1940, the improved SW 10-76 B1 overcame the problem by replacing this panel with a simple yoke and system of web straps. At the same time the collar was slightly remodelled and fitted with a set of snap-fastened chin supports.

The second, more compact type was the inflatable *Schwimmweste pneumatisch* 734 10-30 (SWp 734) developed by Drägerwerke in 1936–37. This was made of soft proofed cotton duck, and activated by means of a 0.06-litre compressed air cylinder mounted on the lower

left front panel, or a rubber mouth inflation tube on the left breast. The SWp 734 had a brown-coloured body with contrasting brick-red shoulder yoke and collar section, and fastened with grey-black webbing straps and double O-ring friction buckles at waist and mid-chest. Although some aircrew wore the inflatable vest in the prescribed manner, under the flight suit, the great majority did not. It was a practical step, therefore, to replace the dull brown with a more visible yellow colour to assist in rescue operations, but the vest remained otherwise unchanged.

The SWp 743 suffered from a design fault similar to the kapok-filled type, in that its back panel incorporated an inflation bladder below shoulder level, causing the same danger of inversion. A simultaneous redesign resulted in the SWp 743 10-30 B1 with open back, yoke and strap arrangement. Early 1941 saw the introduction of the 10-30 B2, differing only in the replacement of some metal fittings with cheaper plastic – in particular the nickel-plated mouthpiece to the inflation tube, which in extreme cold could freeze to a man's lips.

PARACHUTES

Like most contemporary air forces, the Luftwaffe employed three distinctive configurations of parachute; adopted in 1936, these remained essentially unaltered until 1945. The principal models in wartime use were the seat-type *Sitzfallschirm* 30IS-24B (fl 30231); back-type *Rückenfallschirm* 12B (fl 30245); and *Fallschirmgurt* 30-11-24 (fl 30208) harness with quick-attach *Brustfallschirm* 10-3 Dl (fl 30210) chest pack. Selection was dictated by aircraft type and crew position; the aircrew of single- and two-seat aircraft using back or seat types, while the different members of bomber crews needed all three.

All contained an average 7.32m diameter canopy (5m when deployed) of white silk or 'Mako' synthetic weave; this could be safely deployed at speeds of up to 400km/h, giving an average descent rate of 6.5m/sec. Much pre-war development had been shared between Germany and Great Britain and all three models bore striking resemblances to their RAF counterparts, not least in the use of the quick-release *Schloss-Autoflug* (SA) buckle copied from the British Irvin design. Like Allied types, but unlike the *Fallschirmjäger* pattern, the harness featured webbing risers from the shoulders which kept the centre of gravity high for a safer landing.

ADDITIONAL EQUIPMENT

A broad range of survival equipment was provided for aircrews, dictated by environment. This included highly nutritious *Absprungverpflegung* ('bail-out subsistence' rations), Model 9 'Esbit-Kocher' folding field cookers with solid fuel tablets, *Sanitatspack* (medical kits), quilted kapok-filled *Schlafsack* (sleeping bags), and high-quality machetes.

Two-, three- or four-man *Rettungsschlauchboote* (inflatable rescue dinghies) could be stowed in larger aircraft, or an individual *Einmannschlauchboot* was carried in a special pack on the man himself. The battery-powered NSG1 *Funkgerät* (radio transmitter) originally stowed with these boats was superseded, from 1941, by the smaller generator-powered NSG2 & 4 models; these hand-cranked versions offered far greater duration, with the added benefits of keeping men active, focused and warm. Recognition equipment included the *Farbbeutel* (dye-marker pouch), *Sichtfahne* (signal flag) and *Rauchsichtzeichen* (smoke marker).

Crewmen routinely carried a *Leuchtpistole* (flare pistol) with a generous supply of coloured *Signalpatrone* and *Leuchtpatrone* (signal and flare cartridges), along with *Fallschirmsignalpatrone* and *Fallschirmleuchtpatrone* 41 parachute types. The initial practice of carrying cartridges loose in a pocket was unsatisfactory. Various commercially produced *Taille-Riemen für Leuchtpatronen* (waist straps for flare cartridges) saw limited use but were awkward to wear with the parachute and life vest. By far the most practical method was the ten-round *Patronengurt* worn round one or both lower legs.

The gravity-activated *Flieger-Kappmesser* 37 knife was primarily to enable bailed-out airmen to cut themselves free of entangled parachute risers and shroud-lines. Some standard flight equipment, such as the *Armbandkompass* 39 (wrist compass) and *Luftnavigationskarte* (air navigation maps), could be equally useful on the ground. The durable plasticized-linen maps were often printed on yellow background cloth that gave a clear, less reflective image under red night-lights.

Thus organized, clothed and equipped, the Luftwaffe personnel served in both peace and war. In the latter, service took them to every imaginable type of landscape and theatre, from the tropical heat of North Africa to the crushing winters of the Soviet Union, from idyllic service in France in 1941 to a death-battle above the Reich in 1944 and 1945. Our next chapter turns to the heaviest element of their warfighting capability – the bomber.

BOMBERS —
STRATEGIC
REACH

Luftwaffe ground crew on the Eastern Front attempt to warm up the engines of Ju 88s prior to operations, erecting protective heated tents around each engine. The Ju 88 served on every German front, forming the core of the German tactical bomber force.

As noted in Chapter 1, the Luftwaffe was never graced with a bomber arm comparable to that fielded by the British or the Americans. The strategic penalties of this structure have already been discussed, but we should never downplay the fact that the German bomber arm was, nevertheless, able to inflict massive damage when it sought to do so. More than 40,000 British civilians were killed in the Blitz of 1940–41 and Stalingrad was virtually razed to the ground in the early autumn of 1942 by relentless air attacks. As a support arm to land forces, the bombers were an integral element of *Blitzkrieg*, pounding enemy troop concentrations to prepare the way for an advance. The bomber arm may have been ultimately overshadowed in importance by Hitler's fighters, but it still provided the Wehrmacht with its most significant tactical and strategic reach.

BOMBER AIRCRAFT

Forming the heaviest element of the Luftwaffe's medium bomber arm, the He 111 has quite rightly been described by one noted aviation historian as 'one of the most outstanding warplanes of the mid-1930s'. Like its two contemporaries, the Dornier Do 17 and Junkers Ju 88 (all three types would make their maiden flights within weeks of each other in the late autumn/winter of 1934/35), the He 111 stemmed from specifications secretly drawn up by the German Army's Ordnance Bureau in July 1932. This was in the days before Adolf Hitler's rise to power, and the then ruling Weimar Government was still at pains to pay at least lip service to the restrictions imposed on German rearmament by the Treaty of Versailles.

Consequently, the Dornier, Heinkel and Junkers companies were each required to produce a design for a high-speed, twin-engined all-metal monoplane that would be presented to the outside world as a prestigious new passenger/mailplane for Germany's national airline, Deutsche Lufthansa, but which, at the same time, could also be developed as a modern and state-of-the-art medium bomber for the country's fledgling – and as yet still clandestine – military air arm, the Reichsluftwaffe.

The first prototype flight of Heinkel's new aircraft took place on 24 February 1935, after which the He 111 went through a whole raft of mechanical, powerplant and aerodynamic modifications. It was combat-ready enough, however, to fly in the Legion Condor during the Spanish Civil War, working alongside Ju 52 transports co-opted into the bombing role. By the beginning of World War II it had emerged into its defining version – the He 111H, fitted with two 1,350hp Junkers Jumo 211 piston engines. Instantly recognizable through its asymetric glass nose, the five-crew He 111 had a top speed of around 436km/h, a service ceiling of 6,700m and a range of 1,950km. Although the He 111's bomb-load varied according to its model, it could typically carry an internal bomb-load of 2,000kg, and the same externally (over the internal bomb bay). Defensive armament came in the form of assorted cannon and machine guns, set in the nose and in dorsal and ventral positions.

The sheer variety of models and purposes of the He 111 is impossible to boil down into concise form. The aircraft's roles included glider tug, paratroop transport, pathfinder, night bomber and even the platform for aerial launch of the Fi 103 flying bomb. What it was not, however, was equal competition for the best of the Allied heavy bombers.

The He 111 was emphatically a medium bomber, and fell a long way short of the capabilities of the Lancaster or B-17. The former, for example, could fly to a range of 4,070km with a 10,000kg bomb load, and at an altitude of 7,470m. There was only one German bomber that offered similar potential, and that was the Heinkel He 177 'Greif' (Griffon), design of which began in 1938 following an RLM request for a heavy long-range bomber. The He 177 was a long, slender aircraft, with an innovative powerplant.

A He 111 unleashes its bombs over the target area. Depending on the variant and configuration, the He 111 could carry around 4,000kg of bombs internally and externally, the external ordnance often being of types too large to fit into the bomb bay.

ABOVE: Ju 88A-5 'L1+GN' of 5./LG 1, Grottaglie, Italy, April 1941. Some doubt still exists as to the colour of the Balkans theatre markings applied to a number of LG 1 aircraft during the brief Yugoslav and Greek campaigns. Photographic sources seem to suggest the colouration depicted here. (John Weal © Osprey Publishing)

Instead of having four engines (two per wing), it featured four DB 601 engines coupled in pairs within single engine nacelles, driving single propellers. The system was powerful but problematic, and was known for overheating. When the going was good, however, the He 177 could take a 6,000kg bomb-load to 5,500km, and it saw service from mid-1942. Missions included raids over Britain, and supply missions to Stalingrad in 1942/43. More unusual variants included a version designed to carry three Hs 293 anti-ship missiles, the He 177A-5 fitted with 33 rocket-firing tubes, and even a model intended to carry a future atomic bomb. Yet ultimately, only 1,160 He 177s were built, and the limited numbers and troubled maintenance meant they could never make a significant contribution to the Luftwaffe's wartime capabilities.

The He 177 was not the only heavy bomber constructed by the Luftwaffe in World War II. Other aircraft in this category include the Junkers Ju 390, the Messerschmitt Me 264 and several prototypes, some intended to become the transatlantic 'Amerika Bomber', another of Hitler's impractical plans for technological vengeance on his opponents. Yet such aircraft were only built in either single-digit figures or never left the prototype stage. The Luftwaffe would, therefore, remain a medium- or light-bomber force, but in this regard it excelled with three aircraft in addition to the He 111 – the Dornier Do 217, the Junkers Ju 88 and the Dornier Do 17.

The origins of the Ju 88 medium bomber began almost exactly a year before the outbreak of war when the then Generalfeldmarschall Göring was on an earlier visit to the Junkers aircraft factory. By that time the Luftwaffe was irrevocably committed to becoming a wholly tactical air force, whose main role was to support the Army in the field. Wever's successors were all staunch advocates of tactical air power, who thought solely in terms of dive-bombers and twin-engined medium bombers. No machine fitted the latter bill more perfectly than the *Schnellbomber* – or high-speed bomber – under development in the late 1930s at Junkers' Dessau works.

The Ju 88 was a twin-engined bomber with a crew of four and a payload of 3,600kg of bombs. It was a fast aircraft – max speed was around 450km/h, depending on the variant – and it had manoeuvrability to match. So impressed was Göring by this new aircraft that within days of his visit he had written to Junkers' managing director, Dr Heinrich Koppenberg, granting him full authority to begin series production at once. This missive, dated 3 September 1938, ended with the words, 'And now build me a mighty bomber fleet of Ju 88s in the shortest time possible'.

The Junkers Ju 88 was undoubtedly an excellent design, well deserving of the term *Wunderbomber* which was soon bestowed upon it. The first prototypes were unarmed, the original intention being that the Ju 88 – like the RAF's later Mosquito bomber – would rely entirely on its superior speed to escape the attention of enemy fighters. In March 1939 the fifth prototype demonstrated the Ju 88's potential when it established a new world air speed record for its class, completing a 1,000km closed circuit between Dessau

Two Dornier Do 17s seen during the German campaign against the Low Countries in early 1940. The slender profile of the Do 17 earned it the nickname 'flying pencil'.

and the Zugspitze – Germany's highest Alpine peak – at an average speed of 517km/h. However, mass-production of the Ju 88 in the 12 months following Göring's letter of September 1938 did not go entirely according to plan. In fact, it hardly went at all. The prototypes that had made such an impression on the Generalfeldmarschall had been far from ready to enter series production. Also, to add to the usual assortment of teething troubles which inevitably beset any new design, reactionary elements within the RLM had since decreed that the *Wunderbomber* was to be equipped with defensive armament after all. Even more damaging was the decision to fit the Ju 88 with dive brakes, thereby allowing it to operate both as a high-speed level bomber and as a dive-bomber.

The net result of this official tinkering with the basic design concept was not only a 65km/h reduction in maximum speed, but the dashing of Göring's hopes for a steady stream of deliveries of the new bomber to his operational units. Thus, on 1 September 1939, in place of the expected 'mighty bomber fleet of Ju 88s', the Luftwaffe embarked upon World War II with exactly 12 examples of the Junkers' twin in first-line service.

Production of the Ju 88 increased in earnest from 1940, and hence the aircraft's operational contributions increased. During the *Blitzkrieg* against France and the Low Countries, the Ju 88 *Kampfgruppen* of Luftflotte 2 showed the aircraft's versatility. They were employed for their proven dive-bombing abilities, but not against shipping. Instead, they were to perform pinpoint attacks on the AA defences protecting Dutch and Belgian airfields.

The Ju 88 demonstrated low loss rate in combat, a reflection less on the thinly stretched nature of the enemy defences than on the aircraft's own turn of speed and manoeuvrability. Throughout the entire Battle of Britain, of the trio of Luftwaffe twin-engined bombers involved, the Ju 88 would continue to suffer far fewer casualties per sortie than either the He 111 or the Do 17. Pilots of RAF Fighter Command also readily conceded that the Junkers was the hardest of the three to bring down, and despite their best efforts, the daily claims for Ju 88s destroyed over Great Britain remained stubbornly low. On only ten days during the four months from July to October did Ju 88 losses exceed three aircraft. More often than not there was just a single casualty, if any at all. Only on four occasions did the total of Ju 88s lost climb into double figures – nearly every time as a result of exceptional circumstances.

It was a sobering fact that, in July, the number of aircraft written off in training accidents, crashes and as a result of malfunctions over mainland Europe exceeded the 20-odd lost to direct enemy action. It could almost have been argued that, once they were masters of their machine, the safest place for a Ju 88 crew to be in the summer of 1940 was on one of their fast hit-and-run raids over southern England.

The Ju 88 went on to deliver outstanding service throughout World War II. Its performance gave it great tactical flexibility, and hence it found itself in all manner

of roles – dive-bomber, night-fighter, torpedo-bomber, heavy fighter – as well as in a conventional medium bomber capacity. More than 15,000 were produced, far more than the *c.* 6,500 He 111s, essentially making it the backbone of the Luftwaffe's bomber arm.

The Luftwaffe's emphasis on manoeuvrable tactical bombers was nowhere better expressed than in the Dornier Do 17, affectionately known as the *Fliegender Bleistift* ('flying pencil') on account of its slender contour. The Do 17 was also designed during the 1930s, but was very much a light bomber, with just a 1,000kg bomb load. It could

A Ju 88 is 'bombed up' and checked by its ground crew before a mission. The bombs are SC 250 types, one of the Luftwaffe's standard bombs used by both dive-bombers and level bombers.

develop a maximum speed of 410km/h from its two Bramo Fahir radial piston engines, and its manoeuvrability was superb, often evading fighters by pulling lightning-quick wing-over turns and dives. It was a principal Luftwaffe bomber during the campaign over Poland in 1939, but gradually the Ju 88 stole its thunder and only 2,139 were produced during the war.

The Do 17 did, however, spawn the Do 217, a heavier variant that was eventually (in the Do 217M model) able to carry four times the bomb load of the original aircraft. Nevertheless, increasingly powerful engines could not overcome the fact that the Do 217 had lost the nimble performance of the Do 17, and pilots had a frequently lukewarm relationship to the aircraft. Just under 2,000 were produced, and many served not only as medium bombers but also as night-fighters and reconnaissance aircraft. The Luftwaffe's bomber arm, like other branches of the German Air Force, had very much a multi-tasking approach to its aircraft, which admittedly gave it immense tactical versatility.

The Ju 88/Bf 109 'Mistel' (mistletoe) combination was a desperate measure introduced in 1944. The crewless Ju 88 had its nose filled with explosive, and was piloted to and released over its target by the fighter.

KAMPFFLIEGER

So what of the bomber crews themselves? While many men who joined the Luftwaffe as aircrew were immediately captivated by bombers, a large proportion had initially dreamed of becoming fighter pilots. Those found temperamentally unsuited to this vocation, however, were instead redirected to train on multi-engined types. Although initially a disappointment, this was in fact a great compliment to their technical skills. The Luftwaffe at first saw the bomber arm as the true key to victory, and the best recruits were thus guided to this elite corps. The fighter pilot was an inventive, perhaps impulsive, flyer, while service as a bomber crewman demanded a far more deliberate and calculating approach.

One obvious distinction between the bomber and fighter aircrew was that the former demanded a wider range of specializations, including observer, wireless operator, flight mechanic and air gunner. Men chosen to fulfil the many complex duties of *Beobachter* (observer) originally attended *Navigations-* or *Aufklärungs-Schule* (reconnaissance school) until the formation of four dedicated *Kampfbeobachterschulen* (battle observers' schools) in autumn 1942. During their 9- to 12-month stay, they became proficient in navigation, cartography and map reading, photography, basic gunnery and aerial tactics. They learned to operate all manner of navigational instruments, ranging from simple flight computers to the latest radio guidance systems. Low-tech but effective methods were also employed: sextant-reading practice was carried out in chairs that the instructors shook to simulate aircraft vibration and turbulence. A great deal of time was naturally devoted to bomb-aiming, using *Luftbildkameras* (aerial cameras) in place of bomb-sights. In 1937 it was decided that the *Beobachter* would also serve as the 'aircraft commander'. (In practice this was a very flexible title; although *Beobachter* had overall command in flight, and usually senior rank, all personnel habitually referred to 'the pilot and his crew'.) These men now had to possess suitable authority and leadership skills and therefore attended either *Unteroffizier-* or *Offizierschule*, generally graduating as *Feldwebel* or *Leutnante*.

Trainee *Bordfunker* (wireless operators) were required to undergo an intensive and demanding nine-month course at *Luftnachrichtenschule* (air signals school), alongside trainees destined for service in AA and other units. They studied ground wireless reception and transmission and had to attain a proficiency in Morse code of at least 100 letters per minute (sending and receiving). They also mastered theoretical navigation and instrumentation, but were sent to another school (with airfield access) for actual flight experience and practical navigation, map reading, and radio direction-finding exercises.

Flight mechanics held a special status within an aircrew, with the fundamental responsibility for keeping the aircraft up in the air. The trainee *Bordmechanik* learned his trade at *Fliegertechnischeschule*, over a period of around nine months. He studied internal combustion engine theory and elementary aerodynamics, and gained practical experience

OVERLEAF: The realities of bomber navigation. Navigators would find their way to a target through a mixture of time marking, landmarks, mapwork and often sheer luck. On many occasions entire squadrons of bombers missed their primary targets by kilometres.

FIRST FLIGHT (RIGHT)

A wireless operator prepares for his first operational flight. From May 1937 special outer thigh pockets were added to the K So 34 *Kombination*, for two *Verbandpäcke* first aid packets and the gravity-activated *Flieger-Kappmesser* aircrew knife, enabling entangled airmen to cut themselves free of parachute lines. The chest pocket could hold maps and target photographs, but was often used to stow the oxygen mask. Detail shows *Luftwaffe-Bekleidungs Amt* (clothing administration) acceptance stamp and typical makers' label inside the suit. Most units added their own identification marks, here denoting 3. Staffel (I. Gruppe) StG 1, but this practice quickly fell from use. The *Armbandkompass* 39 proved difficult to see at night, prompting the introduction of the more visible white-dial version. Of interest is the commercially produced leather 'holster' for pencil and notepad, the lower edges of which are secured by a few stitches. Designed to ease fitting over bulky flight clothing, the twin-zipped *Fliegerpelzstiefel* were expensive to manufacture and subsequent boots used a perfectly adequate single zip. A standard belt supports a P-08 Luger pistol but, with no practical alternative, the flare-pistol and cartridges are secured wherever convenient; an unsatisfactory situation that was not rectified until early 1941. (Adam Hook © Osprey Publishing)

on many types of aero engines. Students were sometimes sent to work at aircraft factories for practical experience. Although this may have initially seemed slightly demeaning, it gave them invaluable and detailed experience of various aircraft systems, as well as inside advice from the factory engineering staff themselves, for which the '*Bord-Wart*' and his comrades might someday be very grateful. (The various '*Wart*' nicknames were derived from *Wartung*, meaning maintenance.)

Bordschützen (air gunners) perfected their particular craft at *Fliegerschützenschule* (re-named *Bordschützenschule* from January 1942), during a rigorous five-month marksmanship and gunnery course. This involved a great deal of range work and familiarization with small arms and machine guns of various types, principally 7.92mm *Mauser* rifles and the infantry version of the MG13 machine gun. Regular 9mm pistol shooting helped maintain rapid sighting accuracy. After camera gun practice on trainer aircraft, they progressed to air-to-air machine gunnery against towed targets (which many found particularly enjoyable), firing tracer-ammunition as an aid to developing 'lead' skills. Assessed by instructors, they tracked obsolete fighters in dummy passes, but later progressed to Me 109 'attacks', which forced home the startling reality of modern fighter speeds.

A high degree of cross-training was incorporated into each curriculum, with every crewman receiving instruction in navigation, radio-telegraphy and aero engine

principles. This would enable crews to remain effective in the event of casualties. Even after a long day's training there was plenty of homework to be done, with virtually every waking hour devoted to learning every aspect of their trade. The *Bordmechanik*, *Bordfunker* and *Bordschütze* generally held relatively junior grades, the majority serving as *Gefreite* or *Unteroffiziere*.

It should be noted that the numerous trade schools were not always autonomous establishments, but were commonly housed within shared bases, airfields and buildings. Furthermore, they routinely shared aircraft and even flight time. Groups of student pilots, observers and gunners (each with their respective instructors) squeezed aboard the same aircraft for simultaneous training.

To alleviate frontline fuel shortages, training school supplies were cut by almost half in 1942. Consequently, pilots began qualifying with drastically reduced flight time, usually reaching an operational unit with between 220 and 270 hours. Accident rates duly rose, with an average of 14 per cent of training aircraft destroyed annually, and 8 per cent of flights ending in fatalities. The various training programmes were steadily compressed still further to cover the resulting replacement deficiencies; the *Beobachter*

The pilot and navigator/bombardier sit side by side in the cockpit of a Heinkel He 111. The flight engineer stands behind. Bomber crews would have to stay in their positions for many hours during operations, enduring cold, discomfort and the threat of sudden, violent death.

course was reduced to six months or less, sometimes incorporating less than 70 hours' flight time.

Upon completion of the specialist training, each man was awarded an aircrew licence, the *Fliegerschein*, accompanied by the appropriate aircrew badge. The qualified crewmen were then dispatched to one of five *Grosskampffliegerschulen* (higher bomber schools), numbered 1–5, established at Tutow, Hörsching, Greifswald, Thorn and Parow respectively. Wireless operators among them might alternatively be sent for dive-bomber training at a *Sturzkampffliegerschule*.

COMRADES IN ARMS

Throughout the early war years, Göring made great efforts to visit every *Kampfgeschwader* and most crewmen saw, if not actually met, him at some point in their careers. The majority found him a comical and slightly ridiculous figure in one of his self-designed and liberally decorated sky-blue uniforms (he often changed several times during each visit). He had the general aspect of a fat, overgrown schoolboy, but was positively brimming with confidence and enthusiasm. Like most airmen, StG3 wireless operator Obergefreiter Hans Wiedemann, 'didn't even talk about him', but what popularity Göring did enjoy soon waned, as increasingly unreasonable wartime demands were heaped upon the *Kampfgeschwader* and their over-stretched fighter escorts. Directives were issued preventing all leave and rest. Exhausted crewmen could no longer be relieved from operations to recuperate – everyone had to fly. On average two to three missions were executed per night, regardless of weather conditions, with barely an hour between each. As aircraft were hastily patched-up, refuelled and rearmed, aircrews were debriefed, then re-briefed, and perhaps able to grab a rushed meal before take-off. OKL grew evermore obsessed with numbers, and was seemingly detached from the limitations of worn-out men and aircraft. Even inexperienced crews had to join night operations, with predictable results. The combination of tired air and ground personnel, hurried maintenance and unproven pilots operating under strict light discipline, inevitably culminated in disastrous runway accidents and mid-air collisions. Units sometimes lost more men and machines on their own airfield than they did during the mission itself. Nevertheless, confidence in *Geschwader* and *Gruppe* commanders generally remained high.

Crews routinely spent off-duty periods together, but were not always accompanied by their officers, military protocol dictating two very different relationships in the air and on land. While the differences of rank were instantly forgotten and irrelevant in flight, for some crews, as they dismounted, the 'natural order' of officer and other-rank forced its way between them once more. Officers from different crews who had developed particular friendships in the mess would invariably meet to share experiences of the

Engineers work on the futuristic-looking Ju 287, a testbed for a four-engine jet bomber. Only two examples of the forward-swept wing aircraft were built, with many parts scavenged from wrecked aircraft.

mission. Meanwhile, the NCOs and enlisted members of their respective crews, perhaps slightly uneasy in the presence of unfamiliar officers, would likewise gravitate towards each other. Despite the equally close bonds that grew between them, a similar segregation sometimes existed even among Stuka pilots and their gunners. This must not imply any falseness in the depth of their friendships; it was simply the result of proper military behaviour.

By mid-1941, however, a notable degree of separation was emerging in the relationship between air and ground crews. This was in no small part due to the rapid turnover in aircrew (new crews were lost after an average of only three to four missions), leaving little time or inclination for such friendships to develop. Furthermore, the steady decline in training standards meant that inexperienced new pilots frequently reported mechanical faults and concerns to the already over-burdened crew chief that, upon investigation, proved insignificant or downright incorrect. Time and effort had by then been expended for no good reason, sometimes removing a perfectly serviceable aircraft from an operation, and leaving the mechanics' opinion of the aircrew significantly marred. The situation was so detrimental to squadron efficiency that attempts were made to reintegrate the two groups by standing-down a crewman from a mission while a ground crewman covered for him. This not only gave the aircrews some much-needed rest, but also allowed the mechanics to evaluate aircraft systems, defences and shortcomings in action (which occasionally resulted in the design and installation of improved armour or weapon mounts). The excitement of combat, as a 'reward' for seemingly unnoticed efforts on the ground, highlighted the importance of the ground

BELOW: This illustration depicts various training camp activities that *Kampfflieger* would undergo to qualify as air crew. These include assault courses, weapons maintenance, parachute training, aeronautics study and training in ditching procedures. (Adam Hook © Osprey Publishing)

crews' work and heightened their respect and understanding of the aircrews' tasks. They, in turn, came to regard their ground crew colleagues as more than just simple mechanics. While they were a valuable means of team building, these job swaps were only made on relatively short and simple operations. These exercises were generally successful and some very close friendships evolved.

Other replacements were far less welcome. The occasional appearance of a *Kriegsberichter* (war correspondent) was deeply resented and commanders often flatly refused to tolerate their presence on operational flights. Aircrew were contemptuous of *Propaganda-Kompanie* (PK) reporters for the wildly inaccurate newspaper and radio claims they had to endure, boasting great success for 'minimal losses'. In fairness, much of the reporters' original text was corrupted (for dramatic and political purposes) by Propaganda Ministry officials who seldom ventured anywhere near an aircraft, let alone the front line. Goebbels quickly decreed that PK men must first undergo appropriate training, as air gunners or even bombardiers, and some took a very active dual role in campaigns from mid-1940 onwards. By far the greatest contempt was reserved for the (thankfully rare) accompaniment of a '*Sandsack*' (sandbag) – a completely useless staff officer who contributed nothing to the operation, thereby endangering the whole crew, and whose sole intent was to qualify for a year's flight pay and an Iron Cross.

Any change to normal routine, caused by illness, leave, replacement, injury or death, could have a profound impact upon the cohesive operation of the entire bomber crew. Their effectiveness demanded complete trust and familiarity, and these were characterized by subtle practices and signals unique to each crew and developed since their days at *Grosskampffliegerschule*. It was in everyone's interest that replacements settled in quickly, encouraged and aided by their new comrades.

By 1943–44, with massive Luftwaffe losses over both the Western and Eastern Fronts, the odds seemed so heavily stacked against survival that airmen invariably developed some degree of superstition. They carried lucky charms or observed certain rituals (similar to the USAAF fear of placing a hat on a bed), but the precise nature of each man's rite of course, varied tremendously. Friday 13th had the same significance as for the British and Americans, while other chance events were considered lucky omens. An airman who was presumed killed, with his family duly notified, but who later returned to his unit, was apparently assured of survival, for example.

ON CAMPAIGN

The *Kampfgeschwader's* wartime service was a painful and slow degeneration. For the first three years of the war the bombers formed the Luftwaffe's premier combat arm, the aerial tip of the spear. Bombers were sewn into the very fabric of *Blitzkrieg*, intended as

LEFT: A particularly famous image of an He 111 flying over the Thames River in London in 1940. Major rivers, roads and similar landmarks were crucial navigational aids for bomber crews.

OVERLEAF: The He 111's glass nose and cockpit provided a remarkable degree of visibility to its three occupants: pilot, bombardier/navigator and nose gunner. Here we see the nose gunner training his MG15 machine gun.

A top view of three Dornier 215s during an operation over Britain. A very small number of these aircraft were built – only just over 100 – and they were used as reconnaissance aircraft as well as bombers.

a form of aerial artillery that could pave the way for the advances by armoured ground forces. Luftwaffe air liaison detachments would be emplaced amongst the advancing troops aboard SdKfz 251/3 communications vehicles, using radio communications to identify immediate forward targets and guide the bomb runs in. The medium bombers would also range further afield to hit sites deep behind enemy lines or across national boundaries, causing immense destruction in urban zones. Typical targets to receive the attention of the bombers included troop concentrations, railway marshalling yards, airfields, supply convoys and logistics centres.

When the bombers were first unleashed, in Poland in 1939, the world had never seen such an effective coordinated use of bomber power. As the campaign began, the bomber element included 370 He 111s and 527 Do 17s, in addition to the precision-bombing capability offered by the Ju 87s. The Polish capital, Warsaw, received its first air raids by 0600hrs, but the city would later experience much worse. The raid of 25 September, for instance, was little more than a terror attack delivered as Poland's knees buckled, but it demonstrated the cruel possibilities of strategic air power. In more than 1,000 sorties, the German bombers dropped 500 tonnes of high-explosive bombs and added 70 tonnes of incendiaries, raising a pall of smoke over Warsaw that climbed to 5,500m. Hundreds of civilians were killed.

The *Kampfflieger* would continue to demonstrate their tactical and strategic confidence during the subsequent campaigns in the West, North Africa, the Balkans and on the Eastern Front. However, as the years went by some of the gloss started to rub off the prestigious bomber arm. The Battle of Britain and the Blitz in 1940–41, for example, certainly showed that the Luftwaffe was capable of inflicting serious infrastructural damage. During September and October 1940 alone, German bombing killed 13,000 British civilians and wounded 20,000 more. Yet the Luftwaffe was still unable to bring the country to its knees, or to impair industrial production to critical levels. Furthermore, substantial losses during daylight operations meant that by early October – finding no protection in numbers against the tenacious, and seemingly inexhaustible, RAF fighters – the Luftwaffe was beginning to despatch bombers singly, or in small groups, to make hit-and-run raids on specific targets. Although this new tactic reduced October's losses to little more than a steady trickle, it did not stop them altogether.

From late 1940 onwards almost all German bomber activity over the United Kingdom was to be shrouded in darkness. The bombers would be often heard, but seldom seen – except by the electronic 'eyes' of British radar, or as twisted piles of wreckage in the cold light of morning. At first, however, during the winter months of 1940–41, the Luftwaffe bombers left little evidence of their nightly passage other than the damage – often severe – which they themselves had inflicted on London or on some

The Junkers Ju 86 was one of Germany's early bombers, introduced into service in 1936. It was originally designed as a civilian airliner, but like several German aircraft of the 1930s was fairly easily converted to military roles.

unfortunate provincial town or city. Very few of their own number were brought down, for the RAF's night-fighter arm was still in its infancy, and the thousands of shells sent up by the AA guns did more good for civilian morale than harm to the enemy overhead.

For example, in arguably one of the most infamous raids of this period – the attack on Coventry on the night of 14/15 November – only one of the 300 raiders was brought down, the hapless Do 17 of KG 3 which was struck by AA fire. Although the one enduring image of this night's raid will always be the hollow, burnt-out shell of the city's St Michael's cathedral, other, more legitimate, targets were also hard hit. Coventry housed the Fleet Air Arm's main stores depot, and whether by chance or design, this was heavily bombed and completely destroyed. The effects, according to one informed source, 'were felt by Swordfish squadrons all over the world'.

Although weather conditions were still far from perfect, mid-March 1941 was to witness an upsurge in activity as Luftwaffe raids grew in strength and intensity. On the night of 15/16 March 100+ bombers were despatched against London. The following night close on 200 Heinkels and Junkers made a two-pronged attack on Bristol and the neighbouring Avonmouth docks. The sole casualty to come down over the United Kingdom was a KG 51 machine which suffered a double engine failure. There followed major raids on Hull, Southampton, Plymouth and London before the weather closed in again at month's end and brought a virtual halt to all nocturnal activity. April began quietly but soon escalated into a nightly succession of devastating attacks. Once again provincial towns and cities, particularly the ports and harbours, suffered heavily. Clydeside, Tyneside, Liverpool, Bristol and Belfast were all targeted, as too were Birmingham and Coventry.

However, again and again the raiders returned to London. On the night of 16/17 April Luftflotte 3 mounted a major attack on the capital. Over 500 bombers (nearly 300 of them Ju 88s) were despatched in three waves. Severe damage was caused in this, the heaviest raid of the war to date. It cost the Luftwaffe five Ju 88s – a quarter of the month's total Junkers casualties – plus a solitary He 111. Three of the Ju 88s, all

BELOW: A German bomber crew in Germany, 1942. Newly qualified airmen were divided into *Kompanien*, assembled into four- to five-man crews and thereby introduced to the men with whom they would theoretically remain throughout their service lives. Three months of intensive training ensued, during which crews gained around 40–60 hours of flight time together, involving formation work, long-distance navigation exercises (to airfields hundreds of miles away) and short-range bombing practice over countryside ranges. (Adam Hook © Osprey Publishing)

A striking night-time image of an He 111 warming up on a French airfield in 1940. During nocturnal operations, an unguarded flash of white light in the cockpit would disrupt the crews' night vision for several minutes.

from KG 77, may have succumbed to flak. The other two, from KG 1 and KG 76, were both claimed by No. 219 Sqn Beaufighters, as was the Heinkel.

By now the night Blitz was rapidly approaching its climax. The past weeks and months had been a testing time for those living in the larger urban areas of Great Britain. Thousands had been killed. However, the Luftwaffe's nocturnal offensive had done little to further Germany's cause militarily.

For the bomber crews it had been a period of sustained effort, interrupted only by the spells of bad weather. Each *Gruppe* had to locate and attack a wide range of targets the length and breadth of a blacked-out Britain. Sometimes they flew more than one mission on the same night and, while the cost had not been prohibitive, their losses had been slowly increasing all the while. They came to a head in May 1941. That month's 40+ aircraft lost was the highest total since the daylight battle of the previous summer.

Seven of those casualties were suffered on the night of 4/5 May alone, aircraft being brought down during, or after, raids as far apart as Belfast, Bridlington and Torquay. However, it was the devastating attack on London, lasting a full seven hours during the night of 10/11 May 1941, which brought to a close the Luftwaffe's almost year-long attempt to subjugate the British from the air. By then, however, the mass move eastwards had begun. The Luftwaffe went on to make an equally futile attempt to achieve over the Russian steppe what it had signally failed to do over the Kentish Downs – blow the enemy's air force out of the sky.

Even by the time of *Barbarossa*, losses of bomber aircraft and crews were becoming a serious issue. In fact, the vulnerability of the unescorted bomber had been noted from the outset of the war. On the first day of operations against Poland, KG 27 lost six aircraft in one raid over Warsaw to a supposedly inferior Polish Air Force. On 10–11 May, the opening two days of the campaign in the West, 69 bombers were lost, and by the time France had fallen, 468 bombers had been destroyed (30 through accidental causes), some 30 per cent of the bomber arm's strength at the beginning of the campaign. The Battle of Britain resulted in similar bomber losses. Such casualties were the beginning of a grim equation that would play out for the German bomber crews, as loss rates climbed towards exceeding production rates. The attrition continued and indeed intensified in 1941 as the theatres of

A Ju 88 bomber receives an SC 500 bomb ready for a raid over England in the summer of 1940. The blast effect generated by the bomb meant that it was generally unsafe to be within 500m of the point of impact.

AWARDS

The *Frontflugspange fur Kampfflieger* (Operational Flight Clasp for Bomber Crewmen) was introduced on 30 January 1941, for level bomber and dive-bomber crews. The clasp was awarded in three classes: bronze for 20 missions, silver for 60 and gold for 110. Operational flights made from 1 September 1939 were considered in these totals, but because of the wide variations in type and duration of missions undertaken, not all were counted. On 22 April 1941, precise criteria were laid down for what constituted a frontline flight: crews were required to venture a minimum of 30km into enemy airspace, or 100km overseas (this measurement was taken from German-held borders). It is worth noting that of KG 4 pilot Leutnant Elmar Börsch's first 200 missions (his final total was 312), only about 8 per cent lasted more than ten minutes over enemy territory. Flights that took the crewman over enemy territory for more than four hours counted as double, eight hours triple, 12 hours quadruple and quintuple for those in excess of 16 hours. This last, phenomenal duration was added on 28 January 1944 in respect for the ever increasing ranges the bombers were forced to travel to their targets, from drastically receding German frontline airbases. Following the invasion of the Soviet Union, it soon became evident that the original order had underestimated the speed at which airmen could accrue missions, many far exceeding those represented by the current highest-grade clasp. From 26 June 1942, therefore, this golden clasp could be upgraded with the addition of the *Anhänger zur goldenen Frontflugspange*, a pendant in the form of a star flanked by laurel leaves. When soldered beneath the clasp by a jeweller, the pendant denoted a greatly increased total of operational flights: 300 for bomber and 400 for dive-bomber crewmen. By 29 April 1944, it was realized that even these upgraded clasps were insufficient and, moreover, imprecise; a man with more than 600 missions to his credit wore the same badge as those with 'only' 300. A new range of hangers was thus designed to keep pace with each airman's achievements. The *Anhänger zur goldenen Frontflugspange mit Einsatzzahl* (... with Operational Number) was a simple lozenge, again supported by laurel leaves, displaying black-lacquered numerals appropriate to the missions flown, commencing with 200 and rising in increments of 100.

war widened. Total bomber losses for 1941 were 1,339, added to which were the hundreds of aircraft rendered temporarily unserviceable by mechanical failure or combat damage.

The campaigns – particularly that on the Eastern Front – also illustrated the Herculean demands of bomber unit logistics. Movement of an air unit was a major logistical exercise, requiring meticulous timing and coordination to ensure operational capability in the shortest time possible. Once *Fliegerhorst* (air station) boundaries had been confirmed, a few of the more experienced pilots would immediately scout the surrounding countryside, usually in Fiesler 156 Storch liaison craft, locating and mapping suitable emergency landing and aircraft dispersal sites.

RIGHT: The crew of an He 111 prepare themselves for take-off, the setting suggesting a Western European theatre. Mission briefings were typically held outdoors, only retreating to cover in poor weather.

A *Kampfgeschwader-Fliegerhorst* obviously demanded a great deal of space. Geographical restrictions and the need to deny enemy attackers a prime target generally prevented an entire *Geschwader* (with around 126 aircraft) operating from one field. Despite the additional logistical demands, various *Staffeln* would be located at separate *Frontflugplätze* (frontline airfields), often many kilometres apart. Advance units of pioneers, maintenance crews, supply, administration and command personnel would be dispatched by road to prepare the infrastructure of each airbase. Wherever possible, existing military and civil airports were simply taken over, and extended to cater for the numerous support and storage facilities vital for operations. As soon as the airstrip was ready to accept traffic, aircraft would begin to arrive, bringing with them the leading mechanics and essential stores that would enable the *Staffel* to function, and even execute missions, prior to the rest of the unit arriving by road.

Each *Staffel* required access to equipment stores, machine shops, parachute drying and packing sheds, and secure but isolated ammunition, bomb and fuel dumps. Several units could share some of these facilities wherever their respective fields were close enough, and any tree-shielded minor roads within the area served as convenient pre-camouflaged bomb-dumps. The initially open airfields naturally had to be secured against sabotage, and so brick walls and fencing would be erected around the entire perimeter, with the addition of regularly spaced machine-gun towers and sometimes pillboxes. Concealed dispersal pens and hard standing also had to be constructed. Overly tall trees surrounding the airstrip (which were extremely hazardous in poor visibility) were felled in the interests of safety, and warning lights were fitted to the tops of high buildings. Civilian construction companies were frequently employed to assist Luftwaffe pioneer units in such tasks. One Belgian contractor, employed to extend the runway for II./KG3 at Antwerp-Deurne, also obligingly removed the spire of a church, which was unfortunately in direct line of take-off. Sheep were often allowed to roam the flattened grass airstrips, as a simple lawn-mowing expedient.

In addition to all these demands was the need to accommodate 2,500 men. The owners of nearby houses might be ordered to vacate their homes with only 48 hours' notice, to be replaced by squadron personnel. Where sufficient buildings could not be found, barrack huts had to be hastily constructed by *Luftwaffen-Bau-Battalionen* (construction battalions), again often assisted by locally drafted craftsmen and labour. Any available personnel, including aircrews, were employed in the construction of slit trenches – a chore made instantly worthwhile by the first air raid.

A frontline *Kampfgeschwader* consumed around 112 tonnes of bread, 12 tonnes of meat, 13 tonnes of sausage and 12 tonnes of peas every day. The administrative section, therefore, purchased a great deal of agricultural produce from local farmers at government expense, easing a sizeable part of the logistics train. Daily meals produced at the *Kuchhaus*

(cookhouse) were usually of a high standard and the individual airman could often supplement his diet with regional delicacies and merchandise. Unlike some liberating Allied units who later battled their way through mainland Europe, the occupying German soldier always expected to pay for such services and many farmers and restaurateurs did lucrative business with their new (if otherwise unwelcome) customers.

Ground crew take MG15 machine guns aboard an He 111 bomber to install. The MG 15 had a calibre of 7.92mm and a cyclical rate of fire or 1,000–1,050rpm. Feed was from a 75-round drum magazine.

The sheer strain of supplying the bombers was never greater than on the Eastern Front, the hazards of which are explained below. Transporting spare parts and fuel, plus the squadron's human needs, across hundreds of kilometres of Russian or Ukrainian wilderness had a wearing effect on serviceability, as it became an ever greater strain to keep aircraft in the air. In September 1939, the Luftwaffe bombers had a 99 per cent actual (operational) strength, but by the end of 1941 the change was profound, as Luftwaffe historian Williamson Murray explains:

> In December 1941, the bomber force possessed only 47.1 per cent of its authorized strength: only 51 per cent of that force was in commission. Thus, from an authorized strength of 1,950 bombers, the Luftwaffe had only 468 in commission on December 6 1941, or 24 per cent of authorized aircraft.
>
> – Williamson Murray, *Strategy for Defeat: The* Luftwaffe *1933–1945*,
>
> Eagle Editions, Royston (2000)

Production of bombers did jump from 2,952 in 1940 to 3,373 in 1941, but there would be only two more years of increases in bomber output – 4,502 in 1942 and 4,789 in 1943. Given the huge volumes of fighters German factories turned out in these years (nearly 11,000 in 1943 alone), it was evident that the German commitment to maintaining a viable bomber force was waning. Bomber output fell to fewer than 2,000 units in 1944, and by the late part of the year the bomber arm was virtually dissolved altogether. Pilots were retrained on single-seat jet aircraft (with more than 200 men killed in the process) and their crews transferred to other duties, frequently becoming infantrymen taking part in savage street-fighting against advancing Soviet armour. Such was the nightmarish, and frequently fatal, experience for men who had already given hard service to the Reich.

BATTLE

For bomber crews, all operational orders originated at the *Gefechtsstand* (battle headquarters). The *Kartenstelle* (map room), chiefly responsible for updating and issue of appropriate aerial maps, selected the general routes in and out of the target area according to calculated range, as dictated by aircraft type and bomb load.

The *Wetterstelle* (weather office) provided planners with constant reports and forecasts, before and throughout each mission. Meteorological personnel were affectionately known as *Wetterfrösche* (weather frogs; in German folklore, frogs are renowned for their forecasting prowess), or, less kindly, *Falsche prophete*. Under command of the *Funk- u. Navigationsoffizier* (wireless and navigation officer), the *Bodenleitstelle* (ground control centre) informed aircrews of available radio frequencies

and take-off and landing signals. Constant communication would be maintained with the formation throughout the flight, via the *Geschwaderluftnachrichtenkompanie* (air signals company), advising of any weather updates or last-minute amendments to orders. In turn, they received regular reports from aircraft wireless operators, relaying any critical information back to the *Gefechtsstand*, who could decide the required course of action and issue new orders as necessary. From this basic information, the *Staffelkapitän* fixed the precise approach, bomb-run sequences and exit routes, finally briefing the squadron observers.

From 1940, a necessarily generous 400 RM bonus and extra leave privileges were granted to specially selected, sometimes voluntary, *Zerstörerbesatzungen* (destruction crews). Written orders and target descriptions came directly from *Fliegerkorps* headquarters, and although no time was specified, assignments were expected to be completed as soon as possible. The aircraft commander theoretically decided the exact method and time, based on prevailing conditions and crew readiness, but was occasionally detailed to execute a mission immediately, regardless of these factors. The near-suicidal

A German bomb store in the south of France, 1942. Ammunition and fuel stores were extremely dangerous if the airbase suddenly received an air attack. In November 1942, one well-placed bomb on a fuel dump at Armavir airfield on the Eastern Front destroyed or damaged almost 100 He 111s and Ju 88s.

BOMBING MOSCOW

From the opening days of *Barbarossa*, the Soviets had been expecting the Germans to launch an all-out aerial offensive against Moscow. The 195 bombers that participated in the first raid on the night of 21/22 July faced formidable defences – a belt of 300 searchlights 29km in front of the city, backed up by AA batteries, both heavy and light, plus 170 fighters. It is not known how many of the attackers fought their way through to the target – certainly more than the 'ten or fifteen' noted in one Soviet publication, for another admitted heavy losses among the city's civilian population. The Luftwaffe clearly failed in its stated aim of reducing the Kremlin to rubble, although one crew did come close – a single bomb crater in Red Square caused 'quite a stir among the locals the following morning'.

Despite the strength of the defences, this first raid resulted in the loss of only six bombers. A second flown on the night of

Winter presented all manner of problems to bomber crews. Snow and sub-zero temperatures extended aircraft maintenance times dramatically, as even tools needed to be pre-warmed before use in the extreme conditions.

22/23 July cost the 115-strong attacking force five of its number, including three Ju 88s claimed by I-16s. The attacks were to continue on a nightly basis for some time to come, but they quickly declined in intensity – 100 raiders on the third night, 65 on the fourth, until the assault finally petered out in mid-September. Moscow neither suffered a single devastating blow such as that inflicted on Belgrade, nor was subjected to a sustained aerial Blitz of the type endured by London. It has been estimated that of the 76 night raids flown against Moscow in 1941, all but 17 were little more than pinpricks carried out by small groups of from three to ten aircraft.

raids against vital installations, principally aircraft factories, engine works and airfields, were flown without fighter escort. Crews were obliged to destroy their targets, in addition to regular operations.

PREPARATION

Bomber crews themselves frequently knew little of the precise nature of their target, sometimes not even the name of the city, and were often not interested. Their only real concerns were to know about the levels and type of defence they might expect to encounter. Only the *Beobachter* needed to know that much detail, and even he received only the shortest of briefings, with target descriptions often limited to little more than map references. As the *Staffel* grew evermore familiar with their operational areas and routes, information could be reduced to an airfield or factory name only. Before long this was perfectly adequate, as veteran crews could navigate by sight and memory alone.

Beobachter were initially under very strict orders to avoid civilian casualties wherever possible, to the extent of aborting an entire mission if necessary. Enemy reports of deliberate 'terror raids' prompted investigations by Führerhauptquartier (Führer Headquarters) itself. The offending aircrews were traced and interrogated to ensure they had exercised all practical precautions.

On 24 August 1940, British jamming of the *Knickebein* radio-navigation signals caused He 111s inadvertently to strike blacked-out central London, believing it to be Shorts' aircraft factory. The Luftwaffe continued to concentrate on military targets, but five seemingly 'unprovoked' RAF raids on Berlin eventually incited retaliation on 7 September, intended to force a return to military targeting. Hereafter, mission briefings could not have been more succinct: London, Bristol, Coventry. Escalating casualties merely ensured a bitter duel, killing 60,000 British and 600,000 German civilians by 1945.

Before a mission, crews gathered their gear for the long trek to dispersal. Civilian buses had originally been commandeered for this purpose, but ever present fuel shortages curtailed such luxuries and most had to walk (sometimes well over a kilometre) to the flight line. Ground crews helped airmen into their flight suits, and life-vests and parachute harnesses were adjusted to a tight fit.

The bomber would then board the aircraft, as a *Schwarze* slammed the gondola entry hatch shut. A few minutes later, when everyone was strapped into take-off positions, the pilot enquired over the intercom '*Alles Klar?*' ('All clear?'). Each crewman responded in turn, and the intercom was switched off.

The crew sat in silence, awaiting the signal from the crew chief standing just 10m in front of the nose, while he in turn watched for a signal from the *Start- u.*

Landeaufsichtsoffizier (take-off and landing look-out officer). The signal to go was given, and the *Flugzeugführer* shouted from his open window to the crew chief, '*Voraus alles klar?*', for the chief to confirm all-clear ahead.

Ground control staff and every observer had by this time received a flight plan from the *Gefechtsstand*, detailing take-off sequence and time slots allocated to each aircraft.

A flag, or at night a lamp or green flare, signalled the start of the take-off run. Brakes on, half-throttle and then three-quarter-throttle was applied as the aircraft strained to be released. The *Beobachter* watched the instrument panel and signalled that all was well. The *Flugzeugführer* released the brakes and the machine lurched forward. Full-throttle was piled on to achieve a take-off speed of 220km/h. Judging the precise moment, the pilot wound the trim lever with his left hand, pushing down the tail, and hauling back the control column with his right. The nose and undercarriage began to lift just as the red lamps, marking the final 200m of runway, flashed by underneath. At night, perimeter and runway lights were extinguished as the last aircraft left the field. Limited facilities available to frontline units often called for ingenuity; at Gerbini, Sicily, 7./KG 30 had to illuminate their airstrip with the headlights of strategically parked cars.

In mixed formations, slow-climbing Do 17s and He 111s took off first; the superior climb-rate of the Ju 88 enabled them to catch up easily. The lead aircraft had to maintain constant speed and height for the fleet to assemble on him, until finally the lead *Beobachter* set a course for the target. The formation might stay together for *Grosseinsatz* (massed

BELOW: Ju 88A-4 '5K+EK' of 2./KG 3, Kharkov-West, Southern Sector, January 1943. No need for fancy white outlining on this immaculately winter camouflaged A-4 of 2. Staffel. Such cleanliness in the depths of a Russian winter would seem to suggest that this is either a newly arrived replacement machine, or an aircraft that has been freshly repainted during a recent major overhaul. (John Weal © Osprey Publishing)

attack) against a single target, or split at pre-arranged points, towards individual objectives, in small groups or even individually.

FLIGHT AND NAVIGATION

As the aircraft travelled in formation, in-flight checks were carried out; the *Beobachter* and *Flugzeugführer* examined their shared instrument arrays, the former operating switches and fuel transfer levers, more conveniently located for him than the pilot. At night, the *Bordfunker* maintained constant communication with immediately flanking aircraft, in order to hold position and report any mechanical or medical emergencies. He also monitored ground direction-finding equipment in concert with the *Beobachter*. The *Bordschützen*, meanwhile, attended to their weapons and ammunition supplies, firing short test bursts over open land or sea. On larger aircraft, the *Bordmechanik* might also assist with some general duties.

At 2,000m, air humidity was quickly evaporated into steam by friction-generated wingtip heat, with the condensation trails, or 'contrails', scratching unmistakable tracks across the sky. Greater danger appeared at 5,500m as the temperature dropped to around -34°C and moisture froze against control surfaces, air-intakes and propellers. Fine, needle-like crystals squeezed through tiny cracks in the Plexiglas nose, peppering the skin with a stinging mist. Unchecked, ice could cause engine seizure, so regular inspections were carried out. Climbing through the damp cloud band nearer the sun melted the ice, but this too could be hazardous. Accompanied by loud cracking noises, chunks of solid ice could break free to slam into the fuselage, occasionally smashing off the radio mast. At higher altitude, the air grew even colder and became so thin that it was necessary for the crew to use pure oxygen, although prolonged dependency on it had a wearying effect, even in healthy young men.

At night, all interior lights were extinguished as the aircraft neared the enemy front, and an almost complete, inky blackness descended upon the aircraft, leaving only the dim glow of luminous instrument dials. Complete radio silence was imposed and the formation spread out to reduce the likelihood of collision. The tension increased with the knowledge that already-alerted defences awaited them.

The *Beobachter* had previously noted distinctive geographical features upon his map, providing accurate datum points throughout the flight. Reaching these points on time confirmed original wind speed and drift calculations. If not, flight time, airspeed and distance covered were used to determine actual conditions. These new calculations would then be applied to future headings.

Experienced crews welcomed the appearance of searchlights and distant flak as a helpful navigational aid. They could recognize cities from their searchlight signature

RIGHT: A German reconnaissance photograph of Malta's Grand Harbour. Malta was the Luftwaffe's prime target in the Mediterranean between January and April 1941 and December 1941 and August 1942.

alone, and simply circumnavigate dangerous areas. Certain unconcealable landmarks, such as major rivers and power stations, provided excellent reference points. Large and easily defined towns were familiar features and at lower levels aircraft could simply follow major road and railway lines directly to their targets.

Heavy fog presented great navigational and formation problems, but wing-mounted fog lamps were seldom used, as the reflection generally exacerbated the situation. In such poor conditions, enemy counter-measures on the ground could be remarkably successful. On 30 August 1940 'Starfish' decoy fires lit in British fields to simulate blazing cities, deceived a heavy raid against Liverpool into bombing a Welsh hillside. Even if these massive oil-fed infernos could be distinguished as subterfuge, they occasionally masked the intended target with such dense smoke that an accurate strike was impossible, forcing the fleet to abort its primary mission to seek secondary or opportunity targets. In favourable conditions, however, the *Beobachter* was seldom fooled; regular instrument fixes generally enabled him to find his target.

FLAK AND FIGHTER DEFENCES

When approaching known AA emplacements, the *Flugzeugführer* throttled back both engines to confound predictor crews' attempts to determine his altitude and course. If the gunners heard his muted engines, they might assume from the pitch that this machine was beyond range – a common and surprisingly effective ruse. By sporadically desynchronizing his engines, an experienced pilot could even influence the direction of fire, teasing it away from his planned approach route. The bomber might fly on unmolested, but a swaying searchlight could suddenly find and lock onto its prey, flooding the cockpit with blinding white light. Soon other ghostly fingers would converge on the bomber, 'handing over' the captive aircraft to neighbouring batteries as it entered the next zone. The *Flakwaltz* began with a sudden dive, jerking wildly, before climbing back up to evade the searchlights' grasp.

The first AA-tracers, known as *Bügeleisen* (flat irons), were often closely followed by several innocuous-looking puffs of black smoke by day, or sharp flashes by night, usually inaudible over the drone of engines. As the gunners found the range, aircraft were jolted violently and engines faltered from the blast waves of AA shell-bursts above and below, sending shards of white-hot steel to clatter against the wings like gravel thrown at a tin shed. The metallic bang of a large shell-splinter punching through the fuselage, produced a loud, howling noise to add to the general melee and the acrid, sulphurous smell of explosives.

AA fire could vary from a few haphazard guns firing away at targets of opportunity, to highly controlled systems of aerial artillery. British AA fire, for example, was

LEFT: The Luftwaffe was the first aerial combat arm to demonstrate the true power of strategic bombing by fixed-wing aircraft. Here we see an He 111 unloading its bombs over Poland during the opening campaign of World War II in 1939.

generally restricted to a precise, narrow band. Royal Artillery gunners rightly prided themselves on their fire discipline and accuracy, only rarely resorting to deeper or scattered barrage in desperation. The bright, fleeting muzzle flashes on the ground gave brief warning of approaching AA fire, but aircraft in close formation could do little to avoid it. Instead, the crews had to ride the storm with every muscle clenched, often causing violent, uncontrollable trembling deep within the stomach. It was not unknown for men to wet their trousers, particularly during low-level approaches at around 600–900m. At these heights, reaction and firing times of ground or naval defences were significantly reduced, but the bombers' immediate manoeuvring space was also curtailed in the event of fighter attack. An extremely low-level raid was famously executed by Do 17s of 9./KG 76 against RAF Kenley on 18 August 1940,

Flak pops in the air around a flight of Ju 88 aircraft. Anti-aircraft fire to high altitudes was often more effective for breaking up the flight path of bomb runs than for bringing down enemy aircraft.

skimming across the Channel and English fields at altitudes as low as several metres. Steeple-chasing over woodland, several picked up leaves and branches as they ripped through the treetops.

As terrifying as artillery fire could be, the fighter attacks invoked far greater fears. The fighter pilot, determined to down the bomber and all its crew, introduced a personal element to the encounter. With German aircrews bunched so closely together, a concentrated burst of fire into the cockpit would be devastating. Prolonged cannon fire hammered through the engines and wing-roots would rupture the main tanks. Gushing fuel, combined with explosive rounds and tracers, could easily take the wing clean off.

As enemy territory drew near, every eye was strained for a distant shadow or the slightest movement below. Even at close range it was extremely difficult to define a well-camouflaged profile against the shifting landscape. The contrails that once betrayed the bomber could now become an ally; a sudden break in the tracks above indicated that fighters had commenced their diving attack and would soon be on the bombers. Many gunners were initially dismayed that their own fighter escort denied them the chance to exercise their skills. The first interloper quickly changed their outlook.

A sudden shout of '*Jagdflieger!*' and everyone was braced for the onslaught. Aerial engagements were extremely short-lived occurrences. Most of the fighter's time was devoted to selecting and reaching a suitable starting point for his attack, and repeating the process after every pass. Even if a running battle developed over several kilometres, to the bomber crew it was made up of frantic, terrifying moments. Put simply, it was a brief and uneven confrontation between one man with a single MG15 (and severely restricted vision), and a rapidly closing opponent armed with multiple cannon or heavy machine guns. With a cyclic rate of about 850 rounds per minute, sustained fire on the Rheinmetal-Borsig MG15 ate through a 75-round magazine in just five seconds. Reloading took a similar time. During 1943, MG81 machine guns, fed by 500-round belts, replaced these woefully inadequate weapons.

For all his training and accuracy, an air gunner seldom got to place well-aimed fire at the fighter as it flashed past him at around 233km/h. He could merely throw a wild burst in its general direction, before the blurred apparition vanished completely from view once more. Bombers commonly came under sustained attack, with cockpit and radio sets blasted to pieces by sparking bullets, and yet the entire crew saw nothing of the fighters tumbling all around them. At greater range a gunner had a little more time to aim, but the danger of firing into other bombers in formation could deny him even this fleeting chance. A fired round does not stop when it misses the intended target, of course, and with effective ranges of up to 2km it was inevitable that a degree of damage was caused to friendly aircraft by stray 7.92 and 20mm cannon-fire.

OVERLEAF: The fate of many German bombers and their crews. A Ju 88 burns in a field after being shot down.

BOMB RUN AND OBSERVATION

As the formation reached its target area almost exactly on schedule, the leader waggled his wingtips, signalling the formation to loosen as they began to climb. Moments later a green flare was fired and aircraft broke in all directions to prepare their individual attacks. Each circled patiently, avoiding flak concentrations, while the *Beobachter* selected a suitable start-point for his bomb run. Keeping a close eye on the clock, he observed and recorded the results of the preceding aircraft's strike. Each aircraft had been allocated a precise time over the target, a one-minute slot in which to deliver its payload. (Allied bombers routinely held formation to release cargoes simultaneously on cue from the leader, plastering much of the surrounding area.)

Oblivious to the chaos around him, the *Beobachter* remained transfixed over his *Lotfernrohr-Bombenzielgerät* (perpendicular telescopic bomb-sight), concentrating solely on coaxing the approaching target directly into his cross hairs. Ground wind direction, which might push the bombs slightly off course, could readily be determined from chimney smoke, or even horses and cattle, which habitually stand with their hindquarters to the wind. The pilot's concentration, meanwhile, flickered between instrument panels, busy traffic and his commander's voice. Fighting all natural instincts to heave the machine away from pounding artillery, he had to hold a steady course, listening intently for every subtle correction relayed to him. A Ju 88 pilot could occasionally get to settle the score with his observer: in dive-bombing attacks he became bombardier, aiming the aircraft directly through a *Reflexionsvisier* (reflector sight). The observer then had to sit patiently beside him, checking their 60–70° angle against coloured lines etched on the port window.

The *Beobachter* finally pressed the bomb release switch. The aircraft suddenly lurched upwards with the instantaneous loss of up to 1 tonne of steel and high explosive. If a serial

BALLOON ENCOUNTER

One misty evening in 1940, a crippled Do 17 with one engine dead and the elevator jammed was limping home across England when a maze of balloon cables suddenly emerged from the gloom. With limited power and control, the pilot had no choice but to fly right through the steel labyrinth. Barely managing to heave the Dornier past the entanglements, and losing altitude all the while, he finally emerged just 2m off the ground. Gunning that misfiring engine again, he was barely able to reach France for an emergency landing. In another more bizarre incident, Major Hajo Herrmann's Ju 88 stalled and lurched to a halt right on top of a barrage balloon, only to tumble off one side into an inverted but recoverable dive.

ABOVE: Holland, 1944. Returned Do 217 crews of III. Gruppe-Stabsschwarm gather for interrogation by debriefing officers. A seasoned crewman himself, the Major cross checks the *Gefechtsbericht* (battle reports), collected by motorcyclist from each *Beobachter* directly after landing, building a detailed analysis of the mission. Claims of a particularly successful strike will require confirmation by photo-reconnaissance, usually undertaken by the responsible crew. (Adam Hook © Osprey Publishing)

was being unloaded, a rapid succession of faltering lifts was felt, as the release-interval mechanism dropped each projectile in 10m increments. When the *Bordmechanik*, lying prone in his ventral turret, confirmed all bombs gone, the pilot immediately opened his throttles, side-slipping clear of the target for the following crew. From 2,000m, the bombs took about 20 seconds to hit the ground, but they disappeared from view long before. The *Beobachter* could perhaps squeeze a glimpse at the results of his work, although the *Flugzeugführer* seldom got the chance. Standing orders forbade him from making additional passes and very few wanted to. The *Bordmechanik* in a medium-bomber, or the *Bordfunker* in a Ju 87, had the best views of a strike.

HEADING HOME

A fine view of a Do 17 bomber in a climb. Just over 2,000 Do 17s were built between 1932 and 1945, small numbers compared to c. 15,000 Ju 88s, which largely replaced the Do 17 in frontline service from 1942.

With enemy defences now fully alert, the return journey was often more hazardous than the approach. A sinister black void in the night sky was a chilling discovery, revealing a lurking barrage balloon silhouetted against the stars. The use of searchlights, unaccompanied by gunfire, was often the first clue that the bomber was being set up for one of the most dreaded weapons in the Allied arsenal – the night-fighter, such as a British Beaufighter or Mosquito, or a Soviet Petlyakov Pe-3. Many literally never knew what hit them.

Whatever the cause, the physical demise of a bomber took many forms. A bomber might glide silently past, to be suddenly blown to bits in an oily black cloud. Alternatively, it might simply break up, with large pieces dropping away. Other aircraft flying directly through the trail of debris could be damaged or destroyed by impact with falling engines, fins and stabilizers. Sometimes a seemingly unharmed machine sailed close by, perhaps with dead or dying crewmen aboard. Others were simply unable to escape. An apparently slow and graceful roll to earth actually generated a centrifuge of around 3G inside the fuselage, tripling body weight and pressing the doomed crewmen into the walls of their machine.

Nearby aircraft suffering engine fires had to be avoided because of the danger of explosion. Despite their high state of anxiety, those aboard a stricken craft had to act quickly to shut down the crippled engine. The *Beobachter* instantly engaged the electrical fuel transfer system, drawing fuel from the dead engine to reserve tanks. An emergency manual pump was provided in case of electrical failure, usually operated by the *Bordfunker*. Even with the fire extinguished, the *Flugzeugführer* still had to 'feather' the propeller, rotating the blades into the wind to prevent them turning. Failure to do so would allow them to spin at unregulated speed, which would generate excessive heat within the engine and re-ignite fuel vapour. If the machine began to list, the pilot pushed the 'live' wing down to compensate. In this attitude, the aircraft could be re-trimmed to fly straight and level, hands-free, but the additional burden placed on the remaining engine made further mechanical failure almost inevitable. The over-worked engine had to be cooled, so the pilot climbed, raising the temperature still further, before entering a shallow glide at reduced power. The increased speed fanned the engine, but the process had to be repeated throughout the flight.

With formations routinely broken up, the return route was seldom the one intended, and crews often had to determine their own way home. In cases of severe damage, or with wounded crewmen aboard, the pilot levelled off at 1,000m, while the *Beobachter* located the nearest emergency landing strip or any suitable open ground. Such unscheduled approaches, especially at night, often confused German air warning personnel, and AA emplacements frequently opened fire on already battered Luftwaffe aircraft. When pre-arranged flare signals failed to convince the hapless flak crews, they could incur the wrath of air gunners, who gave spirited return fire in the genuine hope of hitting some of them. One KG 55 He 111 was brought down, and its pilot killed, as they neared the French coast on the way to Liverpool. In the gunners' defence, they were faced with Allied air forces bombing around the clock, so had to assume that all unseen aircraft were hostile.

LANDING

Airstrip lights were illuminated as the first returning aircraft were identified. Priority was automatically granted to crews discharging two red flares, signalling the need to make an emergency landing. Those with wounded aboard pulled to one side of the airstrip immediately after landing, and awaited the removal of casualties by ambulance before taxiing back to revetments. A severely wounded or dead pilot forced the remaining crewmen to make a '*Schwarze-Landung*' (black landing, i.e. without permission, or by an unqualified airman). With luck, the involuntary pilot was flying a He 111, which always gave a positive landing. Its weight made it difficult to bounce, although braking required substantial effort. Compared to the Heinkel's stately 153km/h landing speed, the Ju 88 had to race in at 250km/h to remain under control and was not easy to land at the best of times. It was difficult to get the tail down and it had an unnerving tendency to swing violently if even slightly too much brake was applied by an inexperienced or tired pilot.

A lost engine would slow the electrical lowering of the undercarriage, while damaged hydraulics could prevent it altogether. Assuming the assembly itself was still intact, the gear could be lowered manually by hand-wheel or pump. If this back-up system was inoperable, the pilot had to execute a *Bauchlandung* (belly landing), a procedure that, for obvious reasons, could not be practised, but had to be learned the hard way. Although theoretically identical to a normal landing, control was drastically undermined from the moment of impact. Friction, sparks and bursting fuel tanks often resulted in fire. Exhaustion, misjudgement and poor visibility caused numerous mid-air and runway collisions, as aircraft attempted to land simultaneously. An unexpected torrent of cannon-fire from the blackness, ripping into an aircraft just as it began its landing, at last revealed the insidious presence of night-fighters that had trailed the formation all the way back home. Struck at their most vulnerable time, the crews stood virtually no chance of survival. After making it through countless preceding dangers, the loss of crewmen in these final moments of the mission was particularly cruel.

As soon as the last aircraft was down, all airfield lights were extinguished. Traffic controllers guided each to its *Splitterbüchse* (splinter box) protective pen with green hand lanterns, as ground crewmen set about their tasks. Engines were shut down and silence eventually returned.

EVASION AND CAPTURE

During the early *Blitzkrieg* campaigns over Poland and mainland Europe, shot-down crews made determined efforts to return to their units wherever possible, but those who did fall into enemy hands spent only a matter of days or weeks in captivity before liberation. For those brought down over Britain the prospects for escape to Germany were virtually non-existent, although a loose airman could still be a thorn in the enemy's side, tying up disproportionate resources in the hunt. The longest such evasion was made by Feldwebel Josef Markl, 8./KG 55 Greif, in July 1940, only ending when he gave himself up, famished and exhausted after hiding in fields outside Newbury for eight days. While evasion was the accepted duty of the downed airman, very few even attempted to avoid capture, but instead made immediately for the nearest village to hand themselves in. Some were cocky, or mildly irritated by this temporary interruption to their flying careers, certain of liberation by the conquering German Army, but the overwhelming majority were subdued and cooperative, offering little or no resistance. Invariably in shock, they surrendered easily to unarmed policemen or even civilians (although in one case, near Portsmouth, a child's toy pistol was brandished by the local pub landlord). Having miraculously survived a high-speed air-crash, they viewed the prospect of incarceration as of little concern. While some took a few punches and kicks, most Luftwaffe airmen received reasonable treatment from their captors – and usually a cup of tea. Their own treatment of British prisoners was sometimes even more hospitable. In 1941 the crew of one shot-down RAF Blenheim were first plied with coffee and beer in a KG 26 mess and shown around the base, eventually winding up in the cockpit of a Ju 88.

Encounters with Americans were not always so genial, however. Flugzeugmechanik Karl-Heinz Mewes was deeply hurt when one POW camp guard ripped the Iron Cross from his tunic, feeling the GI had no right to it.

A forced landing on the Eastern Front could be an extremely hazardous affair, and finding sanctuary with any Axis unit was the overriding priority. Many Red Army soldiers, brutalized by years of savage conflict and the bestial behaviour of certain Waffen-SS units, had little sympathy for the unfortunate *Fashistii*. Some of those captured by Soviet personnel would not survive long enough to reach imprisonment, and even

A Heinkel He 111 bursts into flames following an attack by enemy fighters. Unescorted He 111s were relatively easy prey to fighter attack, being slow and unmanoeuvrable and having limited defensive armament.

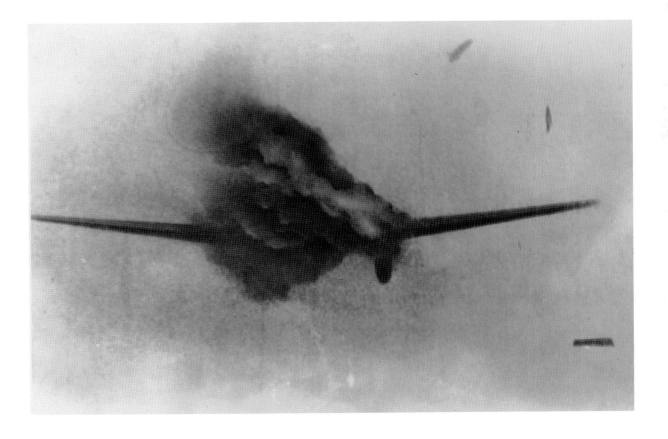

The Dornier Do 17 was a light bomber known for its agility and structural toughness. Its bomb load was minimal, however, being a maximum of 1,000kg.

those that did faced an uncertain future. Such was their fear that several bomber pilots were compelled to land alongside crashed aircraft, risking death or capture themselves in order to rescue their comrades from advancing infantry. Others less fortunate were forced to undertake epic journeys on foot, private odysseys lasting many days or even months, back towards German lines. Reliant on their wits or assisted by courageous anti-communist locals, downed crewmen first had to pass through Russian frontline positions. Rescuing Army units promptly lavished medical treatment, food, alcohol and adulation upon any dazed airmen before returning them to their squadron.

Tales of daring escape attempts often overshadow the mundane and distressing reality of prolonged incarceration, but during their years as POWs, the calm and rational characteristics that ensured selection as bomber crewmen in the first place almost certainly influenced their behaviour in captivity. Those airmen who were most keen to escape, and persistently uncooperative, were nearly always the fighter pilots.

CASUALTIES

People, like aircraft, can sustain remarkable levels of damage while remaining operable. Medical treatment in flight was somewhat restricted by space (particularly in the Ju 88), although the crew was well equipped. Death, however, could sometimes come from unexpected quarters. With aircraft in the hands of the autopilot, the monotonous drone of the engines could have a soporific effect upon the crew, and several *Kampfflieger* confessed to having succumbed to tiredness. Sometimes the entire crew would be fast asleep for several kilometres, bypassing their last available airstrip or heading out across an ocean. It is impossible to know just how many (if any) crews met their end in this way, flying into mountains and hillsides or simply running out of fuel, but it is not inconceivable. KG 30 Beobachter Uffz. Hans Fecht and his crew narrowly avoided just such a disaster over the North Sea in 1941. On occasion, the circumstances were shameful. On 15 September 1940, an already badly wounded Oberleutnant Robert Zehbe, KG 76, came down near the Oval cricket ground in London. An angry civilian mob descended upon him, beating him mercilessly before the police could rescue him. He later died of his injuries.

Throughout the war, German and British air forces upheld the traditions of according full honours to each other's dead whenever possible. Onlookers gathered in respectful silence, as honour guards presented volley-fire over the flag-draped casket. Where an original could not be found, copies of the *Kriegsfahne* or the 'Union Jack' were specially produced. Many Luftwaffe *Kampfflieger* still lie in British and Commonwealth military cemeteries, not separately, but shoulder to shoulder with their former adversaries.

FIGHTERS — SKY WARRIORS

The Luftwaffe fighter ace Franz von Werra examines the kill record on this tailplane of his Bf 109. The Bf 109 and the Fw 190 were the main vehicles of the leading *Experten* (aces) during the war years.

Ironically, given its overwhelming importance during the last years of the war, the Fighter Arm was initially regarded as the lesser branch of pre-war Luftwaffe airpower: the bomber – particularly the dive-bomber – was to be the war-winning element. The primary function of the Jagdwaffe was to achieve and secure air superiority, without which all strategic operations would suffer heavily, if not fail. This goal was achieved over Poland in 1939, France in 1940 and Russia in 1941; it was very nearly achieved over England in 1940, and later over Malta, but in those cases the prize was ultimately lost through German underestimation of the fighter arm's achievements, and untimely switches of target.

Invariably starting campaigns in style, the fighters were before long pushed onto the defensive, becoming and remaining over-tasked. Although the pilots were consistently able to inflict heavy casualties upon their enemies, these were short-term victories of little or no strategic value, since the Allies' greater resources allowed such losses to be replaced. The destruction of enemy day-fighters, even in great number, had diminishing effects, and as the strength of the US Army Air Forces (USAAF) bomber force in England steadily increased in 1943–44 even the occasional slaughter of these 'heavy babies' ceased to threaten Allied strategic aims. The achievements of the night-fighters, in their struggle to prevent British bombers from reaching their targets, were of far greater value to the defence of German industry, military capability and civilian population; yet these victories, too, were of limited effect against such overwhelming odds. The Fighter Arm was constantly forced to evolve and adapt, and met every challenge that was thrown at it (and not always by its enemies).

FIGHTER AIRCRAFT

Between 1939 and 1945, the Luftwaffe fielded two of the greatest fighters ever to take to the skies – the Messerschmitt Bf 109 and the Focke-Wulf Fw 190. These two superlative single-engined machines were, in the daylight hours at least, a scourge of Allied pilots on every front, hence we will give them lengthy consideration here. (Note that twin-engined fighters are covered in the discussion of night-fighters below.)

BF 109

Undoubtedly the most famous German fighter ever, and built in greater numbers than any other aircraft except the Ilyushin Il-2, the Messerschmitt Bf 109 fought in both the Spanish Civil War and World War II. The aircraft's origins can be traced back to the fledgling Luftwaffe's desire to modernize its fighter force in the early 1930s.

On 6 July 1933, the RLM issued Tactical Requirements for Fighter Aircraft (Land). This document stated that the Luftwaffe needed a single-seat daytime fighter armed with two fixed machine guns (1,000 rounds) or one fixed cannon (100 rounds). It had to have a radio for air-to-air and air-to-ground communication, as well as a safety harness, oxygen system, parachute, and heating for the pilot. The fighter had to be able to maintain a speed of 400km/h for up to 20 minutes at 6,000m, possess at least an hour's flight duration and take no longer than 17 minutes to reach this height. Its ultimate ceiling was to be 10,000m.

From a handling perspective, the aircraft had to be capable of diving and turning without losing altitude, and be easily recoverable from a spin. The fighter also had to be operable from the average German airfield, which was 400m × 400m in size, by an average frontline pilot. It would also be required to fly in cloud and fog, and to perform

The Messerschmitt Bf 109E was the mainstay German fighter during the Battle of Britain and the early war years. The 'Emil' was replaced in 1941 by the F variant, then in turn by the superb G variant in mid-1942.

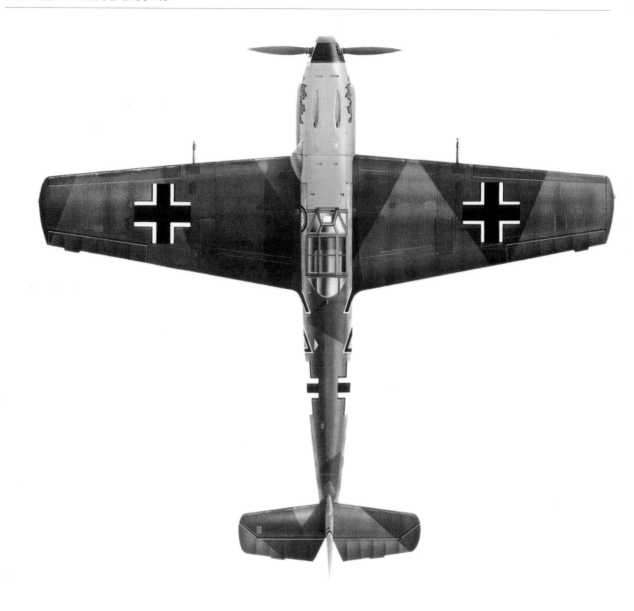

ABOVE: Bf 109E-4 'Black Chevron and Triangle' of Hauptmann Hans von Hahn, *Gruppenkommandeur* LtJG 3, Colombert, August 1940. Von Hahn oversaw LtJG 3's redesignation into II./JG 1 early in 1942, before undertaking a series of staff appointments. He ended the war with 34 victories as *Jafü Oberitalien* (Fighter Leader Upper Italy). (John Weal © Osprey Publishing)

group (up to nine aircraft) take-offs and landings. Finally, the design had to be small enough to enable it to be transported by rail.

Having already built fighters for the Luftwaffe, Arado, Heinkel and Focke-Wulf were seen as front runners to win this lucrative contract, and Messerschmitt, which had no experience in designing fighters, was seen as the rank outsider. The company had a long history of aircraft construction, however, having taken over the Udet Flugzeugbau in July 1926. Bayerische Flugzeugwerke AG had merged with fellow aircraft manufacturer Messerschmitt Flugzeugbau at this time, and company founder Dipl.-Ing. Willy Messerschmitt assumed design control within the new enterprise.

Its series of fast sports aircraft from the late 1920s and early 1930s, boasting low-set, cantilever wings, gave the RLM the confidence to instruct Messerschmitt to build a four-seater touring aircraft to compete in the 1934 European Flying Contest. The M 23 design by Willy Messerschmitt had won this prestigious international competition in 1929 and 1930, and the new aircraft produced by the company was eventually designated the Bf 108.

Design work on the Bf 109 commenced in secret in March 1934 at the Bayerische Flugzeugwerke AG facility in Augsburg-Haunstetten, in Bavaria. Many features embodied in the Bf 108 would find their way into the Bf 109 prototype, including flush-riveted stressed-skin construction, cantilevered monoplane wings, equipped with Handley Page 'slots' along the leading edges, and a narrow track undercarriage attached to the fuselage and retracting outwards into wells forward of the main spar.

The Bf 109F, seen here, had improved aerodynamics over the Bf 109E, with a smoother and more streamlined shape and a redesigned wing. Armament, depending on the subvariant, was a mixture of 7.92mm MG17 machine guns and MG151 15mm cannon.

Ground crewmen servicing a Bf 109E in France, 1940, are temporarily distracted by the *Staffelhund*; one mechanic, still absorbed in his work, wears *Gummiüberschuhe* (rubber boots) to protect the airframe.

Buoyed by the success of the Bf 108, Messerschmitt pressed on with the Bf 109, which incorporated all of the features previously mentioned. Aside from the wing slots, the aircraft also had trailing edge flaps, and the two combined with the flying surfaces' small surface area (made possible by the growing power of aero engines) to give the Bf 109 unmatched manoeuvrability. The fuselage itself was made of light metal as a

monocoque structure of roughly oval section, constructed in two halves and joined along the centreline.

Right from the start, Messerschmitt had planned that the lightweight Bf 109 would be powered by one of the new generation inverted-Vee 12-cylinder engines under development by Junkers and Daimler-Benz. The former's 680hp Jumo 210 was ultimately selected because it was at a more advanced stage in its development than the 960hp DB 600Aa. As it transpired, delivery of the Junkers powerplant was delayed to the point where the first prototype Bf 109 V1 had to be fitted with a 695hp Rolls-Royce Kestrel VI engine.

Construction of the V1 was completed by early May 1935 and, following a series of taxiing trials, on the 28th of that month Messerschmitt's senior test pilot, Hans-Dietrich 'Bubi' Knoetzsch, made the fighter's first flight from Augsburg-Haunstetten airfield. Following initial factory trials, the aircraft was sent to the Rechlin-based *Erprobungsstelle* (testing centre) for service evaluation, where it was soon proved that the Bf 109 was much faster and more manoeuvrable than its primary rival for the fighter contract, Heinkel's He 112 V1 (which was also Kestrel-powered).

A formation of Bf 109s head over to Britain in the summer of 1940. Contrary to popular myth, the Bf 109 was not inferior to the Spitfire, and indeed inflicted heavy losses on all forms of Allied aircraft.

BF 109E-4 WING GUN (ABOVE)

The Oerlikon MG FF 'M' 20mm cannon made its frontline debut in the Bf 109E-4. This version of the weapon fired *M-Geschosse* (Mine) shells, which inflicted more damage than a standard round. Boasting a low cyclic rate of fire, pronounced recoil and oversized *Trommel* T60 drum magazine, the weapon was replaced by the superb MG151 from late 1940. (Jim Laurier © Osprey Publishing)

BF 109E-4 COWLING GUNS (LEFT)

Like previous versions of the 'Emil', the Bf 109E-4 was fitted with a pair of Rheinmetall MG17s immediately above its DB 601 engine. Each weapon had a magazine holding 1,000 rounds per gun. Note how the guns are staggered, with the port MG17 being set slightly forward the width of the ammunition feed chute. (Jim Laurier © Osprey Publishing)

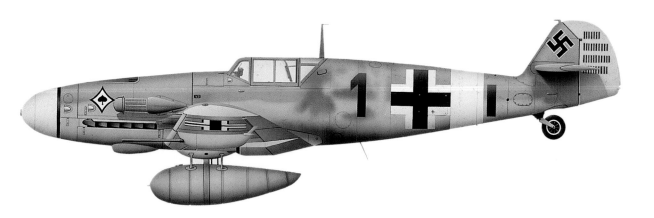

ABOVE: Bf 109G-4/Z Trop 'Black 1', Oberleutnant Franz Schiess, Staffelkapitän 8./JG 53, Tunis-El Aouina/Tunisia, *c.* February 1943. The 38 victories depicted here had mostly been gained during Schiess's previous year's service as Geschwader-Adjutant. Schiess added a further 29 kills during his six months at the head of 8./JG 53, before falling victim to P-38s off the Gulf of Naples on 2 September 1943. (John Weal © Osprey Publishing)

The Jumo 210A-powered Bf 109 V2 took to the skies in October 1935 and joined the trials programme three months later. This aircraft also boasted two 7.92mm MG17 machine guns in the fuselage upper decking. The V3, which had provision for an engine-mounted 20mm MG FF/M cannon firing through the propeller hub, flew for the first time in June 1936, and a short while later both Messerschmitt and Heinkel received contracts from the RLM to build ten pre-production aircraft.

In the autumn of that year the official trials culminated in a series of tests at Travemünde, where the Bf 109 proved its superiority in a memorable flight demonstration that included tailslides, flick rolls, 21-turn spins, tight turns and terminal dives. Being faster in level speed and in the climb than the He 112, and easily able to outdive the Heinkel, the Bf 109 could also perform much tighter turns thanks to its leading-edge slots. From rank outsider, Messerschmitt had become the obvious choice for the contract, and the Bf 109 was duly announced the competition winner.

Production Bf 109Bs entered service in Germany in February 1937, these early aircraft being built at Messerschmitt's Augsburg-Haunstetten plant. It soon became clear that a larger factory would be required, however, so a new site at Regensburg was developed, and production of the 'Bertha' was duly transferred there. The company's design offices remained at Augsburg.

In June 1937, the Bf 109 V10 flew for the first time with the promising 960hp Daimler-Benz DB 600Aa fitted. This new powerplant was much longer and heavier than the Jumo, and in order to offset the shift in the aircraft's centre of gravity, Messerschmitt redesigned the fighter's cooling system. A shallow radiator bath was fitted

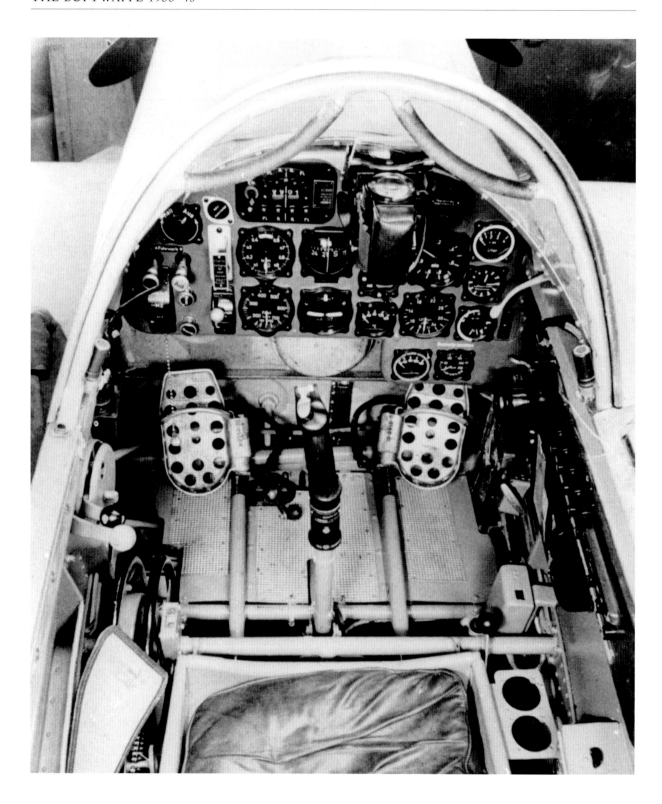

under the nose and two radiators were positioned beneath the wings. A three-bladed VDM propeller also replaced the two-bladed VDM-Hamilton airscrew fitted to the Jumo-powered Bf 109B. Due to the fighter's increased all-up weight, its fuselage and undercarriage were also strengthened. This aircraft would effectively serve as the prototype for the Bf 109E.

In the early spring of 1938 deliveries of the Bf 109C, fitted with the 730hp fuel-injected Jumo 210Ga engine and wing-mounted machine guns, commenced, with the first aircraft being issued to I./JG 132. Only 58 were built before production switched to the four-gun Bf 109D, which was powered by the 680hp carburettored Jumo 210Da engine. Some 657 were built, with aircraft also being constructed by Erla Maschinenwerk in Leipzig and Focke-Wulf Flugzeugbau of Bremen.

By 19 September 1938, the Luftwaffe had 583 Bf 109B/C/Ds on strength, but limited availability of the Daimler-Benz engine stymied plans for the rapid fielding of the Bf 109E. This was because bomber production had priority over fighter procurement in the late 1930s, and most DB 600 production was allocated to the He 111.

Finally, in 1938, the focus shifted to fighter production, and by then the much-delayed DB 601A was at last reaching maturity, so Daimler-Benz switched its efforts to perfecting this powerplant. This new engine was very similar to the DB 600, but crucially it featured fuel injection rather than a float carburettor. This meant that

LEFT: The cockpit of the prototype Me 209 fighter aircraft. The Me 209 was an experimental attempt to create a new fighter from the Bf 109 lineage that could deliver clear air superiority over the Spitfires encountered in the Battle of Britain. The project never reached production stage, however.

The Messerschmitt Me 209 had an unusual profile, with the cockpit set well back along the fuselage. It was designed for speed and manoeuvrability, but once stability issues were solved its performance was no better than that of the Bf 109.

the Bf 109 could perform negative G flight, and also increased the fighter's range through improved fuel economy.

With its DB 601A engine rated at 1,175hp for take-off, the Bf 109E-1 (with phonetic name 'Emil') finally entered series production in December 1938, the new aircraft boasting unmatched take-off and climb performance. The higher wing loading of the 'Emil' increased the fighter's turning circle and stall speed, but it was still very much a pilot's aircraft.

Like the D-model before it, the E-1's armament consisted of two 7.92mm MG17s in the upper fuselage decking and two more machine guns in the wings. The latter had 500 rounds per gun, and the fuselage guns had 1,000 rounds each.

In early 1939 the first Bf 109E-3s began rolling off the production line, these aircraft having their wing MG17s replaced with MG FF 20mm cannon as initially trialled in the Bf 109C-3. Each weapon had only 60 rounds, but their destructive punch was unrivalled. Once in frontline service, the E-3 *Kanonenmaschine* was rated as the best early generation Messerschmitt by those who flew it, with the aircraft enjoying a greater margin of superiority over its rivals than any other Bf 109 variant.

Between 1 January and September 1939, 1,091 'Emils' were delivered. Four engine plants had been established to allow production of the DB 601 to keep apace with airframe construction, with Bf 109s being built by Messerschmitt, Erla and Fieseler in Germany, and by the Wiener-Neüstadt Flugzeugbau in Austria.

By the time the Wehrmacht advanced east into Poland on September 1, 1939, no fewer than 28 *Gruppen* were operating Bf 109B/C/D/Es. The Messerschmitt fighter was now well placed to dominate the skies over Europe. In the autumn of 1940, Messerschmitt's E-model replacement in the form of the Bf 109F-1 began rolling off production lines in Germany. This aircraft differed from its predecessor primarily in its weaponry. The F-model saw the wing guns deleted in favour of a single engine-mounted cannon firing through the propeller hub, in addition to two upper cowling-mounted machine guns. Various hydraulic and cooling system improvements were also incorporated, as was additional pilot and fuel tank armour. Externally, the fighter was also more streamlined around the nose, and lengthened overall. The tail section was tidied up aerodynamically, with the deletion of the horizontal stabilizer bracing. Finally, the F-model's wing was completely redesigned, with the wingtips extended and rounded.

Production of the Bf 109F numbered 3,300+ airframes built over four sub-variants (F-1 to F-4), and ran from September 1940 through to May 1942. Like the 'Emil', the 'Friedrich' performed both fighter and fighter-bomber missions in Eastern and Western Europe, the Mediterranean and in North Africa.

The F-model was replaced on the production line in June 1942 by the Bf 109G, which combined the 'Friedrich's' refined airframe with the larger, heavier and considerably more powerful 1,475hp DB 605 engine. Cockpit pressurization was also introduced for the first time with the G-1 ('Gustav'), although most later sub-variants lacked this feature. Produced in staggering numbers from mid-1942 through to war's end, some 24,000+ Bf 109Gs were constructed in total – including an overwhelming 14,212 in 1944 alone.

Numerous modifications to the basic G-1 were introduced either in the factory (as *Umrüst-Bausätze* factory conversion sets) or in the field (*Rüstsätze*), and these included the provision for extra armament, additional radios, introduction of a wooden tailplane, the fitting of a lengthened tailwheel and the installation of the MW-50 water/methanol-boosted DB 605D engine. In an attempt to standardize the equipment of the frontline force, Messerschmitt began production of the Bf 109G-6 in February 1943, and this model included many of these previously ad hoc additions. The G-6 would ultimately prove to be the most important variant of Messerschmitt's famous fighter, with 12,000+ examples being built – more than a third of the overall production run for the Bf 109.

Unfortunately, the continual addition of weighty items such as underwing cannon gondolas, rocket tubes and larger engines to the once slight airframe of the Bf 109 eliminated much of the fighter's once legendary manoeuvrability, and instead served to emphasize the aircraft's poor slow-speed performance, tricky lateral control and ground handling.

Yet in the late-war Bf 109G-10 model, fitted with the Erla Haube bulged canopy, tall wooden tailplane and DB 605D engine, Messerschmitt had a fighter capable of achieving speeds up to 690km/h at 7,500m. Confusingly, although the G-10 appeared numerically after the lightened G-14 in the sub-variant list for the Bf 109G, it was in fact the last production G-model to see service!

The last main operational version of the Bf 109 was the K-series, which was developed directly from the 'Gustav'. The K-4 was the only sub-variant to see frontline service, and this aircraft boasted a DB 605DM engine, wooden tail construction and single cannon and twin machine gun armament. The continual reinvention of the Bf 109 meant that mooted replacements, such as the Bf 209 proposed by Willy Messerschmitt in 1943, were never required.

RIGHT: Seen here sporting the Oak Leaves to his Knight's Cross, awarded on 21 September for his 40th victory, Major Werner Mölders is wearing standard officer's service dress of tunic and breeches, together with the *Schirmmütze* (officer's peaked cap) and *Pelzstiefeln* (flying boots). Note too the woollen inner gloves. The only non-regulation item is the sheepskin jacket.
(Mike Chappell © Osprey Publishing)

ERICH HARTMANN

The son of a physician, Erich Alfred Hartmann was born in Weissach, Württemberg, on 19 April 1922. Following in his father's footsteps, he had intended to study medicine had the war not intervened. Instead, he left school at the age of 18 in September 1940 and joined the Luftwaffe the following month.

Hartmann was two years in training, spending time at both the cadet college in Berlin and the fighter school at Zerbst, before joining his first operational unit – 7. Staffel of JG 52 – at Soldatskaya, on the southern sector of the Eastern Front, in October 1942. His first victory – an Il-2 – was achieved over the Caucasus on 5 November 1942, but it would be nearly three months (27 January 1943) before he doubled his tally by downing a MiG-1 fighter. Although something of a slow starter, Hartmann claimed his first double – a brace of LaGG-3s – on 30 April 1943 to take his score into double figures. Six months later almost to the day, on 29 October 1943, Leutnant Erich Hartmann was awarded the Knight's Cross for a total of 148 kills! His star was very much in the ascendant, and multiple daily victories had become commonplace. By this time he had been appointed Kapitän of 9./JG 52, the famous Staffel 'Karaya'.

The Oak Leaves followed on 2 March 1944 for his reaching a total of 200, and the Swords on 4 July – three days after Hartmann's promotion to Oberleutnant – for 239. On 18 July he became only the fourth pilot to achieve 250 victories, and his 11 kills on 24 August took his score to 301. The first pilot in the world to be credited with a triple century, this feat earned Hartmann the Diamonds the following day. Promoted to Hauptmann on 1 September 1944, he duly took over as Staffelkapitän of the reformed 4./JG 52 a month later, and also served as acting Kommandeur of II. Gruppe. Invited to join Adolf Galland's Me 262-equipped JV 44, Hartmann declined, preferring instead to return to JG 52 on the Eastern Front for the remaining weeks of the war, which he saw out as Kommandeur of I. Gruppe. On 8 May 1945 – the day hostilities ceased in Europe – Erich Hartmann scored his 352nd, and last, kill, and was promoted to Major.

Despite surrendering his unit to the US Third Army, Hartmann was handed over to Soviet troops and subsequently spent the next ten years in a series of prison camps, where he endured innumerable hardships. In 1955 he at last returned home to his wife, and joined the newly formed West German air force. He remained with the new Luftwaffe until 1970, when he retired with the rank of Oberst. Subsequently joining the Federal Aviation Authority, Hartmann also managed several flying schools in the Württemberg area. Opting for full retirement in the late 1980s, he passed away on 19 September 1993.

It is impossible to say how many Allied aircraft were downed by Bf 109s, but the numbers are certainly in their thousands. Many Bf 109 pilots achieved astonishing kill rates in their aircraft, particularly on the Eastern Front. The greatest of all the *Experten* was Erich Hartmann, who achieved no fewer than 352 kills in his wartime career in

Bf 109s (see feature box opposite), a testimony as much to the flying qualities of the aircraft as to the bravery of the man.

FOCKE-WULF FW 190

In late 1937, a development contract was issued to Focke-Wulf Flugzeugbau GmbH for a single-seat interceptor fighter to supplement the Messerschmitt Bf 109. Under Kurt Tank's direction, a design team led by Oberingenieur Blaser created a low-wing monoplane with a fully retractable undercarriage that could be powered by either the Daimler-Benz DB 601 12-cylinder vee liquid-cooled inline engine (as fitted to the Bf 109) or the BMW 139 18-cylinder two-row radial.

A radial engine typically causes drag and is bulky, and the latter trait reduces the pilot's forward visibility during take-off and landing. However, the RLM surprisingly ordered the radial-engined fighter to be developed so as not to overburden Daimler-Benz – a decision which amazed Tank and his colleagues. Detailed work on the fighter began the following summer.

The Focke-Wulf Fw 190 transformed the capability of the Luftwaffe's fighter force, particularly with the introduction of the main service version, the Fw 190D, in the autumn of 1944. It offered superior manoeuvrability and a top speed of more than 650km/h.

A Focke-Wulf Fw 190D stands partially camouflaged by surrounding trees. Compared with previous variants, the Fw 190D had a longer nose, which accommodated a Junkers Jumo 213 liquid-cooled engine.

Flugkapitän Hans Sander, in his capacity as Focke-Wulf's chief test pilot, flew the first prototype from the company's Bremen facility on June 1, 1939. It was powered by a fan-cooled 1,550hp BMW 139 radial which was fitted with a special ducted spinner to reduce drag. After five test flights, the aircraft was transferred to Rechlin, where a speed of 595km/h was achieved. During October 1939 a second prototype was completed, this machine being fitted with two 13mm MG131 and 7.92mm MG17 machine guns.

In June 1939 the BMW 139 engine was abandoned and work began on the 14-cylinder BMW 801. In an effort to compensate for the greater weight associated with this new engine, the fighter's cockpit was moved farther aft.

Despite its bulky powerplant, the Fw 190 was small, the BMW engine being neatly faired into a slim fuselage. In stark contrast to the Bf 109, the Focke-Wulf fighter was fitted with an extensively glazed cockpit canopy which afforded the pilot with an excellent all-round view.

Early in 1940, Göring visited the Focke-Wulf factory and inspected the Fw 190V2 second prototype. He was very impressed, and told Tank that he 'must turn these new fighters out like so many hot rolls!' The success of the BMW 801-engined aircraft led to the construction of 30 pre-production machines, designated Fw 190A-0, and 100 Fw 190A-1 production models were also subsequently ordered. Early trials were carried out at Erprobungsstelle Rechlin, and in March 1941 pilots and engineers from JG 26 prepared to introduce the new fighter into Luftwaffe service. In August the first Fw190A-1s were delivered to 6./JG 26 at Le Bourget.

On 18 September, when RAF Spitfire Vs and Fw 190s clashed for the first time, it soon became obvious that the German fighter was more manoeuvrable in almost every respect, and also possessed a higher maximum speed. Fw 190As fought their first major action in early February 1942, when they were among the fighters used to cover the battlecruisers *Scharnhorst* and *Gneisenau* and the heavy cruiser *Prinz Eugen* as they sailed

Luftwaffe Fw 190s lie scorched and destroyed at their airbase in Germany, the base having been captured by US forces in 1945. In addition to being a pure fighter, the Fw 190 was also successfully employed as a ground-attack aircraft and night-fighter.

from Brest to the safety of north German ports. Jagdwaffe fighters fought off British attempts to destroy the ships, and Fw 190A-1s from III./JG 26 shot down six Swordfish torpedo-bombers.

Orders soon followed for the improved Fw 190A-2, which was powered by the BMW 801C-2 engine and armed with two 7.92mm MG17 machine guns above the engine cowling and two 20mm MG FF cannon in the wing roots – the aircraft also often carried an extra pair of MG17 guns in the outer wings. The A-2 was followed by the Fw 190A-3, which was powered by a 1,700hp BMW 801D-2 engine and had the MG FF cannon moved outboard and replaced by two of the much faster firing 20mm MG151/20 cannon. The cockpit canopy could be jettisoned with the aid of explosive bolts and the pilot was protected by 8mm and 14mm armour plating.

By early 1942 more than 250 Fw 190s were being produced every month. In March 1942 II./JG 26, which was often in the forefront of attacks on American day-bombers and their fighter escorts, was re-equipped with the Fw 190A-3. In April JG 2 was also equipped with the Fw 190A-3 in the west. Four months later the Fw 190A-4, powered by the BMW 801D-2 engine (fitted with water-methanol injection that provided 2,100hp for short periods), entered production.

Although the Fw 190A had proven itself to be an extremely effective fighter, operational experience revealed that the power of the BMW 801 engine tended to drop off at altitudes in excess of 7,000m. Attempts were therefore made to improve the high altitude performance of the aircraft during the subsequent production of Fw 190A, B and C variants.

In June 1942 Fw 190s were issued to JG 1 to combat American bomber formations appearing over the Reich, as well as to IV./JG 5 in Norway. The following month the first Spitfire IXs entered RAF service, and these aircraft met the Fw 190 on almost equal terms. However, on August 19, when the Fw 190s went into action against Allied fighters and landing craft during the ill-fated Dieppe operation, the RAF lost 106 aircraft, of which JG 2 and JG 26 claimed the lion's share. By the end of the year, with the American daylight bombing raids increasing in their intensity, several more Luftwaffe *Gruppen* were equipped with the Fw 190.

Early in 1943 the Fw 190A-5, which was essentially similar to the A-4, appeared. This version differed from its predecessor by having a revised engine mounting to allow the BMW 801D-2 to be fitted 15cm farther forward of the cockpit. This arrangement was designed to eliminate engine overheating problems that had consistently plagued the aircraft since its service introduction almost two years earlier.

By the start of 1943, the Eighth Air Force in East Anglia had became a potent threat, conducting raids on targets in the Reich. The situation had become so serious by July that Luftwaffe fighter units had to be transferred to airfields in the west from the Eastern

RIGHT: The pilot of an Fw 190A watches an aircraft turning over its engine. The survivability of Luftwaffe fighter pilots dropped significantly as the war went on. By 1944, the life expectancy of replacement pilots was in the region of two to five weeks.

MORTAR ARMAMENT

Many Fw 190s were fitted with Werfergranate (WGr.) 21cm mortars. These were modified infantry weapons intended to break up an enemy bomber formation by blast effect, thus diminishing their defensive fire. One 1.3m-long rifled mortar launching tube was suspended from beneath each underside wing surface of an Fw 190 by means of four bracing lugs and a central hook with a suspension bracket. Three retaining springs, located near the rear end of the tube, held the 112kg shell (with its 40kg warhead) in place, and a screw bolt, also at the rear end of the tube, prevented the shell from sliding out. In an emergency, the launching tube could be jettisoned by activating an electrically primed explosive charge which severed the central hook. The mortars were controlled from a cockpit armament panel containing two armament switches and a Revi 16B reflector sight. Two spin-stabilized shells were fired simultaneously when the pilot depressed a button on his control column. The mortar shells were fitted with a time fuze, pre-set at 800m prior to delivery to an operational unit, and they were not subsequently adjusted. The firing range was therefore invariable, and the weapon's low velocity meant that for it to be effective, it had to be aimed 60m above its target, and a shell had to detonate within 28m of a bomber. (Jim Laurier © Osprey Publishing)

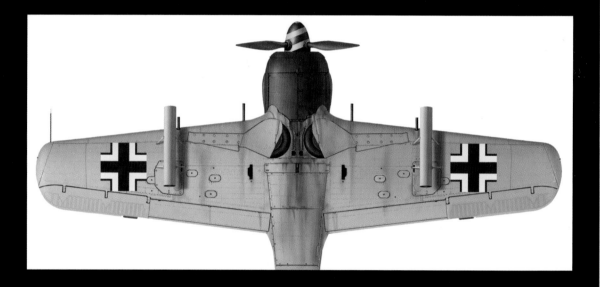

Front and the Mediterranean. From late August 1943 onwards, six *Jagdgruppen* equipped with Fw 190A-4/5s were available for operations against the Allied air forces flying from Britain. On 17 August, when the Eighth Air Force attacked Regensburg and Schweinfurt, more than 300 Fw 190s met the four-engined bombers. The Americans lost 60 'heavies', with almost all of them falling to German fighters. On 14 October, when the Eighth Air Force attacked ball-bearing factories in Schweinfurt, Fw 190A-5/R6 fighters shot down a high proportion of the 79 bombers that were destroyed. A further 120 'heavies' were damaged.

The next major variant of the Focke-Wulf to enter service was the Fw 190A-6, which had a redesigned wing that was both lighter and could carry four 20mm MG151/20 cannon – two MG17 machine guns were also mounted above the engine. The A-6/R1 carried six 20mm MG151/20 cannon and the Fw 190A-6/R3 two 30mm MK 103 cannon in underwing gondolas. In December 1943 the Fw 190A-7 entered production.

The final large-scale production version of the A-series was the Fw 190A-8, which was fitted with an additional 115-litre internal fuel tank and other refinements. One of the last production variants of the A-series was the Fw 190A-9, which was similar to the A-8 but was powered by a 2,000hp BMW 801F engine. Although the radial-engined Fw 190A series was the principal variant to see service with the Luftwaffe, thousands of Fw 190F/Gs eventually replaced the Ju 87 Stuka as Germany's chief close-support aircraft. Essentially these planes were ground-attack versions of the basic Fw 190A series serving as fighter-bombers. Due to their ground-attack roles neither variant can be regarded as a direct opponent of the Merlin-engined P-51.

As good as the BMW radial-engined Fw 190A was, its performance fell away badly at high altitudes. It would struggle to be a premier air superiority fighter once the P-51D appeared in the ETO from June 1944. Following two years of development, the first of some 700 Junkers Jumo 213 inline-engined Fw 190D-9s began pouring off the Cottbus assembly line in August 1944. Although a match for the P-51D, the 'Dora-9' was only ever considered 'an emergency solution' by chief designer Tank, whose ultimate high-altitude fighter was the inline-engined Ta 152H. Also built at Cottbus, production examples of the Ta 152H started to leave the Focke-Wulf plant in November 1944, and by the time the factory was abandoned in early 1945, 150 examples had been delivered to the Luftwaffe. Most of these aircraft were issued to JG 301. Although the Fw 190D-9 and Ta 152H were clearly better air superiority fighters, their paucity in numbers meant that the radial-engined Fw 190A series machines remained in the vanguard of the Jagdwaffe through to VE-Day, opposing the thousands of Mustangs that ruled German skies in the last year of the war.

JETS AND ROCKETS

Hitler's Germany was, for better and for worse, a technologically innovative environment. In the field of aviation, this innovation led to the Luftwaffe being the first of the world's air forces to introduce production jet and rocket fighters into significant frontline service. Although this introduction came too late in the war to save Germany from aerial defeat, the appearance of aircraft such as the Messerschmitt Me 262 sent ripples of shock (and cannon fire) through the ranks of the Allied bomber and fighter crews.

Professor Willy Messerschmitt's state-of-the-art fighter had first taken to the air using pure jet power on 18 July 1942 when company test pilot Fritz Wendel made a

OVERLEAF: The Messerschmitt Me 262, when it entered Luftwaffe service in late 1944, offered levels of performance unobtainable by traditional prop-driven aircraft. It had a maximum speed of 870km/h and was armed with no fewer than four MK 108 30mm cannon.

An Me 262 undergoes
maintenance. The nose-mounted
radar indicates that this aircraft is
an Me 262B-1a/U1 night-fighter.
Other experimental interception
versions were armed with
air-to-air rockets.

trouble-free flight from Leipheim. Following a delayed gestation, largely attributable to
setbacks and problems with engine development and supply from BMW and Junkers,
Wendel was able to report generally smooth handling during the maiden test-flight,
during which he achieved an unprecedented airspeed of 720km/h. Despite misgivings,
Wendel also recorded that the Junkers T1 engines had 'worked well'.

Germany now possessed the technology it needed to respond to the ever-growing
threat of Allied air power in the West. From then on, until mid-1944, development on
the Me 262 forged ahead using a series of prototypes to test all aspects of the aircraft.
The first series production aircraft were plagued by technical problems, but the Luftwaffe
had been advocating the potential benefits of the Me 262 for some time. Persuaded by
Messerschmitt, as early as 17 April 1943, Hauptmann Wolfgang Späte (a 72-victory
Knight's Cross holder and former *Staffelkapitän* of 5./JG 54) flew the Me 262 V2 – the
first Luftwaffe pilot to do so. Two days later he reported to the *General der Jagdflieger*,
Generalmajor Adolf Galland:

Flight characteristics are such that an experienced fighter pilot would be able to handle the aircraft. In particular, the increase in air speed when compared to the fastest conventional fighter deserves attention. This is not expected to decrease markedly when armament and radio equipment have been fitted.

Characteristically, jet engines will not only maintain this speed at altitude, but increase it. The climbing speed of the Me 262 surpasses that of the Bf 109G by five to six metres per second at a much better speed. The superior horizontal and climbing speeds will enable the aircraft to operate successfully against numerically superior enemy fighters. The extremely heavy armament [six 30mm guns] permits attacks on bombers at high approach speeds with destructive results, despite the short time the aircraft is in the firing position.

This was music to Galland's ears. On 22 May 1943, he flew the Me 262 V4 himself at Lechfeld (after an attempt to start the engines of the V3 resulted in a fire) and made his famous report to Göring in which he enthused 'It felt as if angels were pushing!' Galland became a firm advocate for the further development of the jet, and wrote to his superiors that all measures should be taken to ensure swift and large-scale production of the aircraft.

A top view of the Me 262. Messerschmitt continued to produce large numbers of the twin-engine jet during the early months of 1945, although relatively few of them actually saw combat with frontline units.

In a report to Generalluftzeugmeister Erhard Milch he wrote: 'The aircraft represents a great step forward and could be our greatest chance. It could guarantee us an unimaginable lead over the enemy if he adheres to the piston engine.'

The Me 262 eventually emerged as a twin-engined jet fighter powered by two Jumo 004 turbojet units. At the heart of each engine was an eight-stage axial compressor with single-stage turbines producing 8.8kN of thrust at 8,700rpm. In the standard Me 262A-1a fighter/interceptor configuration, it was to be armed with four formidable MK 108 30mm cannon mounted in the nose.

With the engine/airframe combination at last sorted out, however, political interference from no less a figure than the Führer himself saw the programme side-tracked for a number of months as he insisted that the aircraft be developed as a bomber. Sense finally prevailed in early 1944, and the first aircraft to reach the front line saw combat in June of that year. Despite Germany being bombed virtually 24 hours a day during the final 12 months of the war, 1,400+ Me 262s were completed by Messerschmitt, and a further 500 were lost in air raids. Engine reliability, fuel shortages and unrealistic operational taskings restricted the frontline force to around 200 jets at any one time but these, nevertheless, accounted for more than 200 Allied aircraft (Jagdwaffe claims exceeded 745 victories for the Me 262!) during day and night interceptions. A total of 28 pilots 'made ace' flying the jet with the seven units that saw combat.

The Me 262 was the most famous and effective of many jet and rocket designs to emerge from Germany in the late war years, more than can be considered in individual

The Heinkel He 162 Salamander was an indulgent experiment late in the war, an attempt to create a turbojet-powered single-seat interceptor. The aim was to produce 2,000 units per month by May 1945, but by the end of the war only 275 aircraft had been completed.

Gerhard 'Gerd' Barkhorn was second only to Erich Hartmann in terms of aerial kills. Flying both the Me 109 and Fw 190 (he also briefly piloted the Me 262 just before the end of the war), he destroyed 301 aircraft in air-to-air combat, all on the Eastern Front.

FAR LEFT: Hauptmann Gunther Lützow rings the changes completely in his summer combination flying suit (Model K So/341) with its multitude of zippered pockets worn with the officer's gabardine *Feldmütze* field service forage cap. Note too the officer's pattern belt and holster, the latter housing any one of the various small 7.65mm automatics which were issued to aircrew, and the cloth sleeve patch denoting Lützow's rank and his Knight's Cross, awarded on 18 September 1940 after he had achieved 15 aerial victories. (John Weal © Osprey Publishing)

LEFT: Major Joachim Müncheberg wears a 'Mae West' inflatable lifejacket over his flying overalls. The Knight's Cross is worn at the throat and the rank pennant is sewn on the sleeve. The uniform trousers were sometimes worn loose as shown, rather than tucked into flying boots, and were made roomy enough to contain a sidearm, knife and maps. A tropical issue cap is worn, and among the lifejacket attachments is an oxygen mask lead and map reading torch. (Mike Chappell © Osprey Publishing)

detail here. They included the Arado Ar 234, a single-seat tactical light bomber powered by twin 800kg-thrust BMW 003A-1 turbojets, and with a maximum speed of 742km/h. There was also the Heinkel He 162 Salamander interceptor fighter and Henschel Hs 132 dive-bomber, both with top-mounted BMW turbojets blasting over a twin tailboom.

Other designs were more outlandish. Junkers developed a prototype of the Ju 287, a twin-turbojet heavy bomber with forward-swept wings and the potential to carry a 4,000kg bomb. Conversely, the Me 163 Komet was a single rocket interceptor armed with two 30mm MK 108 cannon. Technologically, the Me 163 helped to develop high-speed, swept-winged, tailless aircraft aerodynamics and the use of liquid-fuelled rockets for aircraft propulsion. In October 1941, the aircraft was flown at more than 1,000km/h, setting an unofficial world record at a speed which the Me 262 did not achieve until 1944. Its attack profile required strong nerves on the part of the pilot. It took off from a dolly undercarriage, which was jettisoned after launch, then began a steep rocket-powered ascent at an astonishing climb rate of 3,600m per minute. The pilot took the aircraft to a height of around 9,000m, above the US bomber stream (the Me 163 was suitable for daylight operations only), then turned into a dive for its combat run, zipping through the bombers and opening up with its cannon. During this phase of the flight it was effectively a blur to enemy gunners, who found it almost impossible to get a bearing on the aircraft. Eventually, the rocket motor would cut out, and the Komet now began a glide back to earth, landing on a retractable skid. Naturally, during the glide phase the Me 163 was easy prey for Allied fighters.

A total of 300 Me 163s were produced, but like many German jet and rocket designs, the effort was not worth the return – there were only nine confirmed Me 163 victories. The operation of the Me 163 also required the almost simultaneous development of handling and storage techniques for the highly volatile rocket fuel, special protective clothing for the pilots, high-altitude training for the pilots and radio navigation homing and interception methods. Apart from the Me 262, and notwithstanding the legacy to future jet aircraft design, the German jet and rocket fighters were largely a technological distraction from the production of more valuable fighter aircraft.

JAGDFLIEGER

The Luftwaffe produced all of the world's leading *Experten*, a small number achieving three-figure totals of aerial victories that are never likely to be equalled. Even by night, a few were able to out-perform the best Allied pilots' daylight achievements. These men represented a tiny percentage of Luftwaffe fighter pilots, but today they too-frequently monopolize the attention of commentators. The average fighter pilot was no ace.

Like all fighter pilots of the day, he had undergone up to two years of training before his first combat mission. Many did not survive that first engagement; and for those who did, most of their subsequent combats were inconclusive. At best, the average pilot may have inflicted some damage on a few enemy aircraft, but he seldom brought one down. In time he might develop the necessary instincts to do so, but this was generally a slow process.

The one key difference between the *Jagdflieger* and his foreign contemporaries was the duration of his frontline service. Assuming he survived, he had no option but to continue in a task that most others endured for only a limited period; those Allied pilots who returned to squadron service after completing a tour of several months, and a period instructing or performing some other rear-area task, did so by choice. The odds were stacked against the German aircrews' survival; nevertheless, to most of the pilots, radio-operators and gunners, supported by their ground crews, all that mattered was to be *Jagdflieger*.

RECRUITMENT AND TRAINING

Between the ages of 10 and 14, many German boys joined the Deutsche Jungvolk (German Youth; DJ) movement, which replaced German participation in the World Scouts Organization (rejected as a 'Jewish-led spy network'). The DJ encouraged the acceptance by the new generation of order and authority, vital to the planned regeneration of Germany. From the DJ they progressed to the more overtly political Hitler Jugend (Hitler Youth; HJ); originally voluntary, from 1936 membership became compulsory for all 14-year-old boys. Regular drill and marches engendered discipline and team spirit, and an annual two-week camp encouraged leadership potential. The great majority seem to have taken pleasure in the opportunities available to them in the HJ, which included mountaineering, sailing, orienteering, and – of particular interest to those aspiring to Luftwaffe service – the chance to qualify as pilots at *HJ-Segelschule* (glider school).

The Fighter Arm consistently enjoyed a ready supply of young hopefuls from which to choose. Some felt a strong sense of duty, others a wish to take a kind of personal revenge against the Allied nations for the hardships following World War I; but for many

the personal challenge was the major spur. All shared the curiously innate human desire to fly, and responded to the appeal of the perceived 'glamour' of the fighter pilot's life (few could honestly have denied that the guaranteed interest of girls was a factor). None of these incentives, honourable or superficial, were sufficient to ensure success, of course: aircrew selection was a particularly rigorous process.

A ground crewman paints the 32nd victory on the tailplane of a Bf 109 in September 1940. The great limitation of German fighters during the Battle of Britain was that fuel constraints allowed for only 15–20 minutes of combat/loiter time over the UK.

Pilots eventually selected for short-range fighter and dive-bomber training each had their specialist schools, at which flying time totals were initially raised to some 150–200 hours over a leisurely 13-month period. By the close of 1943, however, a potential fighter pilot could expect to be forwarded directly from A/B-*Schule* to *Jagdfliegerschule* (fighter school; JFS), where special attention was paid to formation flying and gunnery, to accrue the same 50 hours' flight time in just three to four months. The intensity of the course meant that trainees now received an average 12½ to 16 hours' flying per month – three or four times the peacetime norms. If no space was immediately available at one of the fighter schools proper the trainee might temporarily be assigned to a *Jagdfliegervorschule* (intermediate fighter school), usually amounting to

ABOVE: Fw 190A-4 'Black 1' of Oberleutnant Horst Hannig, Staffelkapitän 2./JG 2, Triqueville, Spring 1943. Hannig's 'Black 1' is adorned with one of the more elaborate motifs applied to disguise the soot deposits that quickly collected behind the Focke-Wulf's exhaust louvres. This striking 'Eagle's head' design was more commonly associated with III. Gruppe machines, although many of the latter later repainted their engine cowlings, removing the eagle's head to make way for 'Assi' – Hahn's far less intimidating cockerel. (John Weal © Osprey Publishing)

around 15 hours of basic aerobatic flying. Upon completion of JFS the late-war pilot would join his future *Geschwader's Ergänzungsgruppe* (finishing group), with a total of 180–250 flying hours amassed over a 9–13 month period.

Those A/B-*Schule* graduates demonstrating sufficient mastery of twin-engined trainers were destined for future service with bomber, transport, reconnaissance and heavy fighter ('destroyer') units; they were immediately advanced to C-*Schule* for an additional 50–70 hours on heavy aircraft over the next two to six months. This included introductions to instrument-flying and direction-finding apparatus on aircraft such as the Ju 52 tri-motor transport. From here, pilots were separated and sent to appropriate schools, with those selected for the heavy-fighter arm attending *Zerstörerschule* for two to three months of gunnery and target flights. It was here that pilots were introduced to their wireless operator/air gunners, with whom they would continue their service. The crews would first attend blind-flying school, for an advanced instrument navigation course involving intensive instrument-flight and landing practice, along with advanced direction-finding technique. With a total of around 220–270 flying hours, after 20 months in training, the pilot and his *Bordfunker* would finally join an operational *Ergänzungsstaffel*, to become a reserve crew.

Until entering this final phase the emphasis had been almost entirely devoted to developing flying skills, with aerial gunnery a secondary concern. Willi Holtfreter, a young *Jagdflieger*, had been in flight training for more than a year before he even began to practise such skills: 'They set up boards on the ground and we had to fly in and shoot. I shot 50 and hit 4 – that was gallery practice' (he added, 'I got better'). While it might seem strange to invest so much time in training a pilot who might later prove a poor marksman, it must be remembered that flying was the tricky part, with take-off and landing accidents far more likely to kill him than aerial combat. 'The more planes you flew', said Holtfreter, 'the more experienced you got at handling the different types. We flew a lot of different types.' Accurate shooting would only come with time and under real combat conditions.

Now fully trained, future combat pilots were originally sent to *Waffenschule* (fighting school), while awaiting assignment to operational units. Training at these establishments, usually staffed by combat veterans, was merely a continuation of instruction on appropriate aircraft types, and lasted from a few days to several weeks. From 1940 the role of the over-stretched fighting schools was largely – and effectively – taken over by the *Ergänzungsstaffeln* (later growing to entire *Gruppen*) attached to most operational *Geschwader*. These 'finishing' squadrons provided new pilots and crews with the best possible introduction to frontline conditions and tactics, in surroundings as close as possible to actual combat. Flying as wingmen to experienced veterans 'resting' from frontline duties, the new pilots carried out relatively safe

An Me 110 provides an aerial escort to an Axis convoy heading to North Africa. The Me 110 was not at its best in such roles, as its optimum performance was at high altitudes.

rear-area patrols, but missions occasionally included attacks on poorly defended enemy transport and reconnaissance machines if the opportunity arose. Transfer to one of the *Geschwader*'s operational *Staffeln* was initially made only when a new man was considered experienced and dependable enough to join the '*alte Hasen*' ('old hares') in combat; latterly, the pressure on manpower saw *Ergänzungsstaffeln* as a whole increasingly being committed to combat at need. By 1943 aircrew shortages had left many *Ergänzungsstaffeln* undermanned with suitable instructors, leading to their disbandment and the eventual reintroduction of the *Waffenschulen* (primarily for single-engined fighter pilots). The fledgling pilots thereafter often suffered from a lack of practical mentoring before joining their combat squadrons.

Even when a pilot was fully qualified the training process was continuous, with new aircraft types and variants constantly entering service, and aircrews reassigned to new tasks.

TACTICS

The fighter war was as much an exercise in tactics as it was in flying ability. Each front and each enemy air force brought its own particular set of tactical challenges, and it was down to fighter commanders to design formations and manoeuvres that would give the advantage in combat. The tactical evolution over six years of war was a complicated one, but can be understood by looking at the fighter war in two distinct contexts – the battle against the RAF during the Battle of Britain in 1940, and the air war over the Reich in 1943–45.

TACTICS OVER BRITAIN

The German fighter force that engaged the RAF during 1940 was by far the most experienced and tactically advanced anywhere in the world at that time. Although less than a third of its pilots had seen action in Spain, the lessons learned there had been introduced throughout the Jagdwaffe. Werner Mölders was the most influential of all Legion Condor veterans, and what he had learned fighting Spanish Nationalist aircraft was officially institutionalized in training in the lead up to World War II.

His philosophy for success in combat saw the emphasis placed more on fighting than flying. Experience had taught Mölders that the best way to achieve this was to abandon the three-aircraft 'vic' formation and go with the two-aircraft *Rotte* (pair), which in turn formed the basic fighting unit for all Jagdwaffe formations. Within the pair, the *Rottenführer* (pair leader) was responsible for making the kills and his wingman (the *Katschmarek*) protected the leader's tail. The wingman did not worry about where he was flying, or what to do next – he simply had to follow his leader. He usually held position some 200m away from the *Rottenführer*, flying almost in line abreast formation. Each pilot concentrated his search of the sky inwards, so as to cover his partner's blind spot.

Two *Rotten* made up a *Schwarm* (flight), flying some 300m apart – roughly the turning radius of a Bf 109E at combat speed. The leading *Rotte* typically flew to one side and slightly ahead of the other, and a *Staffel* formation comprising three *Schwärme* either stepped up in line astern or in line abreast. The Jagdwaffe also devised the 'cross-over turn' to avoid aircraft on the outside of a *Schwarm* becoming stragglers when the formation turned at high cruising speed in an area where contact with the enemy was likely. Each pilot held his speed going into the turn and the *Rotte* simply changed position in the formation during the manoeuvre.

During the early stages of World War II, the Bf 109E enjoyed a superior altitude performance to all the fighters it came up against, so the favoured tactic of the Jagdwaffe was to get above their opponents and attempt to bounce them, if possible using the sun to mask their approach. After a single firing pass, the *Jagdflieger* would use the speed gained in their diving attack to climb back up into a position from which to perform any repeat attacks. With enemy fighters usually being slower and more manoeuvrable, German pilots tried to avoid turning dogfights wherever possible.

Bf 109s escort He 111 bombers on a raid. Escort duties were tactically onerous. If the fighters stayed too close, they sacrificed their performance, in which lay their survivability. If they strayed away to tackle enemy fighters, they risked leaving the bombers exposed.

BF 109E-4 COCKPIT

1. Machine gun firing button
2. Control column
3. Rudder pedal
4. Fuel cock
5. FuG VII radio control switch
6. Fuel contents gauge
7. Cockpit light control
8. Pitot head-heating warning lamp
9. Circuit breaker
10. Airspeed indicator
11. Engine starter switch
12. Turn and bank indicator
13. Altimeter
14. Compass
15. Instructions for flap settings, landing speed, etc.
16. Clock
17. Revi C/12D gunsight
18. Boost gauge
19. Compass deviation table
20. Tachometer
21. Propeller pitch indicator
22. Undercarriage position indicator
23. Fuel and oil pressure gauge
24. Undercarriage control lever
25. Undercarriage emergency control lever
26. Mechanical undercarriage position indicator
27. Filter pump control lever
28. Coolant temperature gauge
29. Oil temperature gauge
30. Low fuel warning lamp
31. Elevator control wheel

32. Landing flap control
33. Oil cooler flap control
34. Throttle control
35. Main instrument light
36. Engine instant-stop lever
37. Engine ignition lever
38. Starter coupling lever
39. Canopy release lever

40. Seat height adjustment lever
41. Tailplane incidence indicator
42. Circuit breaker panel
43. Oxygen hose
44. Main instrument light
45. Radiator flap control

46. Fuel pump auto switch
47. Map holder
48. Pilot's seat
49. Seat harness adjustment lever
50. Fuel injection pump
51. Remote control ventilator
52. Oxygen apparatus

If bounced, the *Rotte* or *Schwarm* would typically turn individually to meet the attack, and if there was no time for this, they would take advantage of the direct injection system fitted to their Bf 109Es by bunting over into a dive. The *Abschwung* (American 'Split-S') was also used as an alternative escape route, the pilot performing a half-roll pulled through into a steep dive at full throttle – this manoeuvre could only be done with plenty of altitude in hand, as up to 4,500m in height would be lost.

These formations and tactics served the Jagdwaffe well over Dunkirk and for much of the Battle of Britain, with *Rottenführer* having just one job to do – find and destroy the enemy. When they were found, the formation leader was the one who went in for the kill, leaving his wingmen to cover his tail. By sticking to the *Freie Jagd* ('free hunting') tactic, pilots of the calibre of Mölders, Galland, Ihlefeld, Oesau and Wick all racked up impressive scores. Lesser-known pilots were also well served by these tactics, including 3./JG 52's Oberleutnant Ulrich Steinhilper on 26 September 1940:

We were approaching Dover when we saw a whole squadron of Spitfires spread out in line astern below us, with a weaver on either side at the back. They were so well defined against the blue-green of the sea that we couldn't have missed them. My *Staffelführer*, Oberleutnant Helmut Kühle, instructed me to take one of the weavers and he said that he'd take care of the other. When the rest of the squadron saw that this had been accomplished, they could then pick their own targets. These were good tactics, as the weavers were there to protect the rear of the flight, and if they could be taken out without raising the alarm, there would be a good chance of the rest of the squadron bagging the majority of the enemy aircraft. This was what was so foolish about flying this kind of formation.

We peeled away and I began to position my fighter. The red ring of the Revi gunsight was projected onto the windscreen, and I'd already flipped over the trigger for both the nose guns and the wing cannon, ready for the attack. Gradually, the Spitfire filled the ring of the sight and I increased the pressure on the triggers. Four lines of tracer hosed out towards the target and I saw strikes, the aircraft spinning away. Instead of chasing it down, I altered course slightly and went for the next Spitfire in line. Again I saw hits before I broke away to safety.

As the Battle of Britain progressed, however, the tactical advantage enjoyed by the Jagdwaffe was steadily eroded by the unbreakable spirit of Fighter Command, its radar coverage of the Channel and its efficient fighter control system. The Bf 109E's short range also became more of a problem as the *Kampfgeschwader* started to go after targets farther inland from the south coast. Oberstleutnant Adolf Galland, *Geschwaderkommodore* of JG 26 by the end of the Battle of Britain, wrote at length about this problem in his autobiography *The First and the Last*, stating that the Messerschmitt fighter's lack of range was critical to the outcome of the Battle of Britain:

> It used to take us roughly half an hour from take-off to crossing the English coast at the narrowest point of the Channel. Having a tactical flying time of about 80 minutes in the Bf 109E, we therefore had about 20 minutes to complete our task. This fact limited the distance of penetration, German fighter squadrons based on the Pas de Calais and on the Contentin peninsula barely being able to cover the south-eastern part of England. Circles drawn from these two bases at an operational range of 125 miles [200km] overlapped approximately in the London area. Everything beyond was practically out of our reach. An operating radius of 125 miles was sufficient for local defence, but not enough for such tasks as bomber escort, which were now being demanded of us.
>
> It was assumed that the appearance of German fighter squadrons over England would draw the British fighters into the area within our range, where they would be destroyed,

Bf 109Es in production in 1940. Germany produced 55,772 fighters during the whole period of the war, an astonishing figure but still one that did not stem the tide of attrition in the later years of the war.

beaten, or at least decimated in large-scale air battles. Things turned out differently. Our fighter formations took off. The first air battles took place as expected and according to plan. Due to the German superiority, these attacks, had they been continued, would certainly have achieved the attempted goal, but the RAF fighters were recalled from this area long before this goal was achieved.

The weakened squadrons left their bases near the coast and used them only for emergency landings or to refuel and rearm. They were concentrated in a belt around London in readiness for our bomber attacks. Thus they evaded the attack in the air in order to encounter more effectively the attack from the air, which would logically follow. The German fighters found themselves in a similar predicament to a dog on a chain who wants to attack the foe but cannot harm him because of the limitations of the chain.

As losses to both German fighters and bombers mounted, and Fighter Command's resolve seemingly remained intact, senior officers in the Luftwaffe sought to lay the blame at the feet of the *Jagdgeschwader*, as Galland recalled:

We had the impression that, whatever we did, we were bound to be wrong. Fighter protection for bombers created many problems which had to be solved in action. Bomber pilots preferred close screening in which their formation was surrounded by pairs of fighters pursuing a zigzag course. Obviously, the visible presence of the protective fighters gave the bomber pilots a greater sense of security. However, this was a faulty conclusion, because a fighter can only carry out this purely defensive task by taking the initiative in the offensive. He must never wait until attacked because he then loses the chance of acting.

We fighter pilots certainly preferred the 'free chase during the approach and over the target area'. This in fact gives the greatest relief and the best protection for the bomber force, although not perhaps a sense of security for the latter.

Reichsmarschall Göring, however, did not side with *Jagdflieger* when it came to allowing them to continue to wage the Battle of Britain on their terms. Indeed, in late August he ordered that all *Jagdgeschwader* were to remain close to the bombers that they were escorting, and on no account were they to engage enemy fighters unless they or their bombers came under a direct threat of attack. With the bombers cruising at a much slower speed than the fighters, the *Jagdflieger* had to weave in order to maintain station, and yet still retain a high cruising speed in the combat area. By ordering the Jagdwaffe

OVERLEAF: A Spitfire of No. 603 Sqn engages a Bf 109 on 30 August 1940. The Messerschmitt, piloted by Feldwebel Ernst Arnold, was badly shot up, but its pilot managed to perform a controlled belly landing in a field near Faversham. (Mark Postelthwaite © Osprey Publishing)

to fly close-formation missions, Göring totally nullified the effectiveness of the previously superior German fighter tactics, thus surrendering the initiative in the skies over southern England to the RAF.

Losses amongst the Bf 109E *Geschwader* rose steeply once they were 'chained' to the bomber formations, and one of those men shot down was six-victory ace Feldwebel Heinrich Hoehnisch of 1./JG 53:

On my last mission, on 9 September 1940, our task was to give direct fighter cover to the rear of an He 111 bomber formation. One *Kette* [three aircraft in a 'vic' formation] of bombers got separated, so our *Staffel* looked after them. We had only seven Bf 109s, and I was tail-end Charlie with Oberfeldwebel Mueller. Approaching London Docks, there was no contact with the enemy, but I was sure that we could expect attacks out of the sun as soon as we turned 180 degrees for our return flight. To my surprise, I saw, when I was looking towards the rest of my *Staffel*, six Spitfires on a reciprocal course in line astern about 50 metres above me. To avoid the inevitable attack, I tried to come up with my *Staffel* flying in front and below me. When I was level with my *Staffelkapitän*, I thought I had made it.

However, there was a rattle like an explosion in my aeroplane and, with the pressure of a blowtorch, flames hit my face. With the greatest difficulty, I got out of my aeroplane. I landed with severe burns to my face and bullet wounds to my right calf. I stayed in the hospital in Woolwich for two months.

German airmen relax on a French airfield between operations, their Bf 109 fighters standing ready in the background. The glory days of 1939–41 were distant memories by 1944, when the Luftwaffe was fighting a largely defensive war against overwhelming numbers of Allied aircraft.

Hoehnisch had been shot down by No. 19 Sqn Spitfire ace Flight Lieutenant Wilf Clouston in an engagement that had lasted just a matter of seconds, a typical example of the Spitfire-versus-Bf 109E clashes that occurred throughout the Battle of Britain.

DAY-BOMBER INTERCEPTION

Commencing summer 1942, US B-17 Flying Fortresses began attacking targets in occupied France and, from January 1943, in Germany too. Learning the same hard lessons as the RAF, the USAAF nevertheless chose to stick to daylight bomber operations; the much vaunted (and somewhat overstated) accuracy of its Norden M-series bombsight would be squandered if forced to follow the British into the night. Initially cursed by the same lack of long-range fighter cover as the RAF, American crews would suffer terribly for this choice; but the arrival of disposable auxiliary fuel tanks in late 1943, coupled with the appearance of the superb P-51D Mustang, allowed bombers to be escorted throughout their missions deep into the heart of Germany.

Luftwaffe tacticians quickly realized that it was no mean feat to bring down just one heavily armed B-17. Breaking through a fighter escort in a Bf 109 or Fw 190 so as to get close enough to the bombers to ensure success was a difficult and draining task. The *Jagdflieger*'s primary goal was to strip away the escorts as soon as possible, drawing them into the fight. Initial contact forced the American P-47s and P-51s to jettison their range-extending 'Tokyo-tanks' immediately if they were to stand anything like an even chance in the mêlée. Their endurance instantly cut, the fighters would thus be forced to make for home early, abandoning the bombers to fend for themselves later in the mission.

Attacks against bombers took two basic forms. The first of these, the 'Fly-Through', was as simple as it sounds: the fighter flew an essentially straight line towards the bomber formation, pouring as much cannon-fire as possible into a point ahead of his selected target, into which the bomber would fly – a simple deflection shot. This form of attack might be commenced at right angles to the bomber, from any elevation, but was most often presented directly from the front, concentrating fire upon the pilots and control deck. A side-on or rearward approach would give the pilot the most time – but that extra time was shared by the American air-gunners. Whichever direction was taken, the fly-through attack meant that a pilot's aim was good for only a fraction of a second, much of his fire going wide. The fighter would attempt to align as many bombers into his direct line of sight as possible, often closing to a few hundred yards before opening fire on his selected victim. If apparently sufficient strikes were seen to register upon his primary target, a slight flick of the stick or pressure on the rudder pedals might slip the guns just enough to pick up a second and, perhaps, even a third target beyond it, before

he flashed right across the top of the box formation only a moment later. Catching these other targets demanded great skills in the complex art of deflection shooting, as the precise degree of deflection required altered rapidly (and in many different ways) with his approach rate, and the varying ranges, courses and speeds of the individual targets. For the most part, causing sufficient damage to just one machine was a great achievement, and even that was primarily down to luck. In a head-on approach at 600km/h, a fighter would pass over a 300m-deep box in less than two seconds, since the converse heading of the 500km/h bomber produced closure and departure speeds of around 1,130km/h.

The second method of attack was the 'Pursuit Curve'. Commencing from any direction, this gentle curve towards the bombers permitted the fighter to unload a constant and prolonged stream of firepower into the length of his target. He must, however, keep turning into the direction of the bomber stream if his fire was to remain effective. This had the undesirable effect of presenting a predictable and rapidly enlarging target to the bomber's air gunners as he flew ever closer. Visibly seeming to slide sideways to the rear, in a straight line towards the bomber's tail (its 'apparent motion', as opposed to its 'real motion'), the fighter passed directly through the azimuth of the beam-guns – often rewarding a well-calculated deflection shot on the part of the waist-gunner and upper turret. While fleeting, this was possibly the defender's best chance of a 'kill'. Nevertheless, this dangerous second technique soon became a standard method of cutting bombers out of the box, enabling the fighters to slice the formation apart. Bombers that suffered critical damage could not hold station in the mutually protective formation for long, and as they lost power and altitude they became comparatively easy prey.

Studies of gun-camera footage have revealed that an average of 20 rounds of 20mm ammunition were required to bring down a bomber; and since only 2 per cent of shells fired actually hit their intended target, 1,000 rounds would be required to be absolutely sure of

LEFT: The Bachem Ba 349 'Natter' (Viper) was one of the more alarming Luftwaffe attempts to counter the Allied bombing campaign. The aircraft was launched vertically by ten seconds of rocket thrust, after which the pilot would fire 24 7.3cm unguided rockets at enemy aircraft, before deploying an aircraft parachute and floating to earth. Needless to say, the Bachem was not a success.

BELOW: Fw 190D-9 'Yellow 11' of II./JG 2, Stockheim, March 1945. Based on photographs of a wrecked machine (found on a small airstrip south of Nidda), the aircraft depicted in this profile undoubtedly wore Defence of Reich bands – and they were reportedly yellow-white-yellow (note how the break in the white band has been used to create a II. Gruppe horizontal bar). (John Weal © Osprey Publishing)

Ground crew work hard on a Bf 109 to ready the aircraft for operations. Typically, about half a *Staffel*'s total inventory of 12–15 aircraft (including reserves) were operational at any one time.

a kill – demanding an impossible 23 seconds of continuous fire. In reality, the fleeting moments available to a fighter pilot, combined with enemy fire, ensured the chances of successfully engaging the target were slim. However, just one 20mm cannon-shell in the right place was capable of destroying a bomber; an exploding engine or fuel tank could rip a wing apart with terrifying ease, causing the bomber simply to fold in half, break into pieces, or fall engulfed in flame. The frightening 30mm MK 108 could complete the task with just three rounds, and could kill a fighter with just one.

Soaring over Germany in July 1944, P-51 pilot Lieutenant Arthur C. Fiedler (317th FS, 325th FG) was perplexed by a curious '8x8 staggered-box' formation approaching the B-17 fleet far beneath him. Initially taking them for more Mustangs, he was horrified to see what he now recognized as 64 Fw 190s hacking about six Fortresses down in a single pass from the rear. However, both sides routinely believed their opponents to have the upper hand in these engagements; *Jagdflieger* always hated engaging the B-17 formations, with their heavy concentrations of defensive firepower, and invariably sustained damage whenever they got close enough to attack. The Americans flew a carefully meshed defensive combat wing, comprising three 'boxes' of 18 bombers each, arranged to uncover as many guns as possible for mutual protection and maximum visibility. Simply getting near the formation seemed near-suicidal. Wilhelm Holtfreter: 'When I was posted back to Lippspringer, we flew against four-engined bombers a lot, but I wasn't able to shoot anything down, because I was always too outnumbered.'

After much costly experimentation, it became clear that the best technique was to fly as close as possible, in a perfectly straight line, directly over the central axis of the bomber, from either front or rear. The former was favoured, to inflict maximum damage to cockpit and crew or, at least, to shatter the nerves of the pilots, perhaps forcing them to collide. The fighter's close proximity to its target ensured minimum opportunities for the gunners; the engineer's top turret had the best chance of hitting the fighter in approach, but was unlikely to traverse fast enough to track his exit; nose- and tail-gunners were granted extremely brief chances during the approach or escape; the waist-gunners never got a shot, and supporting fire from flanking bombers was theoretically curtailed by the danger of hitting comrades. With each fighter racing full-throttle at and over its assigned Fortress, the opening salvo would ideally rip out at least one of the '*Dicke Autos*' ('fat cars'); but a *Staffel* might suffer over 50 per cent losses in return.

OVERLEAF: Major Walther Dahl, *Kommodore* of Jagdgeschwader 300, in his Fw 190A-8 Wk-Nr 170994 'Blue 13', and his wingman, Feldwebel Walter Loos, in 'Blue 14', lead their *Gruppe* to attack the 39 B-17s of the 303rd Bombardment Group (BG) over Bitburg as they make their way home from a mission to bomb Wiesbaden airfield on 15 August 1944. (Gareth Hector © Osprey Publishing)

Conversely, the bomber men often underestimated the damage they inflicted, and considered themselves outgunned by the fighters. Watching their formation being broken apart as the 'bandits' flashed through their ranks with cannon blazing, gunners were frequently unaware of the devastating effect of their own combined firepower. Every bomber seen to falter and shudder was inevitably seen as another victim of the Luftwaffe, but this may not have always been the case. A fleet of 1,000 B-17s and B-24s, sprawling over many kilometres of sky, had a total defensive armament of some 10,000 heavy machine guns, with a staggering 7 million rounds of .50-cal ammunition between them. While it is impossible to research, given the massive volume of lead being sprayed in all directions throughout the formation, to an effective range of 1,000 yards, it is inevitable that a fair proportion of the damage suffered was from 'friendly fire'. The danger was obvious to USAAF planners, who devised the formations to reduce the risk to a minimum while placing the echelons close enough for effective mutual support. Fields of fire had to overlap, eliminating any safe corridors between the boxes. This was a difficult and dangerous compromise, but one that had to be accepted.

By mid-1944, *Ergänzungsgruppe* instructors had largely given up teaching the classic 'finger-four' fighter formation in favour of the long-discarded arrowhead.

During the powered phase of its flight, the Me 163 could reach a maximum speed of 960km/h, a speed that actually made it difficult for the pilot to bring the guns to bear on the enemy. Partly for this reason, the Me 163 type secured only nine confirmed kills during its few months of wartime service.

The '*Staffel-Pfeilspitze*' comprised all 12 aircraft in two tight 'V's (seven in high lead, the second wave of five immediately below). Holding formation in a head-on pass demanded nerves of steel, but such a tactic could unleash the devastating fire of 24 × 12.7mm heavy machine guns and 48 × 20mm cannon on the word of the *Staffelkapitän*. Destruction of the bombers now took precedence over even basic survival techniques. Flying specially up-armoured Fw 190s, *Sturmgruppen* (assault groups) were raised within three of the home defence *Jagdgeschwader*, and were solely devoted to the destruction of bombers, by whatever means necessary. This level of desperation reached its nadir in the formation of volunteer *Rammjäger* units, in which pilots swore an oath to bring down at least one bomber per mission, by ramming if all else failed; a well-positioned wing could easily slice off a tailfin or stabilizer. Unlike the Japanese *Kamikaze* – and as contradictory as it sounds – the *Rammjäger* were not expected to be suicidal, but were instructed to bale out after impact. (How many such attacks were ever actually made is the subject of some controversy.)

The *Jagdflieger* on the Eastern Front had no need to devote such attention to bomber interception. The Red Air Force lost a staggering number of aircraft on the first day of Operation *Barbarossa*, including much of its antiquated bomber fleet.

In the last months of the war, some fighters were needlessly wasted in improbable experiments. Here we see an Fw 190 used in the ineffective '*Mistel*' combination, the bomber beneath being an unpiloted, unguided bomb.

TOP RIGHT: Bf 110C '2N+BB' of Oberleutnant Siegfried Wandam, *Gruppenadjutant* I./ZG 1, Vendeville, May 1940. Wandam achieved no kills as a *Zerstörer* pilot, but went on to score ten in night-fighters. He served first with NJG 1, but was killed in action over Belgium in the early hours of 4 July 1943 as a *Hauptmann* flying with the *Stab* of I./NJG 5. (John Weal © Osprey Publishing)

MIDDLE RIGHT: Bf 110C 'L1+IH' of Feldwebel Herbert Schob, 1.(Z)/LG 1, Jesau, East Prussia, September 1939. Wearing standard early war camouflage and a textbook set of national insignia of the period, 'Ida-Heinrich' was the mount of Herbert Schob at the start of the Polish campaign. He downed one of two P.7 fighters which fell to his *Gruppe* on the first morning of hostilities. The success was marked with a victory bar below the windshield. (Mike Chappell © Osprey Publishing)

BOTTOM RIGHT: Bf 110C 'L1+LK' of Oberleutnant Werner Methfessel, *Staffelkapitän* 14.(Z)/LG 1, Mannheim-Sandhofen, May 1940. Although no *Zerstörer* ace emerged from the Polish campaign, 2. Staffel's Werner Methfessel came close with four. He was to claim his fifth during the 'Phoney War', and scored more during the opening phase of the *Blitzkrieg* in the West. (John Weal © Osprey Publishing)

Thereafter, Soviet long-range bombing missions would remain modest in scale and scope; the Red Air Force adopted instead a policy of defence in depth, luring German bombers deep into Soviet territory to be met by the eventually massive fighter force. By far the greatest aerial threat to German ground forces came instead from precision strikes by fast, heavily armoured ground–attack aircraft. Best approached from low and

An Me 110 aircraft is fitted with a new propeller in the North African theatre. The sand and grit of the desert environment was punishing to engines and other moving parts of aircraft, increasing the demands of regular maintenance.

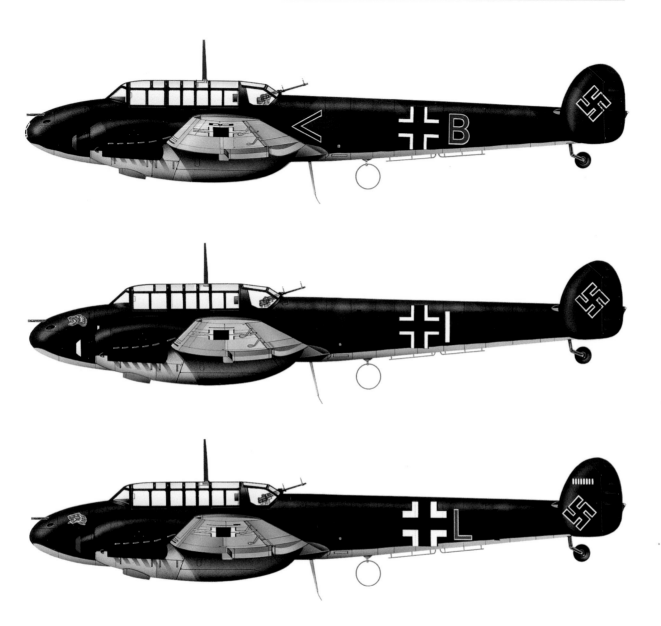

behind, within the dorsal gunner's blind-spot, the legendary Il-2 Sturmovik was so apparently bulletproof that the Luftwaffe christened it 'Iron Gustav'. Entire *Schwärme* are known to have taken turns to empty their guns into a single Ilyushin, only to watch it carry on in a straight line, unperturbed. The crews were not always of equal quality. The leader was often the only experienced flyer among them, and the only one briefed on the target; if he could be singled out for attack the rest might simply scatter for home.

A Ju 88C night-fighter fitted with the FuG 202 Lichtenstein aerial radar. These radar sets could detect Allied bombers at distances of up to 3km, and they dramatically improved detection and kill rates when first introduced in 1942.

NIGHT-FIGHTERS

In the early daylight raids over Germany, with only partial (if any) fighter cover, the RAF had suffered terribly at the hands of the Luftwaffe. Casualties inflicted by fighters and flak were so crippling that the British were soon forced over to night operations, buying much-needed concealment at the cost of greatly reducing their already marginal accuracy. However, the switch from 'point' to 'area bombing' from March 1941 negated the need for much precision.

Although both sides had experimented with a night-defence force, neither had made any serious progress, instead relying on AA artillery. Early Luftwaffe efforts at night interception were extremely scrappy and frightening for all involved. Initially they simply attempted to flood the skies over the targets with as many searchlights as could be mustered, while regular fighters, from hastily raised *Nachtstaffeln* within the *Jagdgeschwader*, tried to line up on bombers temporarily caught in the glare. Since the local flak batteries naturally did not cease fire, the Bf 109s were routinely buffeted by nearby shockwaves, the blast from the heavy 8.8cm rounds sometimes jolting engines to a stall. Attempts to co-ordinate the three elements proved frustrating, with the fighter pilots frequently drifting into the flak gunners' sights. Their rudimentary instrument-flying and navigation skills made any night mission perilous, whether or not it involved combat.

Persistent experimentation with ground-radar control of aircraft and searchlights proved the viability of the *Hellenachtjagd* (bright night-fighting) or *Henaja* system, and the experimental specialist *Nachtjagdgeschwader* began formation from mid-1940. Within two years the night-fighting arm had evolved into the most technologically advanced sphere of aerial combat, and its crews into the most highly trained and skilled.

The Luftwaffe needed dedicated night-fighter types to pursue the war, and found them in repurposing other types of aircraft. One of the most successful conversions was that of the twin-engined Me 110. Designed in 1934–35 to fill the perceived need for a high-speed, long-range, heavily-armed twin-engined fighter, Messerschmitt's Bf 110 *Zerstörer* (destroyer) fulfilled all these criterion. Seen as the ultimate bomber escort, capable of sweeping the sky clean of enemy fighters, the Bf 110 relied more on its firepower than manoeuvrability to survive in combat. Too late to see action in the Spanish Civil War, the Bf 110C made the aircraft's combat debut over Poland, where it dominated the skies in an environment of overwhelming Luftwaffe air superiority. These successes continued throughout the 'Phoney War' and into the early days of the *Blitzkrieg* in the West, but come the Battle of Britain, serious flaws in the *Zerstörer* concept were cruelly exposed. Indeed, by the latter stages of this epic aerial conflict between the RAF and the Luftwaffe, the 'destroyer' was only allowed to venture across the Channel when its own dedicated single-seat fighter escort was available! Following the loss of more than 200 Bf 110s during the campaign, the day-fighter role was given over almost exclusively to the single-seat Bf 109E *Gruppe*, and the Messerschmitt 'twin' was sent to operate on less hostile fronts in the Balkans and the Mediterranean.

Yet the Bf 110 found a new lease of life from 1940, when the first night-fighter wing – Nachtjagdgeschwader 1 – had been hastily formed with Bf 110s. Messerschmitt's twin-engined heavy fighter would remain in the forefront of the night war over occupied Europe through to VE-Day, despite its virtual removal from the day-fighter force. Nocturnal missions were ideally suited to a twin-engined, multi-seat fighter like the Bf 110, and Messerschmitt produced a series of aircraft tailored exclusively to the night-fighting role. These began to replace surplus C-models (issued to the *Nachtjagd* in 1940 following their removal from the *Zerstörergeschwader* in the wake of the Battle of Britain debacle) from early 1942 onwards. The Bf 110G was radar-equipped, and accounted for around 60 per cent of the overall *Nachtjagd* force for the final three years

OVERLEAF: Unteroffizier Ernst Schröder of 5.(*Sturm*)/JG 300 fights for his life in his Fw 190A-8/R2 on 17 September 1944. His opponent in this duel was 2nd Lieutenant Robert Volkman of the 376th FS/361st FG, who was flying a P-51B. Schröder managed to escape after his guns jammed. (Mark Postlethwaite © Osprey Publishing)

Night-fighter crews receive a briefing before heading out to meet the enemy. The night-fighter campaign was one of the most successful strands of the German interception mission against the nightly visitations from Allied bombers.

of the war. The best night-fighter variant of all the Bf 110s was the G-4, which boasted DB 605B-1 engines, FuG 212 Lichtenstein C-1, SN-2 or 221a radar and various cannon fits, depending on the sub-type. So effective was the Bf 110G in this role that the fighter remained in production until March 1945.

The Me 110 was not alone in the night skies. There were also Ju 88, Bf 109 and Fw 190 night-fighters, and together they served as unnervingly successful hunters of Allied aircraft over Germany. Night interception techniques fell into two distinct elements, aptly named *Zähme-Sau* and *Wilde-Sau* ('Tame Boar' and 'Wild Boar'). When incoming raiders were detected by ground radar stations, the 'tame' Bf 110 and Ju 88 heavy fighters were despatched to wait above designated sectors, there to be vectored into the bomber stream as it approached. Precise location of individual targets was then the work of the aircraft's wireless operator and the pilot's naked eye. The fighters went up in turn, relieving each other as fuel ran low, to maintain a constant presence over their assigned area. The most experienced crews invariably went up first, and thus tended to see the most action; the junior crews sat and waited in their cockpits, in *Sitzbereitschaft* (seat-readiness), often until they were finally stood-down at dawn.

The 'wild' Bf 109s and Fw 190s, circling high above, also relied upon purely visual recognition. Against the sweeping searchlights, enemy marker-flares and even burning cities below them, the heavy bombers could be readily picked out. On particularly overcast nights the searchlights were simply fixed across the cloud-base, creating a glowing cushion against which the bombers stood out in sharp silhouette. On cloudless, moonlit nights the RAF usually suspended its operations – under such conditions the *Nachtjäger* could literally see them a mile away.

An important new capability was added from February 1942 with the fitting of the first airborne radar sets to Bf 110s, which thereafter put the 'Wild Boars' out of business for about a year. Although primitive by today's standards, and difficult for the wireless operators to master, these sets freed the *Nachtjäger* from the apron-strings of ground control and transformed the night war over Germany. The initial Lichtenstein BC set was soon updated to the more sophisticated FuG 202, and a technical competition between improved British and German technologies lasted for the rest of the war. Another innovation of 1942 was the augmentation of nose-mounted guns with upwards firing 20mm cannon in dorsal *Schrägemusik* (a colloquialism for 'jazz music') mountings.

From the end of 1942 RAF Pathfinder crews would penetrate German airspace far ahead of the *Möbelwagen* ('furniture vans' – big planes). These picked navigators and master-bombers sought to illuminate the target with flares, incendiaries and some high-explosive bombs; the following waves simply had to pour their loads into the fire. The real prize for a night-fighter was to find and kill this *Zeremonienmeister* ('master of ceremonies'), thus severely hampering the entire mission.

The prospect of closing tightly on a black shadow in the dark sky was unnerving; collision was a constant danger and a not-uncommon occurrence. Drawing ever nearer, the pilot had to manoeuvre smoothly into his optimum attack position, generally directly below the tail. At any moment the blackness could be ripped apart by a burst of fire from the quadruple tail guns just yards away from him. A bold RAF tail-gunner might let him approach, waiting to fire a 'lightning bomb' at his pursuer – a flash-powder charge designed to dazzle the approaching night-fighter and destroy his night-vision – before letting fly with a hail of well-aimed .303in. machine-gun fire. Often derided for their poor armament, the British bombers in fact proved their capability in knocking night-fighters out of the sky (though never often enough to seriously reduce the very high casualty rate among bomber crews). If the *Nachtjäger* could slide in close unseen, his combined battery of 7.92mm machine guns and heavy 20mm and 30mm cannon had a devastating effect upon the thin structure of the British machines. Slamming into the wing-root at close range, his shells would quickly bring flames erupting to engulf the stricken machine, or would simply smash its skeleton to pieces.

Screwing his eyes shut in an effort to preserve his night-vision, the attacker heaved his craft out of the way of the falling giant; some failed, and were destroyed by their own victims. Many had no choice but to fly right through the burning wreckage, badly damaging or setting fire to their own machines. The *Nachtjagd* also suffered from a whole new dimension of danger following the appearance of RAF Beaufighter and later Mosquito night intruders from mid-1943. As the air war turned ever more decisively against Germany, even the night-fighter arm was increasingly pressed into daytime defence against US bombers. Encumbered by their heavy radar equipment,

OVERLEAF LEFT: An Me 109 pilot, stationed on the Eastern Front, paints another kill indicator on his fuselage. The poor training of Red Air Force pilots, plus the prevalence of obsolescent Soviet aircraft types, were conducive to high kill tallies, at least in the first years of the German–Soviet war.

NIGHT-FIGHTER TACTICS

4./Nachtjagdgeschwader 1; Venlo, Holland, 1941. Instructors discuss tactics with experienced day-fighter pilots undergoing conversion to night-fighters. A model Halifax bomber fitted with wire cones (representing defensive arcs of fire) is used to demonstrate the safest approach.

Insets:

Bottom: The 'Pursuit Curve', when viewed from above shows its 'real motion', while the same approach viewed from a B-17 top-turret position illustrates the 'perceived motion'. In the complex art of deflection-shooting, 'lead' is not always given ahead of the target. The gunner's ring-sight is here aimed directly away from the travel of the enemy fighter, the forward motion of the bomber drawing his fire onto that aircraft.

Top Right: Late-1941 trials of appropriately named *'Spanner-Anlage'* ('peeping Tom' installation) infra-red sensors in the noses of Bf 110 night-fighters gave limited success, until replaced by advanced Lichtenstein intercept-radar, with its distinctive antenna-arrays. The rear cockpit section is fitted with twin-mounted 20mm MG151 machine guns. Designed by Hauptmann Rudolf Schönert and Oberfeldwebel Paul Mahle of II./NJG 5, the devastating *'Schrägemusik'* system enabled attack in an RAF bomber's blind spot (the majority of them had no ventral defences), from 30–50m below. (Karl Kopinski © Osprey Publishing)

A Ju 88 night-fighter displays its Lichenstein airborne radar system. When flown with tactical skill, the German night-fighters would only reveal their presence to the Allied bomber target when they began pumping cannon shells into it.

the Bf 110s were terribly vulnerable to escort fighters, and in this role they suffered shocking losses.

The limited nocturnal operations mounted by the Red Air Force did not demand a heavy presence in the East, where only one *Nachtjagdgeschwader* (NJG 6) and two single *Gruppen* (NJG 100 and 200) operated, compared to five NJGs in the West.

Taken together, the Luftwaffe's pilots and aircraft threw up an incredible defence of German air space, and inflicted heavy losses on all fronts. As the introduction to this book pointed out, however, the struggle was an unequal one. Late in the war, the German fighter pilots were badly trained and hastily thrown into the battle against all odds, and only a handful survived in the lethal skies over the Third Reich. Young replacement fighter pilots who joined the Reichsverteidigung (Defence of the Reich) as 1944 progressed had only limited chances to survive in air combat, as they were primarily misused as cannon fodder. In early 1944, 50 per cent of all German fighter pilots were combat experienced veterans, with the remainder being replacement pilots. The majority of the latter category had only a minimum of flying experience in first-line fighters, and no combat experience at all to compensate for the heavy losses from which the Luftwaffe then severely suffered.

It was not uncommon for replacement pilots not to have flown a fully armed fighter prior to reaching the front line. Take-offs and landings in formation were also rarely undertaken in training units, and pilots never fired the MK108 and MG151 cannon prior to entering combat. The tactics employed in the front line were entirely new tasks to be learned as well. All of this occurred during a period of about two months, with severe restrictions on flying time because gasoline supplies were becoming increasingly limited. The tension of a young airman, climbing into his fighter cockpit on a rubble-strewn improvised airfield in 1945, waiting to face impossible odds, can only be imagined.

GROUND ATTACK — STRIKE FROM ABOVE

The Arado Ar 234 was a late-war jet-powered reconnaisance and bombing aircraft. Its twin Junkers Jumbo turbojets could power it to more than 740km/h, making it a tough challenge for Allied fighters to intercept. However, like many German jet project, too few of the aircraft were built to make an impact on the war.

In defeated Germany just after World War I, any arguments for or against the ground-attack and dive-bomber aircraft as opposed to the traditional high-altitude level bomber were perforce purely academic. Shorn of all offensive weaponry by the 1919 Treaty of Versailles, Germany's arms manufacturers were expressly forbidden from producing any replacements. The ink was hardly dry on the hated Diktat, however, before companies began seeking ways to circumvent the strictures imposed upon them.

GROUND-ATTACK AIRCRAFT

One such firm was the Dessau-based Junkers Flugzeugwerke AG which, in the early 1920s, set up the Swedish subsidiary AB Flygindustri at Limhamn-Malmo. Here, they were free to concentrate on military, rather than civil, aircraft production and development. Among the types built at Limhamn was a highly advanced two-seat fighter. Designed by Dipl.-Ing Karl Plauth and Hermann Pohlmann, the two Junkers K 47 prototypes, which first flew in 1929, were subsequently evaluated at the clandestine German air training centre at Lipezk, north of Voronezh, in the Soviet Union.

While a batch of 12 production K 47 fighters was completed in Sweden for export (six being supplied to the Chinese Central Government and four ultimately going to the Soviet Union), the Reichswehr purchased the two prototypes, plus the two remaining export aircraft. Found to be capable of carrying a 100kg bomb-load (eight 12.5kg fragmentation bombs) on their underwing struts, three of these machines were tested at Lipezk for their suitability in the dive-bombing role. Although successful, high unit costs precluded the tightly budgeted Reichswehr from awarding a production contract, and the four aircraft (now designated as A 48s) served out their time in the Reich engaged in a variety of quasi-civil duties.

The seed had nevertheless been sown, and in the predatory shape of the original K 47 – despite the uncranked wing and twin tail unit – the embryonic form of the wartime Stuka, what would become the Luftwaffe's most infamous ground-attack aircraft, could already be seen emerging. A further two aircraft were to play a part in the story of German dive-bomber development before the advent of the Junkers Ju 87. The first of these came about as a direct result of growing Japanese interest in dive-bombing. Although an erstwhile ally of the Western Powers during World War I, Japan herself was now also restricted by international treaty in the number and tonnage of the capital ships she was permitted to build (a ratio of three-to-two in favour of the United States and Great Britain). Seeking ways to redress the balance, and keenly aware of the ongoing dive-bomber experiments being conducted by the US Navy across the Pacific, Japan turned to Germany for assistance, approaching not Junkers, but the reputable seaplane manufacturing firm of Ernst Heinkel AG.

ABOVE: Hs 123A 'Black Chevron/Yellow L' of II./SG 2, Khersonyes-South, Crimea, April 1944. Incredibly, what must surely have been the last remaining operational examples of the venerable Hs 123 reappeared on Luftflotte 4's order of battle late in April 1944. According to that document, they were assigned to II./SG 2 and based alongside the *Gruppe*'s Fw 190s during its final days on the Crimean peninsula. Note the percussion rods fitted to the 50kg SC 50 bombs. (John Weal © Osprey Publishing)

The resulting two-seater biplane design stressed for diving, and initially equipped with floats, was later exported to Japan as the Heinkel He 500, and served as the basis for the Imperial Japanese Navy's own Aichi OIA carrier-borne dive-bomber.

Heinkel then offered a second (landplane) prototype to the Reichswehr. After a demonstration at the Rechlin test centre in 1932, followed by trials at Lipezk, the type was accepted into service as the He 50A interim dive-bomber in 1933, the year that Adolf Hitler came to power. It was thus the Reichswehr under the aegis of the Weimar Republic, and not the new National Socialist regime, which was responsible for preparing the groundwork and introducing the dive-bomber and ground–attack aircraft into Germany's covert, but burgeoning, new armoury. However, Hitler and the head of his still clandestine air force, Hermann Göring, were more than willing to tread the path already laid down for them. Thus, when World War I fighter ace turned international stunt pilot Ernst Udet came back from a tour of the United States in the early 1930s extolling the virtues and dive-bombing abilities of the Curtiss Hawk II fighter then being offered for export, Göring authorized the newly established RLM to provide Udet with the necessary funds to purchase two examples of the type for use in his aerobatic displays. It was a shrewd move, for not only did it give German designers the

OVERLEAF: A moment of fun and fraternization. The pilot and ground crew of a Ju 87 flirt with a group of Norwegian female skiers while they arm the Stuka.

opportunity to examine state-of-the-art American technology, but it also acted as a bribe in tempting the 'freebooting' Udet back into the official Luftwaffe fold.

The dual-role capability of the Curtiss machines prompted the Technisches Amt (Technical Office) of the RLM to issue similar specifications in February 1934 for a single-seat fighter and dive-bomber. The winning design, in the shape of the Henschel Hs 123, made its public debut at Berlin-Johannisthal in May of the following year. Flown by Ernst Udet himself, its performance did much to strengthen the hand of the pro-Stuka (i.e. dive-bomber) lobby within the RLM. Yet, if one discounts its early days in Spain, the Henschel was destined never to see action as such. Throughout the whole of its long operational career – it was still flying on the Eastern Front in 1944 – the 'eins-zwei-drei' or 'one-two-three', was employed to great effect as a low-level close-support aircraft. For despite being the first Stuka design to be ordered in any quantity for the Luftwaffe, the Hs 123 was regarded from the outset as a 'Sofort Lösung' – an 'immediate solution' or temporary measure – to bridge the gap until the second, and final, phase of the dive-bomber programme produced a more advanced two-seater machine, offering an improved performance and heavier bomb-load.

To this end, the RLM turned back to Dipl.-Ing Hermann Pohlmann of Junkers, co-designer of the original K 47 (Karl Plauth had lost his life in a flying accident before the K 47 was completed). Pohlmann had begun design work on the Ju 87 on his own initiative back in 1933 when the subject of a second phase to the Sturzbomber-Programm had first been broached. By the time the official specification was finally issued some two years later, he had already commenced the construction of three prototypes, leaving rival firms Arado and Heinkel well out of the running.

Although obviously a product of the same stable as the K 47, the early Ju 87s were, by contrast, particularly ugly and angular aircraft, characterized by the inverted gull wing which would be the hallmark of every one of the 5,700+ Stukas built. However, the Ju 87 had been designed to fulfil a specific role, and in this it was unsurpassed, even if (when it was in its natural element swooping almost vertically on its intended target) it was likened somewhat fancifully to an evil bird of prey.

The first prototype Ju 87 V1, powered by a Rolls-Royce Kestrel V12-cylinder, upright-Vee, liquid-cooled, engine, featured a twin-tail unit not dissimilar to that of its K 47 predecessor. However, when this failed in flight during a medium-angle test dive, causing the V1 to crash, the remaining prototypes were redesigned with a centrally mounted single fin and rudder assembly.

A fourth prototype was later added to the first three, this, the Ju 87 V4, incorporated all the lessons learned from flight-testing the original trio. With its Junkers Jumo 21 OAa inverted-Vee engine in a revised, lowered, cowling to improve forward visibility, re-contoured cockpit canopy and enlarged vertical tail surfaces, the V4 led directly to the first batch of fully armed Ju 87A-O pre-production models ,which started coming off the assembly line before the end of 1936. These in turn were followed during the course of 1937 by the A-I and A-2 production runs, the latter being equipped with the uprated Jumo 210Da engine.

In 1938, hard on the heels of the last 'Anton' to be built, there appeared the first of the 'Bertas': when compared to the Ju 87A, the B-model featured not just a more powerful Jumo 211 engine with direct fuel injection, but a completely redesigned and reconstructed fuselage, cockpit and vertical tail. The most striking difference between the two, however, was the abandonment of the Ju 87A's huge 'trousered' undercarriage in favour of the slightly less obtrusive, and therefore aerodynamically cleaner, spatted leg. Both aircraft, alongside other nascent Luftwaffe ground-attack aircraft, were soon to receive their first combat testing.

THE SPANISH CIVIL WAR

The outbreak of the Spanish Civil War in the summer of 1936 afforded Hitler the ideal opportunity to test the mettle of the men and machines of his new air arm under operational conditions. He lost little time in despatching the first units of a volunteer force, soon to evolve into the Legion Condor, to fight alongside the insurgent Spanish Nationalist troops commanded by General Francisco Franco.

A trio of early Hs 123s were among the first aircraft to be sent to Spain. Arriving in the autumn of 1936, they were formed into the *Stukakette* of VJ/88, the Legion's then still experimental fighter component. Commanded by Leutnant Heinrich 'Rubio' Brücker, the three Henschels first saw action in support of the Nationalist offensive against Malaga in January 1937. They were then transferred northwards to participate in the attacks on the so-called 'Iron Ring' defences around Bilbao on Spain's Biscay coast.

However, it quickly became apparent that the Hs 123 left a lot to be desired as a dive-bomber, for Brücker and his pilots were unable to achieve the level of pinpoint accuracy that had so impressed Ernst Udet during the Hawk II's demonstration in America six years earlier. The reason for this, it was now discovered, was the Henschel's inability to maintain sufficient steadiness during the dive.

The Legion's chief of staff, Oberstleutnant Wolfram Freiherr von Richthofen (cousin of the legendary Manfred Freiherr von Richthofen of World War I fame) therefore decided to employ Brücker's small unit in the non-diving ground-attack role. And in this they were to prove highly successful. Three more Hs 123s arrived in Spain in the spring of 1937, and 'Rubio' Brücker's now six-strong command set about the business of re-inventing and perfecting the type of low-level ground-attack sorties that had last been flown against the 'Reds' in Latvia nearly two decades before. Brücker's pilots were soon

OVERLEAF: An Me 109 seen outside its hangar in 1940. The Me 109 proved to be a flexible platform, switching readily between fighter and ground-attack roles when necessary.

ABOVE: He 51B '2.78' of Oberfeldwebel Adolf Galland, *Staffelkapitän* 3.J/88, Legion Condor, Calamocha, Spain, January 1938. Wearing one of the many non-standard green and brown camouflage schemes applied 'in the field' after the He 51s had first arrived in Spain (in overall pale-grey finish), '2.78' was Adolf Galland's preferred mount for most, if not all, of his time at the head of 3.J/88. Like many of the Legion's fighter pilots, he personalized his machine by embellishing the black fuselage disc – in his case outlining it thinly in white and adding a large Maltese cross. (John Weal © Osprey Publishing)

reporting that the 'fearsome noise alone' of the Henschels roaring only a matter of metres above the enemy's columns and positions was often enough to cause panic and confusion – sometimes even flight. It was a tactic which would be repeated to great effect during the opening months of World War II.

Despite the Henschel's inherent ruggedness, these early 'experimental' missions cost the unit dearly. By the summer of 1937 it had lost four of its number, and the following year the two survivors were passed to a Spanish mixed *Grupo*. During their service with the Legion Condor the Hs 123s had somehow acquired the nickname '*Teufelsköpfe*' ('Devil's Heads'). Oddly, after transfer to the Spanish Nationalist air arm, which subsequently took delivery of a further dozen improved B-1 models, the Henschels were rechristened '*Angelitos*' ('Little Angels')!

However, the Hs 123 was not the only machine to have its operational deficiencies brought to light by service in Spain. The Heinkel He 51 was to prove an even greater disappointment to the German command. Selected as the standard single-seat fighter of the newly emergent Luftwaffe, the Heinkel biplane had already displayed its gracefully aggressive lines to the World's press in a number of carefully staged demonstrations and fly-pasts long before the first six examples of the type were shipped to Cadiz, in southern Spain, in August 1936.

ABOVE: He 46C '1K+BH' of 3. Störkampfstaffel/Lfl. 4, Eastern Front, Southern Sector, c. April 1943. The He 46 tactical reconnaissance machine, first flown in 1931, was typical of the elderly types equipping the early night ground-attack *Staffeln* on the eastern front. This particular example – tactical number '8' – is carrying 50kg SC 50 bombs (fitted with tail screamers) on its ventral rack and wing support struts. (John Weal © Osprey Publishing)

Here, reality turned out to be very different from the image of Luftwaffe superiority fostered by the propaganda-fuelled aerial parades above the rooftops of Berlin. Despite a few initial successes, it came as a rude shock to discover that the He 51 was, in fact, dangerously inferior to the majority of the (mainly French) fighters flown by their Republican opposition. This was brought forcibly home by an incident in mid-September when just two Republican machines escorting a gaggle of elderly Breguet bombers were able not just to prevent six Heinkels from attacking their charges, but actually to drive the German fighters off! It was only the poor armament of the French aircraft which prevented matters from becoming even worse.

At first the Germans tried to remedy the situation by sheer weight of numbers, and by the end of November a further 72 Heinkels had been despatched to Spain (including 24 to the Spanish Nationalist air arm). However, the arrival in Spain of the first Soviet I-15 and I-16 fighters that same month finally dashed any lingering hopes the German Command may still have been harbouring that in the He 51 – which now equipped all four *Staffeln* of the Legion's J/88 fighter *Gruppe* – they possessed a fighter aircraft of world-class standing.

By the close of the year the position of the German fighter force in Spain was being described as 'farcical', and the humiliation of its pilots was well nigh complete. Hopelessly outclassed as an air-superiority fighter, the He 51s could not even be gainfully employed on bomber-escort duties. It was reported that upon the approach of enemy aircraft the German fighters were often 'forced to take refuge within the bomber formations in order to gain the protection of the larger machines' defensive machine-gun fire'. However, just like the shortcomings of the Hs 123 as a dive-bomber, which soon faded from memory with the advent of the lethally effective Ju 87, so the He 51's near total inadequacy as a fighter was quickly forgotten upon the appearance of its successor – one of the true greats in the annals of fighter history, the Messerschmitt Bf 109.

In the early spring of 1937 the first Bf 109Bs were rushed to Spain, where they re-equipped 2.J/88. The question now was what to do with the Legion's He 51s? It was decided that the 2. Staffel machines replaced by the Bf 109s, plus those of the disbanding 4.J/88, would be passed to the Spanish Nationalists, while the aircraft of 1. and 3.J/88 – pending the arrival of more Messerschmitts – would be redeployed mainly in the ground–attack role.

A Ju 88A-14 was a close-support version of the prolific German medium bomber. Armed with a 20mm MG FF cannon in a pod under the fuselage, it could destroy many tanks and all soft-skinned vehicles.

The Spaniards had already begun to use their Heinkels for such missions. Indeed, it was they who developed the *Cadena*, or 'chain', tactic, which consisted of a formation of He 51s, flying in line-ahead, diving upon an enemy trench and machine-gunning along its length one after the other. When the leader had completed his run he would pull up into a steep half-roll and rejoin the end of the queue. The result was that the occupants of the trench were pinned down by continuous fire. The onslaught would be kept up until either the Heinkels' ammunition was exhausted, or the position was captured by attacking forces. The pilots of 1. and 3.J/88 employed similar tactics during their first ground-attack sorties around Bilbao and Santander on the northern front in the spring of 1937. They also added a ventral Elvemag weapons rack to enable each machine to carry six 10kg bombs.

Meanwhile, the Ju 87 was also forging its reputation as a formidable dive-bomber and ground-attack aircraft. The experience gained from the handful of Stukas sent to participate in the Spanish Civil war was indeed invaluable. Air and ground crews alike practised and perfected their skills and techniques, equipment was honed and numerous modifications made. The Ju 87 proved its ability to hit a precision target from a near-vertical dive, installing terror via the B-1's '*Jericho-Trompete*' ('Jericho Trumpet') dive sirens, or the whistles fitted to its bombs. However, one ingredient had been lacking – serious opposition. In the air the Ju 87s enjoyed strong fighter protection, whilst effective Republican AA fire was almost non-existent except in the immediate vicinity of those targets deemed to be vitally important. A great feeling of confidence in the dive-bomber had therefore been engendered by the Stuka's performance in Spain. No bad thing, and one which would serve the crews well in the opening months of the war that was to come. However, in one important respect the Ju 87 remained untested – its ability to survive in a completely hostile airspace.

LUFTWAFFE *SCHLACHTGRUPPEN*

Although the Ju 87 was a de facto ground-attack aircraft, the creation of dedicated ground-attack formations for service in World War II was centred largely on other aircraft. One of the key names in this work was the great Luftwaffe fighter pilot, 'ace' and commander Adolf Galland. After service in the Legion Condor, Galland had relinquished command of 3.J/88 late in May 1938, shortly before the *Staffel* converted to the Bf 109. The passionate fighter pilot had not managed to claim a single kill during his time in Spain. To rub salt into the wound his successor – one Werner Mölders – quickly made the most of the unit's new Messerschmitts by downing a couple of I-15s. And these were just the first of the 14 victories which would see Mölders emerge as the Legion Condor's highest scorer.

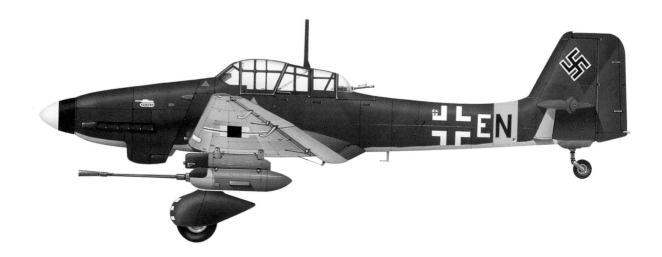

ABOVE: Ju 87G 'S7+EN' (Wk-Nr. 494231) of Feldwebel Josef Blümel, 10.(Pz)/SG 3, Wolmar, Latvia, September 1944. Appropriately displaying the *Panzerjäger* badge on its cowling, this was the machine Josef Blümel was flying when he claimed his 60th Soviet tank on 19 September 1944. On a second mission later that same morning, however, the Ju 87 was damaged by anti-aircraft MG fire and Blümel was forced to land behind enemy lines south of the Latvian capital, Riga. Both he and his radio operator were executed by Red Army troops. (John Weal © Osprey Publishing)

Galland hoped that a return to the Reich would also mean a return to fighters, but he was to be disappointed. With growing confidence Hitler had already marched his troops into the de-militarized zone of the Rhineland and annexed Austria – both actions specifically prohibited by the Treaty of Versailles. Now the Führer had his sights firmly set on the Sudeten territories of Czechoslovakia.

To add weight to his demands, Hitler ordered his ever-growing Luftwaffe to mount a strong aerial presence along the borders with the disputed territories. The Luftwaffe duly obliged by providing over 40 *Gruppen*, predominantly bomber, dive-bomber and fighter. Among the *Stukagruppen* included in this force was Hs 123-equipped III./StG 165, which was then the only unit of its kind not yet flying the Ju 87.

As an additional safeguard, should this show of strength prove insufficient and an actual armed invasion be required to wrest the Sudetenland from Czechoslovakia, it had further been decided that a ground-attack force – similar to, but much larger than, the one that had recently been so successful in Spain – would be the ideal weapon to open up a gap in the Czechs' frontier defences. And who better to help organize such a force than the man who had just spent ten months with the Legion Condor perfecting the very tactics which would be needed to do the job?

His post-tour leave suddenly cancelled, Adolf Galland thus found himself behind a desk in the new RLM building in Berlin, involved in the creation of five ad hoc ground-attack *Gruppen*. Despite the confusion and haste – 'of course, everything was wanted by the day before yesterday at the latest' – the five new units, designated *Fliegergruppen*, were activated in time to participate in a large-scale exercise before taking up station along the Reich's borders with the Sudetenland.

Three of the *Gruppen* were assigned to Lw.Gr.Kdo. 1, the command deployed in Silesia, Saxony and Thüringia to the north and north-west of Czechoslovakia. Fliegergruppen 10 and 50, based at Brieg and Grottkau respectively, were by now both equipped with ex-school Hs 123s, while Fliegergruppe 20, at Breslau, had to make do with the antiquated He 45, long ago rejected as a light bomber, but still soldiering on in the reconnaissance role. The other two units, Fliegergruppen 30 and 40, came under the control of Lw.Gr.Kdo. 3 in Bavaria and Austria to the south-west and south of Czechoslovakia. Fliegergruppe 30's Hs 123s were stationed at Straubing, while the outdated He 45s of Fliegergruppe 40 took up residence at Regensburg.

By the latter half of September 1938, with his ground and air forces fully assembled, Hitler's 'show of strength' was in place. In the event, he was not required to unleash that strength. The British and French governments were united in their apparent desire to follow the path of appeasement at all costs. On 30 September they co-signed the Munich Agreement, ceding the Sudeten territories of Czechoslovakia to the Greater German Reich. Twenty-four hours later Hitler's forces marched virtually unopposed across the now defunct frontier.

Most of the Luftwaffe units gathered for *Fall Grün* (Case 'Green', as the Sudetenland operation had been code-named) were quickly dispersed back to their home bases. Of the five ground-attack *Gruppen*, only one, Hauptmann Siegfried von Eschwege's Fliegergruppe 30, was transferred into the newly occupied zone. Its stay at Marienbad was to be brief, however, and on 22 October it rejoined Fliegergruppe 40 at Fassberg, in northern Germany.

Although their operational careers under the guise of *Fliegergruppen* had been short-lived, the effort expanded in creating these five units did not go to waste. Three were re-equipped with the Ju 87 and redesignated as *Stukagruppen*, a fourth converted to Do 17s to become a *Kampfgruppe*, and the fifth – Fliegergruppe 10 – joined the ranks of the *Lehrgeschwader* in November 1938 to provide a nucleus for the sole *Gruppe* to be formed in furtherance of the science of ground attack. Some sources maintain that it was the He 45-equipped Fliegergruppe 20 which was selected for this role.

The Luftwaffe's *Lehrgeschwader* were mixed-formation units tasked with the operational evaluation of new machines and/or the development of new tactics. Each *Gruppe* within a *Lehrgeschwader* was equipped with a different type of aircraft. Lehrgeschwader 2, for example, consisted of a fighter *Gruppe*, a reconnaissance *Gruppe* and Fliegergruppe 10's Hs 123s. As such, they alone represented the Luftwaffe's entire dedicated ground-attack strength during the final ten-month countdown to war.

HARD LESSONS, NEW ROLES

After helping to establish the five *Fliegergruppen* at the time of the Munich Crisis, Galland had finally been permitted to return to his true love – fighters. However, his tenure of office as *Staffelkapitän* of 1./JG 433 (which became 1./JG 52 on 1 May 1939) was to last exactly nine months. His knowledge of, and experience in, ground-attack operations had not been forgotten by the upper hierarchy and on 1 August 1939, as the war clouds gathered over Europe, he was posted to II.(Schl)/LG 2. It now formed part of Generalmajor von Richthofen's *Fliegerführer z.b.V.* This was the 'special duties' command – consisting mainly of Ju 87 Stukas – which was to provide the aerial component of the world's first *Blitzkrieg* operation: the smashing of a narrow breach in Poland's defences by 10. Armee and its subsequent all-out drive, spearheaded by 1. and 4. Panzer Divisionen, north-eastwards to the enemy's capital, Warsaw.

Ju 87B dive-bombers sit in winter snows. If all else failed, the last resort for coaxing a frozen engine back into life was to light a fire underneath it.

However, von Richthofen, who in Spain – like some field commander of old – had often watched his troops in action from the vantage point of a nearby hilltop, was aware not only of the Hs 123's capabilities, but also of its limitations: 'By the time Spielvogel and his old crates finally reach the front from Alt-Siedel,' he complained, 'they will already have used up nearly half their fuel.' He therefore issued instructions that a forward landing ground be made available for Major Werner Spielvogel's 'crates' close to the Polish border.

It was no accident that the Ju 87 was selected to carry out the very first operation of World War II, which was initiated some 20 minutes before the official outbreak of hostilities! Given the nature of the objective, no other choice was possible.

The easternmost province of the Reich, East Prussia, was cut off from Germany proper by the Polish Corridor. This hotly disputed strip of territory, which afforded the landlocked Poles access to the Baltic Sea, was another product of the Treaty of Versailles, and a contributory factor in Hitler's decision to attack Poland. Across its neck ran a single railway which connected the province to Berlin. This track would be a vital lifeline between the two in time of war. Its weakest link was the bridge at Dirschau (Tczew), where it spanned the River Vistula. Both the Germans and Poles were aware of this, and the latter had prepared the bridge for demolition should they be attacked.

The target for the first bombing raid of the war was, therefore, not the bridge itself, but the demolition ignition points situated in blockhouses at nearby Dirschau station, plus the cables which ran out along the railway embankment on to the bridge. The objective was to prevent the structure from being destroyed before it could be seized by German ground troops being transported into Poland by armoured train. It was a job that only the Stuka could do. Wearing civilian clothes, pilots of I./StG 1 – the unit ordered to carry out the attack – had undertaken their own first-hand reconnaissance by travelling back and forth several times in the sealed trains (inevitably known as 'corridor trains') in which Germans were allowed to traverse the 100km stretch of line that connected East Prussia with the Fatherland.

At exactly 0426hrs on 1 September 1939 a *Kette* (three-aircraft formation) of Ju 87s of 3./StG 1, led by *Staffelkapitän* Oberleutnant Bruno Dilley, lifted off from their forward base in East Prussia for the eight-minute flight to the target. Despite the all-pervading ground-mist that blanketed the area, the trio of Stukas, each loaded with one 250kg bomb, plus four smaller 50kg weapons slung in pairs under each wing, soon spotted the unmistakable iron lattice-work of the bridge looming ahead of them. Flying at a height of just 10m above the flat Vistula plain, the three pilots climbed as one before separating to plant their bombs unerringly on the station blockhouses, severing the finger-thick cables. Despite the successful completion of the mission, it was all to no avail. The armoured train was delayed, and the Poles managed to destroy the bridge before German ground troops could reach it. The first bombing raid of the war had been a carefully planned – albeit ultimately abortive – operation.

Also in the pre-dawn darkness of 1 September 1939, the 39 pilots of II.(Schl)/LG 2 found themselves running up their engines on a small field outside the township of Alt-Rosenberg, less than 15km behind the arm of the River Warthe which marked Germany's frontier with Poland in this region. Despite the swathes of ground mist still clinging to the damp grass of the meadow, all got off safely. From his forward HQ immediately to the south of the border crossing point at Grunsruh, von Richthofen could hear the approaching Hs 123s. Their shapes were just visible as they circled above the river, their engines 'droning angrily like a swarm of disturbed hornets'.

At 0445hrs precisely, Hauptmann Weiss, Spielvogel's senior *Staffelkapitän*, led the Henschels in to the attack. On the far bank of the river he quickly spotted the *Gruppe's* objectives – Polish Army installations, identified by Intelligence as being occupied by forward elements of the enemy's 13th Division, in and around the village of Przystain.

Every one of Weiss's 4. Staffel pilots placed his load of four 50kg explosive-incendiary bombs with precision. Hard on their heels, Galland's 5.(Schl)/LG 2 did the same. By the time 6. Staffel commenced its run, the enemy positions were shrouded in smoke and flames. Despite being taken by surprise, the Polish troops responded with light AA and small-arms fire. However, this opposition was soon suppressed as the Henschels, splitting up into individual *Ketten* (three-aircraft formations), then carried out a series of strafing runs, hedge-hopping over and around trees and other obstacles, and raking the Poles with machine gun fire.

Generalmajor von Richthofen watched the entire proceedings from the near bank of the Lisswarthe. What he was witnessing in the dawn light of 1 September 1939 was the first ground-attack operation of World War II to be mounted by the Luftwaffe in direct support of an advancing army. And it was a complete success. At the end of that momentous day the OKW issued a communiqué summarizing events. It included the phrase, '… in addition, several *Schlachtgeschwader* provided effective support for the army's advance'.

The successful attack on Przystain on the opening morning of hostilities set the pattern for the week ahead. Over the next seven days Major Spielvogel's II.(Schl)/LG 2 continued to blast a path for 10. Armee's Panzers as they drove hard for Warsaw. Whenever an armoured or motorized infantry unit was brought to a temporary halt by strong local enemy resistance, the call went out for the 'one-two-threes' to clear the obstacle. In the process, the Henschels earned a new nickname for themselves. The *Trabajaderos* ('labourers') of Spain became the *Schlächter* ('butchers') of Poland. It was a brave – and rare – enemy column that could withstand the sight, and sound, of a dozen or more Hs 123s roaring along a road just 10m above their heads. Men and horses bolted in panic. Drivers and crews leaped from their vehicles to seek what cover they could. Had they but known it, the more racket the Henschels were making, the safer those on the ground actually were, for at those revs, or so it has been said, the pilots were unable to fire their machine guns for fear of shooting their own propellers off!

However, there were also plenty of opportunities to employ more lethal measures, strafing and dropping a whole arsenal of 50kg high-explosive and incendiary bombs, as the Henschel pilots kept up the pressure, mounting one sortie after the other as long as daylight lasted. The Stuka crews were doing the same, while overhead flew the Heinkels and Dorniers of the *Kampfgeschwader*. Even the Messerschmitt fighter and *Zerstörer Gruppen* were being called upon to carry out low-level ground-strafing attacks. Ground-attack aircraft thus played a central role in the defeat of Polish forces in the autumn of 1939.

With the cessation of hostilities in Poland, II.(Schl)/LG 2 returned to Brunswick, in Germany, for rest and refit. The winter of 1939–40, one of the most severe in living memory, was spent quietly. It was not until 1 February 1940 that two of Hauptmann Weiss's *Staffeln* were moved up to München-Gladbach, just 24km from the Dutch border.

The *Gruppe* still formed part of Generalmajor von Richthofen's 'special duties' command which, by this time, had been raised to the official status of a *Fliegerkorps*. Anticipating that the aerial opposition to be faced in the forthcoming attack in the West would be much stronger than that put up by the gallant, but outclassed, Poles, the new VIII. Fliegerkorps was assigned its own protective fighter force of Bf 109s. A Do 17-equipped *Kampfgeschwader* was also temporarily attached to increase the range of the corps' striking power.

Again, Hitler's ground-attack aircraft were in the vanguard of operations in the West. They supported the pioneering Luftwaffe airborne assault on the Belgian fortress of Eben Emael on 10 May 1940, then provided air cover for the Panzer assault through Belgium. By day's end the *Gruppe* had flown some eight to ten ground-support missions, as indeed had most of VIII. Fliegerkorps' units – even its attached reconnaissance *Staffel* had been armed with 50kg bombs so that it could engage 'targets of opportunity'.

By that time, too, the Panzer and motorized infantry divisions of 6. Armee were starting to pour in an uninterrupted stream through the town of Maastricht and out along the two exit roads leading westwards, across the Vroenhoven and Veldwezelt bridges, into Belgium. Over the next few days Allied bombers made many desperate, near suicidal, attacks on the 'Maastricht bridges' in repeated attempts to stop this flow of traffic.

With the all-important bridges now securely ringed by flak batteries and covered by standing fighter patrols, Weiss's pilots were able to roam slightly further afield on day

ANTI-TANK TACTICS

These trainee crews discuss anti-tank techniques with their *Hauptmann* instructor.

1: A typical approach commences from 4,500m. As the target is acquired through the floor window, the range-timing clock is set. The engine is reduced to idling speed, air-intakes are closed and dive-brakes opened. The nose drops into an instantaneous 80° dive and the timing clock is started.

2: A Ju 87 tended to oscillate in the dive, but the pilot centres the target in the 'Revi-16B' reflector sight, holding it in the crosshairs. A buzzer sounds at 2,100m (*c.* 30 seconds into the dive), and the pilot starts the release and recovery timer.

3: The aircraft continues to plummet at *c.* 560km/h, largely driven by gravity. At 1,000m, the *Einhängung* cradle unlocks to swing the bomb away from the fuselage and clear of the propeller. The bomb slips free as the auto-recovery system commences simultaneously. The crewmen push their heads back against padded restraints to prevent their chins being forced painfully into their chests.

4: Auto-recovery pulls the aircraft out of the dive so steeply that crewmembers usually black out under forces of 3–4G. The bomb continues its line of descent towards the target (approximately 15 seconds to impact). The pilot resumes consciousness and control of aircraft. (Adam Hook © Osprey Publishing)

two of the campaign. This led to their first recorded brush with the expected 'strong' enemy fighter opposition. It came in the form of an RAF Hurricane of No. 607 Sqn, which got in 'four or five bursts' at one of 5. Staffel's machines as they were busy bombing Belgian positions along the River Meuse. Although claimed as a kill, the Henschel returned to base only slightly damaged.

But all this intense early activity on the northern flank of the offensive – spectacularly successful though it was proving to be – was, in reality, a gigantic feint deliberately designed to lure the Allied ground forces up into Belgium in response. The main thrust, to be delivered by the five Panzer divisions of 12. Armee, would then be launched through France out of the Ardennes hills to the south, and would again be capably supported by ground-attack formations, which fought nearly all the way to the French coast.

By early June the campaign in France was virtually over and so, it seemed, was the operational career of the Hs 123. When von Richthofen's Stukas began transferring up to Normandy the following week as part of the preparations for taking the war to England's shores, II.(Schl)/LG 2 did not accompany them. The Henschels had proved themselves rugged and willing workhorses, able to operate from the most primitive of grass fields and capable of absorbing tremendous punishment. They had also provided invaluable support to ground troops at numerous water barriers.

However. the next hurdle facing VIII. Fliegerkorps was no Polish stream, Belgian canal or French river. It was the 112km width of the English Channel separating Cherbourg from the Dorset coast and it was an obstacle the short-legged 'one-two-threes' simply could not overcome.

Otto Weiss, who was promoted to *Major* on 1 July, therefore led his *Gruppe* back to Brunswick-Waggum for re-equipment. It was not just the Hs 123, the 'interim dive-bomber' turned ground-attack aircraft, which was facing retirement. The entire *Schlacht* arm was in imminent danger of dissolution. The elderly biplane's intended successor, the Hs 129, a heavily armoured, twin-engined machine designed from the outset for the ground-attack role, had first flown more than a year earlier. However, it had proved a major disappointment.

Plans had already been mooted to convert II.(Schl)/LG 2 into a bona fide dive-bomber unit equipped with the Ju 87. Many felt that the dedicated ground-attack machine, despite the success of the strafing and bombing aircraft above the trenches of World War I, had no place in a modern war of movement. The new 'wonder weapon' of the *Blitzkrieg* era was the Ju 87 Stuka, which had already demonstrated its abilities – not only by carrying out pinpoint dive-bombing attacks, but also by flying low-level strafing missions. And these latter, to all intents and purposes, were ground-attack operations.

OVERLEAF: Warsaw burns following an attack by Stukas in 1939. The Stuka was capable of precision ground-attack operations, but it was also used in a more indiscriminate capacity, as seen over cities such as Leningrad and Stalingrad on the Eastern Front.

DIVE ATTACK OVER POLAND

Major Oskar Dinort, *Gruppenkommandeur* of I./StG 2 'Immelmann', recalls one of the earliest aerial actions in Poland shortly after midday on 1 September 1939, when air reconnaissance brought back reports of large concentrations of Polish cavalry advancing on Wielun and threatening the northern flank of the German XVL Armeekorps:

'We moved up into Poland. Our new base was some seven kilometres outside the town of Tschensrochau (Czesrochowa). We arrived about midday and the base personnel immediately set about erecting tents and organizing defensive positions. We were, after all, on enemy soil and the woods bordering the field to the north-east were reportedly full of Polish stragglers …

'… sure enough, hardly had darkness fallen before shots rang out from the edge of the woods. Our ground-staff replied with machine-guns and light flak. The whole field was eerily illuminated by flickering searchlight beams and red beads of tracer. The firing continued throughout the night, but died out shortly after 4 am when it started to rain. At last we aircrew could snatch some sleep.'

Dinort and his crews got all the rest they needed. The rain persisted, and they did not take off until 3 pm the next afternoon. Their targets were the bridges over the Vistula near the fort of Modlin, to the north of Warsaw:

'We climbed through the grey clouds and broke out into clearer air at some 1200 metres. Below us the ragged valleys of cumuli, above us a leaden, sunless sky.

'Course north-east. Visibility was still not good. The windscreen streaked with more rain. Only the occasional glimpse of the ground and brief sighting of the Vistula through a break in the clouds to keep us on track. At last I saw the fort below us. It lay in the brown landscape, huge, grey and pointed like some burned-out star. And there too the Vistula bridges. Tiny lighter strips against the dark bed of the river: our target.

'The moment has come. Wing over into the dive! The machine drops like a stone. The altitude unwinds – down 200 metres, 300, 500. The instruments can hardly keep pace with the rate of descent. Then the red veil in front of the eyes that every Stuka pilot knows. 1400 metres from the ground … 1200 metres … press the release. The bomb falls away into the depths below.

'I recover and take the usual evasive measures. Linking away, I look back. Behind me the Stabskette are in the middle of their dive, the first Staffel right on their tails, dark shadows against the lightening sky. Their aim is good … one bomb hits the centre of the target.'

In the event, Major Weiss's *Gruppe* was re-equipped not with Ju 87s, but with Bf 109 fighter-bombers. The reason for the change of policy is not known. The bursting of the Stuka bubble over southern England by RAF Fighter Command was still some weeks away. However, the conversion to Messerschmitts may well have been a lucky escape for II.(Schl)/LG 2.

The advent of the fighter-bomber was a further muddying of the waters as far as the ground-attack concept was concerned. Both Bf 109 fighters and Bf 110 *Zerstörer* had also flown ground-strafing sorties in Poland and the west. Also, an experimental *Gruppe* equipped with the two types was currently undergoing training prior to commencing cross-Channel fighter-bomber operations.

II.(Schl)/LG 2's own re-training for the fighter-bomber role, which was completed at Böblingen in southern Germany, lasted well into August. It thus missed the opening rounds of the Battle of Britain.

Over Poland in 1939, then Scandinavia, France and the Low Countries in 1940, the Stuka seemed to prove both the theory and practice of the dive-bombing ground-attack mission. Precision strikes ahead of the armoured spearheads had a terrifying effect on Allied positions and troop movements, and helped to pave the way for the armoured advance. Ju 87s delivered some of the last aerial attacks on the British evacuation from Dunkirk, on one day assisting in the sinking of 31 Allied vessels off the French coastline. Yet as the Introduction to this book indicated, everything changed during the summer of 1940, with the Luftwaffe's attempt to subdue the RAF in the Battle of Britain.

BATTLE OF BRITAIN

The Battle of Britain actually began with the *Kanalkampf* (Channel Battle) attempts by Ju 87s, Do 17s and other aircraft to interdict British shipping in the Channel. One of the first reported encounters between Ju 87s and British shipping in this latest phase of the Stuka's operational career had been an ineffectual dive-bombing attack (believed to have been mounted by III./StG 51) on deep-sea convoy 'Jumbo', which was attacked whilst approaching Plymouth early on the afternoon of 1 July. Three Hurricane Is of No. 213 Sqn were scrambled from Exeter to engage the Stukas, but by the time they had arrived over the convoy the raiders had long since departed.

Three days later III./StG 51 staged a maximum-effort raid on Portland harbour that resulted in probably the highest military loss of life ever inflicted by a single air attack on the British Isles. Led by their new *Kommandeur*, Hauptmann Anton Keil, some 33 Stukas dived out of the morning mist, which hung over the naval base, totally unannounced. They concentrated their attacks on the largest vessel in the harbour, the auxiliary AA ship HMS *Foylebank*, and within eight minutes 22 bombs had struck the ship, killing 176 of her crew.

With no RAF fighters in the vicinity, the *Gruppe* escaped back to Cherbourg all but unscathed, having also set fire to an oil tanker moored in Weymouth Bay with a direct hit from a 500kg bomb prior to making good their escape – the vessel burned for 24 hours before the flames could be brought under control. The only loss inflicted upon the Ju 87s was one machine brought down over the target area, its wing blown off by a

A Ju 87 Stuka releases its bomb as it pulls out of its near-vertical dive. This was actually the most dangerous moment of an attack for the Stuka, as its speed and manoeuvrability drained away in the climb.

direct hit from one of the *Foylebank's* 4in. AA guns – both Leutnant Schwarz and his gunner were killed in the subsequent crash. A second Stuka landed back at Cherbourg having suffered minor flak damage.

The Stukas continued to inflict a heavy punishment on Allied shipping around the British coastline for the rest of the month, with the British fighters often arriving too late to inflict casualties on the dive-bombers. The weather deteriorated as July drew to a close, but the *Stukagruppen* had already performed to perfection the initial task required of them in the run-up to the planned invasion of England. By 'plugging' the Channel at either end, and neutralizing the Royal Navy's south coast destroyer flotillas (which had lost a dozen vessels since mid-May, plus many others withdrawn from the area for essential repairs), they had secured the cross-Channel sea lanes for the invasion fleet, which was even now being assembled in northern European ports.

Next would come phases two and three of their part in the conquest of Great Britain. In August – repeating the tactics of Poland and France – they would take out RAF Fighter Command's forward airfields in a series of precision attacks in preparation for the landings. And in September, once the German Army was safely ashore, they would resume their classic role of 'flying artillery' as the ground-troops pushed northwards into the heart of England. The relative ease with which they had accomplished phase one (at a cost of only some dozen aircraft lost or written off) had given no indication of the storm that was about to break over them.

The 13th of August 1940 – *Adlertag* – was the opening round of the Luftwaffe's main air assault on the British Isles. For the protagonists, their 'big day' did not get off to a good start for adverse weather conditions in the early morning led to last-minute postponement orders being transmitted. However, not all units received them, and in the resulting confusion some bombers flew missions devoid of fighter cover, while other fighters dutifully flew to assigned target areas without the bombers they were meant to protect!

By the afternoon, however, the weather had improved sufficiently to allow the *Stukagruppen* to launch the second phase of their three-part role in the overall invasion plan – a series of pinpoint attacks intended to neutralize Fighter Command's forward fields. They struck along both flanks of the designated assault zone. In the east Luftflotte 2 despatched II./StG I against Rochester and IV.(St)/LG 1 against Detling. The former failed to locate their target, but Hauptmann von Brauchitsch's 40 Ju 87s caused severe damage at Detling, killing 67 (including the station commander Group Captain Edward Davis), demolishing the hangars and totally destroying 22 aircraft. Retiring without loss, IV.(St)/LG 1 landed back at Tramecourt with justifiable feelings of a job well done. It was German intelligence that was at fault – Detling was not a Fighter Command airfield. Indeed, the only aircraft permanently based there were Ansons of No. 500 'County of Kent' Sqn, which had been seconded to Coastal Command since early 1939. One of the unit's armourers provided this candid description of the oncoming raid as seen from his squadron dispersal:

> The B Flight night-duty ground crew finished their evening meal and waited in and around the Dennis lorry which would take them to the Anson aircraft, parked in fields alongside the Yelsted road at the northeast corner of Detling aerodrome.
>
> Faintly, in the distance, Maidstone's air-raid shelter sirens were heard, and then the drone of aircraft. These aircraft could be seen approaching the airfield from about two miles [3.2km] away to the south-east at a height of about 5,000ft [1,524m]. The formation was much larger than had been seen in the area before – so much so that it prompted one of the squadron armourers, Bill Yates, to announce that he 'didn't know we had so many'. This remark almost qualified for 'Famous last words' as Yates clambered to the Dennis' canvas top and began a count of the aircraft. He had passed the 30 mark when the leading machine dipped its port wing in a diving turn, and became without any shadow of a doubt a Stuka.

To the west, units of VIII. Fliegerkorps suffered diversities of fortune. Elements of StG 77 searched in vain for Warmwell before dropping their bombs at random over the Dorset countryside and returning to their Caen airfields unmolested. Despite being bereft of fighter cover (their 30 Bf 109 escorts from II./JG 53 had been obliged to turn back through a shortage of fuel), Hauptmann Walter Enneccerus' 27 Ju 87Rs of II./StG 2 crossed the coast near Lyme Regis en route for Middle Wallop, but they never made it. Intercepted by 13 Spitfire Is of No. 609 Sqn, they lost five of their number in a one-sided duel over the coast, and a sixth which crashed into the Channel during the return flight – the RAF claimed to have destroyed or damaged 14 Ju 87s and Bf 109s and suffered no losses. This decimation of the Stukas had been witnessed from the Portland cliffs by Prime Minister Winston Churchill and a clutch of senior Army generals. One of the pilots to claim a Ju 87 destroyed, and a second dive-bomber damaged, was leading No. 609 Sqn ace, Flying Officer John Dundas:

> Thirteen Spitfires left Warmwell for a memorable Tea-time party over Lyme Bay, and an unlucky day for the species Ju 87, of which no less than 14 suffered destruction or damage in a record squadron 'bag', which also included five of the escorting Me's. The formation, consisting of about 40 dive-bombers in four-vic formation, with about as many Me 110s and 109s stepped-up above them, was surprised by 609's down-sun attack.

The four-minute massacre off the Dorset coast was the beginning of a terrible period for the Stukas. Their loss rates spiralled upwards – between 8 and 18 August some 20 per

ABOVE: Ju 87G 'Black Chevron and Bars' (Wk-Nr. 494193) of Oberst Hans-Ulrich Rudel, *Geschwaderkommodore* SG 2, Niemes-South, Czechoslovakia, May 1945. Although he had a Fw 190D-9 at his disposal, Hans-Ulrich Rudel remained true to the Ju 87 Stuka until the very end. And it was in the Stuka that Rudel chose to fly his last mission on 8 May 1945, and then lead the seven aircraft of his HQ flight (three Ju 87s and four Fw 190 escorts) to Kitzingen and surrender to US forces. (John Weal © Osprey Publishing)

cent of the entire Stuka force were destroyed over Britain, and 33 other machines destroyed. The dive-bombers did not have the manoeuvrability or the power to survive on their own in a dogfight against the superior British fighters. Their very dive attack profile also left them ideally placed for fighter interception as they crawled out of the dive and attempted to gain altitude. By 18 August, therefore, the Stuka had been effectively pulled out of operational service over Britain, and even the aircraft's staunchest advocates were having to concede that the Stuka was not operable as a strategic weapon if pitted against a determined defence.

By contrast, the results being achieved by the experimental *Erprobungsgruppe* 210 since the start of their low-level precision fighter-bomber attacks on southern England in mid-July were more than encouraging. The success of Erpr.Gr. 210's operations prompted an exasperated Göring to order that one-third of his entire Channel-based fighter force be similarly converted to carry bombs.

In the weeks and months ahead, throughout the winter – weather permitting – and into the early spring of 1941, II.(Schl)/LG 2 kept up its sporadic attacks on southern England. Flying from St Omer and Calais-Marck, the unit's targets included RAF airfields, oil refineries, railways, docks and coastal shipping. Although usually accompanied by a fighter escort – often provided by JG 27, the unit which had been assigned to protect its

Henschels in France – these operations resulted in a dozen or more combat casualties. Fortunately, some two-thirds of the pilots survived to become prisoners of war.

Of course, none of the operations flown by II.(Schl)/LG 2 during its six-month campaign against England were *Schlacht* missions in the truest sense of the word – i.e. ground-attack sorties flown in direct support of the Army in the field. Yet, oddly, the (Schl) abbreviation continued to be used in the unit title. Perhaps Weiss's pilots were to have reverted to their original role once the German Army had set foot on England's shores?

In the meantime, the *Gruppe* had retained both a sense of individuality, and a link with the past, by applying a unique set of markings to its Bf 109s. Each machine was identified by a letter, rather than a fighter-style numeral, and each sported a large black equilateral triangle ahead of its fuselage cross. Such triangles had first been worn by the aircraft of the *Fliegergruppen* at the time of the Munich crisis. Their re-adoption may well have been at the instigation of Major Weiss himself, who had served as a *Staffelkapitän* in Werner Spielvogel's Fliegergruppe 40 during that period.

Between September 1940 and March 1941 these triangles – a few litres of black paint at most – were the only outward sign of what was now, in effect, an all but extinct ground-attack force. However, the triangle would survive to become recognized as the official symbol of the *Schlacht* arm, for a resurrection was about to take place. Less than a fortnight after its last Bf 109 had been lost over England (or, to be more precise, had been shot into the Channel off Dungeness) on 15 March 1941, II.(Schl)/LG 2 was given something far more tangible than mere markings to show that it was still very much in the ground-attack business – a new intake of old Hs 123s.

EASTERN FRONT 1941–43

By the first week in January 1941, II.(Schl)/LG 2's strength at St Omer/Arques had sunk to just 11 serviceable Bf 109s. This was probably the lowest point in the fortunes of the Luftwaffe's ground-attack arm at any time in the war. However, a change of strategic policy by the Führer heralded a reversal in those fortunes and marked the beginning of the *Schlacht* force's emergence and expansion into one of the most important fighting components of the Wehrmacht.

The proposed invasion of England, shelved the previous autumn, was now postponed indefinitely. Hitler's attention was focused instead on Nazi Germany's traditional enemy, Communist Russia. Plans for an attack on the Soviet Union were already well advanced when a popular uprising by the people of Yugoslavia against their pro-Axis government forced the Führer into an unplanned, and unsought, campaign to stabilize his south-eastern borders.

Among the Luftwaffe units hastily assembled for a combined assault on Yugoslavia and Greece (the latter country currently locked in conflict with, and thoroughly trouncing, Germany's ally Italy) was II.(Schl)/LG 2. The *Gruppe's* paucity in numbers was soon made good. By the end of March 1941 they were fielding 30+ Bf 109s. However, as the coming action in the Balkans was to be a repeat of the previous year's *Blitzkrieg* campaigns – an all-out offensive against the enemy's armies in the field – the Messerschmitts were divided between just two of the *Gruppe's* component *Staffeln*. The third was re-equipped with that trusty veteran of ground-attack operations, the Henschel Hs 123, now brought out of retirement for a second time.

In addition, a completely new *Staffel*, 10.(Schl)/LG 2, was formed and likewise equipped with 'one-two-threes'. The two *Staffeln's* total complement of 32 Henschels, taken together with the others' Bf 109s, meant the *Gruppe* was again numerically the strongest of any being committed to the coming campaign. By the first week of April, operating once more as part of General der Flieger von Richthofen's VIII. Fliegerkorps, II.(Schl)/LG 2 had transferred down into Bulgaria. The main body of the *Gruppe* was based at Sofia-Vrazdebna, close to the Bulgarian capital, while 10. Staffel shared nearby Krainici with elements of StG 2.

Operation *Marita*, launched in the early hours of 6 April 1941, began in true *Blitzkrieg* style with heavy raids on the enemy's airfields and frontier defences. More accustomed perhaps to the lengthy approach flights which had preceded their recent cross-Channel fighter-bomber attacks on southern England, some of the *Gruppe's* Bf 109 pilots seem to have been caught off guard by the immediacy and ferocity of tactical ground-support operations. At least three of their number crashed on returning to base, although whether this was a direct result of previous damage from ground fire has not been established. The *Gruppe's* Bf 109s and Hs 123s were soon proving their worth in true *Schlacht* style, clearing a path for their own advancing forces by bombing and machine-gunning any reported pockets of opposition into submission or retreat. The Balkans were in German hands by the end of May 1941, by which point the *Schlacht* forces were readying themselves for a far greater adventure.

On the eve of the invasion of the Soviet Union II.(Schl)/LG 2 was based at Praschnitz (Praszniki) in the far north of German-occupied Poland, just below the Lithuanian border. Its strength comprised 38 Bf 109Es, all but one of which were serviceable, plus 22 Hs 123s (17 serviceable). The Henschels, it appears, were now all operated by the attached and enlarged 10. Staffel.

The *Gruppe* was still part of General von Richthofen's close-support VIII. Fliegerkorps, the bulk of whose units had only recently arrived in the area following their successful participation in the Cretan campaign. Von Richthofen's command was also, itself, one of the two corps which together provided the striking power of Luftflotte 2, the air fleet tasked with supporting land operations on the central sector of the coming Eastern Front campaign.

VIII. Fliegerkorps' specific responsibility was the aerial support of the four armoured and three mechanized divisions of Panzergruppe 3, whose orders were to smash all opposition in the border areas of Soviet-occupied Poland and White Russia, before advancing as quickly as possible on Smolensk, 'the last great fortress before the Soviet capital, Moscow'.

Despite its immense scale – involving three-and-a-half million German troops and their allies assaulting a front stretching some 3,000km from the Baltic to the Black Sea – Operation *Barbarossa* relied on the same basic *Blitzkrieg* formula as before. That meant, first and foremost, neutralization of the enemy's air power. II.(Schl)/LG 2's pilots played an important part in the savage and sustained strafing attacks on the 66 Soviet frontier airfields which marked the opening day of the invasion, which inflicted staggering Soviet losses, including 1,489 aircraft destroyed on the ground. So astonishing were these claims that the Luftwaffe High Command at first refused to accept them, only doing so after subsequent investigation on the ground had confirmed their accuracy.

Despite the enormity of its losses, the Soviet Air Force still managed to mount retaliatory bombing raids, but these were left to the *Jagdgruppen* to deal with as II.(Schl)/LG 2 now began to concentrate on its primary task – the support of the German armoured spearheads. Over the summer and autumn months of 1941, the ground-attack aircraft were shifted between various sectors, in each place exacting a

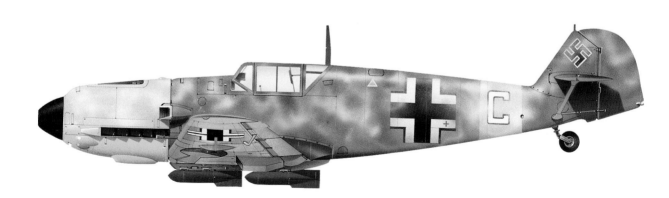

ABOVE: Bf 109E 'White C' of 4.(Schl)/LG 2, Moscow Front, Central Sector, November 1941. Depicted towards the close of II.(Schl)/LG 2's 28-month long operational career, 'White C's' standard Eastern Front finish and markings are all but obscured by a thick and irregular wash of temporary white winter paint. Oddly, this aircraft displays neither a unit badge nor the black ground-attack triangle. (John Weal © Osprey Publishing)

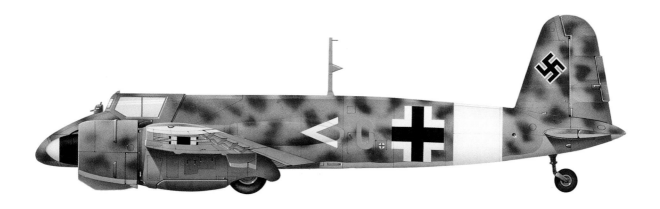

ABOVE: Hs 129B 'White Chevron/Blue 0' of Hauptmann Bruno Meyer, *Staffelkapitän* 4.(Pz)/SchlG 2, El Adem, Libya, November 1942. The second specialized Hs 129 anti-tank *Staffel* to be formed, 4.(Pz)/SchlG 2 was destined from the outset for the North African theatre, as witnessed by the factory-applied camouflage finish of overall tan with disruptive green mottling. Bruno Meyer would later command the Hs 129-equipped IV.(Pz)/SG 9, and would survive the war having flown more than 500 ground-attack and anti-tank missions. (John Weal © Osprey Publishing)

heavy toll on Soviet troops, vehicles and armour. The original plans for *Barbarossa* had envisaged the capture of Moscow well before the onset of winter, but the enforced delay in its launch, brought about by the intervening campaigns in Yugoslavia and Greece, meant that German forces were still short of the Soviet capital when the first snows fell. They were ill-prepared and ill-equipped to face the appalling severity of the winter months that followed.

Even the hardy Henschels found it almost impossible to continue operations from their base close to the River Ruza, some 80km to the west of Moscow. Blizzard conditions and temperatures plunging down to between 20 and 30 degrees below zero kept them firmly on the ground for most of the time. And when the Red Army renewed its counter-offensive around Moscow, using fresh Siberian divisions from the Far East, any last hopes of a quick conclusion to *Barbarossa* were finally dashed. German frontline troops had little option but to dig in and sit tight until the spring.

The end of 1941 also saw the end of II.(Schl)/LG 2. However, the *Gruppe* which had single-handedly kept the flag of the *Schlacht* arm flying – both figuratively and literally – for the past three years was being recalled to Germany not to disband, but to provide the nucleus for the first ever *Schlachtgeschwader*. Major Otto Weiss, who had commanded the *Gruppe* for almost its entire operational career, and who had been the first *Schlacht* pilot to receive the Knight's Cross, now became the first to be awarded the Oak Leaves – on 31 December 1941 – before being appointed *Geschwaderkommodore* of the new unit early in January 1942.

A Luftwaffe Stuka pilot sits astride a destroyed Soviet gun emplacement at Sevastopol in the Crimea. In June 1942, Ju 87s subjected Sevastopol to near-continuous strikes, with the crews flying as many as eight sorties a day from their bases around Sarabuz.

II.(Schl)/LG 2's destination in Germany was Werl, a pre-war fighter airfield to the east of Dortmund. It was here that Weiss established the *Stab* of Schlachtgeschwader 1, and II.(Schl)/LG 2 was redesignated to form the basis of his first *Gruppe* – I./SchlG 1. At nearby Lippstadt (likewise a fighter field of long standing) a second *Gruppe*, II./SchlG 1, was also activated mainly from scratch.

The mainstay of SchlG 1 was the Bf 109, but both *Gruppen* also received the Hs 123 and the heavily armed and armoured twin-engined Hs 129. It was to be used to equip two new *Staffeln*: 4.(Pz) and 8.(Pz)/SchlG 1. As the Pz (*Panzer*) abbreviation in their designation indicates, these two *Staffeln* were designed to operate as dedicated anti-tank units. Despite persistent powerplant problems, the Hs 129 would indeed develop into a potent tank-killer as subsequent models were fitted with ever more specialized weaponry, including large-calibre ventral anti-tank cannon and armour-penetrating hollow-charge bombs.

Operations against the Red Army in the spring of 1942 resumed where they had perforce been broken off late in 1941. However, the new year brought with it a change in the strategic direction of the campaign on the Eastern Front. The blockade of Leningrad in the north would continue. On the central sector, however, the German Army no longer had its sights set on capturing Moscow. The Führer had decreed that the primary objective of the 1942 offensive was instead to be the oilfields of the Caucasus in the far south.

SchlG 1 was therefore ordered to stage the 2,200km journey east south-east from the Ruhr to the Crimea. Unseasonably bad weather en route delayed its arrival, but on 6 May the unit paraded on the airfield of Grammatikovo for inspection by General der Flieger von Richthofen. Von Richthofen's command was part of Luftflotte 4, the Air Fleet responsible for all operations on the southern sector.

Grammatikovo was situated at the base of the Kerch Peninsula. This easternmost part of the Crimea had been occupied by the Germans late in 1941, only to be retaken by the Red Army in a surprise midwinter counter-offensive. Now it had to be captured a second time.

For most of the younger pilots of II./SchlG 1 the two-week battle to clear the Kerch Peninsula was to be their introduction to Eastern Front operations. It was not an altogether reassuring experience. While VIII. Fliegerkorps' Stukas bombarded the Soviet frontline positions, SchlG 1 was sent deep into the enemy's rear to disrupt his lines of supply, both road and rail, and to attack any other reported signs of movement. However, the Red Army was no longer the disorganized, demoralized force it had been during the opening months of *Barbarossa*. Even the veterans of I. Gruppe were surprised at the way the Russian soldier now stood his ground, and at just how much fire – from cannon to small-arms – was thrown up at them. By the time the town of Kerch, on the tip of the peninsula, finally fell on 21 May, both *Gruppen* had sustained a number of losses from the heavy enemy ground fire.

On the surface, *Fall Blau* (Case Blue) appeared to be just the latest in a long line of classic *Blitzkrieg* campaigns. However, by this midway point in the war the cracks were beginning to show. There were clear signs that the Wehrmacht's resources were being outstripped by the growing demands made upon it. For example, the pilots of SchlG 1 were now frequently required to fly their own pre-op reconnaissance sorties, as VIII. Fliegerkorps' sole dedicated reconnaissance *Staffel* was often engaged on more pressing duties.

Nor did the *Schlachtflieger* enjoy the luxury of automatic fighter protection any more. This was something else they often had to provide for themselves. True, the occasional enemy aircraft had been claimed by ground-attack machines since the earliest days of the war, but these had usually been as a result of chance encounters. Now chance was turning

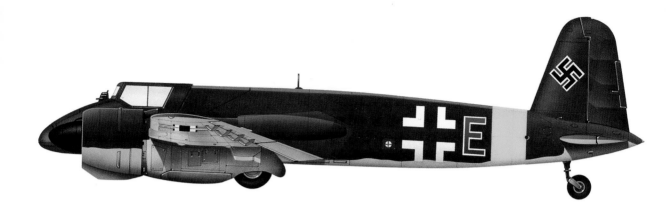

ABOVE: Hs 129B-2 'Blue E' of 4.(Pz)/SchlG 1, Mikoyanovka, Kursk Salient, July 1943. Based upon a photograph purportedly taken at the time of Operation *Zitadelle* (the great tank battle of Kursk), this profile of 'Blue E' offers evidence that the Hs 129, despite its unmistakable shape and form, was also toning down its markings. The black *Schlacht* triangle was long gone, and now the bright yellow nose panels – an ideal aiming point for Soviet anti-aircraft gunners – had, perhaps quite sensibly, been dispensed with too. (John Weal © Osprey Publishing)

into necessity as Red Air Force pilots began specifically to target the *Geschwader*'s bomb-carrying ground-attack Bf 109Es, the former regarding them as easier prey than the Luftwaffe's Bf 109F fighters. In return, however, the Bf 109s often went hunting enemy aircraft themselves, the pilots giving free reign to their design to be fighter pilots as well.

The juxtaposition of duties, combining the ground-attack and the *Zerstörer* arms, was an indication of just how complex the growing assortment of Luftwaffe ground-support forces was becoming. *Schlacht* and Stuka units had long been engaged in essentially similar roles. To them had since been added two wartime creations – fighter-bomber (*Jabo*) and fast bomber (SKG) formations. Now twin-engined *Zerstörer*, whose original deployment as long-range fighter escorts had proved so disastrous during the Battle of Britain, were being categorized as ground-attack aircraft too.

Operationally, the ground-attack forces were playing out their roles against the backdrop of the Stalingrad disaster. With winter 1942/43 operations reduced to a minimum – between the months of November and March suitable flying weather could be expected on average on only one day in ten – the time was used instead finally to re-equip. It had long been acknowledged that the narrow-track undercarriage of the Bf 109 made it less than ideal for use on the Eastern Front's uneven and unprepared grass airfields, particularly when encumbered with ventral and/or underwing racks and stores. The Focke-Wulf Fw 190, currently serving on the Channel front in the fighter-bomber role, offered the perfect replacement, its wide-set undercarriage legs being better able to cope with rough ground. The armoured ring in front of its air-cooled radial engine also provided increased protection against enemy ground fire (many a Bf 109 had met its end with a single bullet hole in its vulnerable coolant plumbing). Also, the Fw 190 was at its best at low to medium altitudes – the natural environment of the *Schlachtflieger*.

Commencing in late autumn, Major Hitschhold's units were therefore rotated one *Staffel* at a time back to Deblin-Irena, in Poland, to convert onto Focke-Wulfs. It was a long drawn out process, which would not be fully completed until the end of April 1943. SchlG 1 did not reappear in full on Luftflotte 4's order of battle until May 1943. Although still consisting of only two *Gruppen* (plus the specialized anti-tank *Staffeln*) upon its return to Eastern Front operations, the *Geschwader* represented a formidable fighting force well over 100 aircraft strong. Figures for mid-May indicate that Major Druschel's enlarged *Stab* flight was made up of six Fw 190s, while 67 more Focke-Wulfs, plus 32 Hs 129s, were divided almost equally between his two component *Gruppen*.

A ground-attack version of the Fw 190. In addition to two 13mm machine guns and two 20mm cannon, the Fw 190D-9 variant also carried a single 500kg bomb on the fuselage centreline.

The Hs 123 may have been nearing the end of its service career, but there was still an urgent and growing need for an aircraft capable of combating the increasing numbers of Red Army tanks now beginning to dominate the Eastern Front battlefields. One answer seemed to lie in that other Henschel design, the Hs 129, which, despite its ongoing powerplant problems, had already claimed a considerable number of armoured kills. It was therefore proposed that, in addition to the established Pz. *Staffeln*, every *Jagdgeschwader* on the Eastern Front should have its own Hs 129 anti-tank *Staffel*. In the event, however, only one such unit – 10.(Pz)/JG 51 – was to be raised and see combat.

Another attempt to solve the problem had led to the activation of the Versuchskommando für Panzerbekämpfung (Experimental Command for Anti-Tank Warfare) at Rechlin late in 1942. This experimental unit was tasked with testing heavy anti-tank weaponry on other aircraft types. It was composed of four *Staffeln* – two of Ju 87s equipped with underwing 37mm BF 3,7 cannon, and one each of Bf 110s and Ju 88s, the former with a single BK 3,7 in a ventral fairing, and the latter carrying a massive 75mm PaK 40 cannon beneath the forward fuselage.

Field trials with the Bf 110s and Ju 88s, operating as Pz.J. *Staffeln* 110 and 92 respectively, proved unsatisfactory. The PaK 40-toting Ju 88s were particularly unwieldy, and one pilot still recalls the cannon's recoil regularly blowing the nose and engine panels off his machine! Although the nose (and propeller blades) were subsequently strengthened, the inner nacelle panels of the armour-protected engines were thereafter always tied on with baling twine as an added precaution.

In contrast, the Ju 87's 37mm underwing cannon were found to be highly effective against Soviet armour. In June 1943, the two experimental *Staffeln*, 1. and 2./Vers.Kdo.f.Pz.Bek., were therefore officially redesignated *Panzerjägerstaffeln* (anti-tank squadrons), one each being assigned to StGs 1 and 2 as specialized frontline tank-buster units.

The then *Staffelkapitän* of 1./StG 2, who had been given the opportunity to fly one of the test machines on operations, was quick to see the possibilities of the new weapon. The BK 3,7-equipped Ju 87G would become the aircraft of choice for Hans-Ulrich Rudel – the most famous and successful Stuka pilot of all – for the remainder of the war.

Many *Kampfgeschwader* set up so-called *Eisenbahn* (railway) *Staffeln*. Those flying He 111s usually just fitted their bombers with additional nose armament to carry out low-level strafing attacks on railway targets. The Ju 88-equipped units were slightly better off in being able to employ cannon-armed Ju 88C heavy fighters for their train-busting sorties. One of the greatest exponents of this latter art was 9.(Eis)/KG 3's Leutnant Udo Cordes. Nicknamed the '*Lok-Töter*' ('Loco-killer'), in one short period during the spring of 1943 Cordes succeeded in destroying not just 41 locomotives, but 19 entire trains – including two carrying fuel and three transporting ammunition. After his unit was disbanded, Cordes spent the final weeks of hostilities flying Fw 190s with

a *Schlachtgruppe*. Indeed it was the Fw 190 that was to be the dominant *Schlacht* aircraft, both in terms of numbers and performance, during the last two years of the war on the Eastern Front. It fulfilled all expectations, meeting every demand made upon it – and more. Under different circumstances it could well have had a significant influence on the course of the campaign. As it was, it was thrown into the maelstrom of Kursk in July 1943 – to great effect – but then began the final, gruelling retreat of German forces back to the Reich.

By the winter of 1943, a new era was about to begin. Just as, on the ground, the German Army was attempting to stabilize and organize its forces along the *Ostwall* (East Wall), so, in the air, the Luftwaffe was finally beginning to recognize the value of its hitherto woefully neglected *Schlacht* arm. Some sort of order had to be created of the bewildering assortment of ground-support units – *Stuka, Schlacht, Zerstörer, Schnellkampf, Jabo, Panzerjäger* – which had been allowed to accumulate during the first four years of

A Bf 110 undergoes maintenance to its nose-mounted machine guns. In the Bf 110E and 110G variants, armed with a powerful 30mm or 37mm cannon, the Luftwaffe had a potent anti-armour weapon that accounted for dozens of tanks in North Africa and on the Eastern Front in 1941–42.

the war, but which, by this present stage of the conflict, were now all performing essentially the same tasks.

The initial step – the establishment of a unified command – had already been taken. On 1 September 1943, Oberstleutnant Dr Ernst Kupfer had been appointed as the Luftwaffe's first *General der Schlachtflieger*. A Stuka pilot of long-standing, and latterly *Geschwaderkommodore* of StG 2 'Immelmann', Dr Kupfer had recently led the *Gefechtsverband Kupfer*, a mixed-force battle group – including the Fw 190s and Hs 129s of SchlG 1 – which had come to the rescue of 9. Armee at Orel after the collapse of the Kursk offensive.

On 11 October Major Alfred Druschel had then relinquished command of SchlG 1 to assume the post of *Inspizient der Tag-Schlachtfliegerverbände* (Inspector of Day Ground-Attack Units) on Dr Kupfer's staff.

Exactly one week after that, on 18 October 1943, the confusing mix of Luftwaffe ground-support units, together with their many, varied, and often complicated designations, was finally done away with. For on that date all were reorganized into *Schlachtgeschwader* – henceforth to be identified by the simplified abbreviation 'SG' – and incorporated into the framework of a new and greatly enlarged *Schlacht* arm.

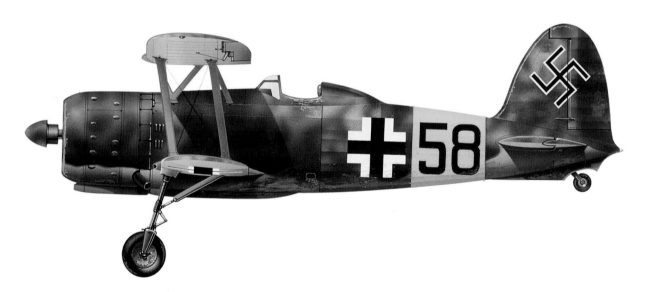

ABOVE: Fiat CR.42 'Black 58' of 3./NSGr 7, Agram (Zagreb), Croatia, July 1944. Another unit to be equipped with Italian machines (together with a miscellany of other types) was NSGr 7, which was operating on the other side of the Adriatic under the control of Fliegerführer Kroatien. Flying both nocturnal ground-attack missions and anti-partisan operations by day, 3. Staffel's Fiats appear to have retained their original Regia Aeronautica camouflage, to which was added Luftwaffe theatre markings and national insignia (including an oversized swastika). (John Weal © Osprey Publishing)

ABOVE: Me 262A-1a/U4 (Wk-Nr 111899) of Major Wilhelm Herget, JV 44, Munich-Riem, April 1945. Formerly a Messerschmitt works test vehicle based at Lechfeld, this is the Me 262 armed with the 50mm Mauser MK 214A nose cannon which 'Willi' Herget brought with him to JV 44 in January 1945. (John Weal © Osprey Publishing)

NORTH AFRICA AND ITALY

By the time Kursk ended, the Wehrmacht had already experienced disasters on other fronts, including in North Africa. It was not until November 1942, by which time the battle of El Alamein had been fought and lost, and his forces were in full retreat, that Rommel was able to call upon the services of a *Schlachtgruppe*. By then, no single *Gruppe* had a hope of turning the tide of the war in North Africa.

Like its Eastern Front counterparts, I./SchlG 2 – the unit in question – was made up of three *Staffeln* of single-engined fighters (in this instance Bf 109Fs) and an attached *Staffel* of Hs 129 tank-busters. The latter was the second Hs 129 Staffel to be formed (after 4.(Pz)/SchlG 1's activation at Lippstadt early in 1942). Set up late in September 1942 at Deblin-Irena in Poland, reportedly around a cadre of personnel supplied by the short-lived Pz.J.St. 92, 4.(Pz)/SchlG 2 was initially equipped with a dozen of the twin-engined Henschels. However, by the time the *Staffel*, commanded by Hauptmann Bruno Meyer, arrived at El Adem, south of Tobruk, on 7 November, this number had shrunk to eight, only four of which were serviceable. The Hs 129s nevertheless claimed a dozen British tanks knocked-out during their first reported action just one week later.

However, not renowned for their reliability at the best of times, the mixing of the Hs 129s' Gnome-Rhône engines with Libya's all-prevailing dust and sand was a certain recipe for disaster. After only a few more operations, during which two machines were lost when forced to land behind Allied lines, the *Staffel* was withdrawn to Tripoli. Here, attempts were made to produce a satisfactory sand filter for the recalcitrant powerplants, but without much success. When the advancing Eighth Army entered the Libyan capital on 23 January 1943, the remaining unserviceable Henschels were reportedly destroyed and the *Staffel* evacuated to Bari, in Italy, for re-equipment.

Erwin Rommel, the famous commander of the Afrika Korps, prepares to make a reconnaissance flight in a Focke-Wulf 'Weihe' (Harrier). Rommel never managed to secure the volume of air support he needed in North Africa, and the Allied armies there were eventually able to operate under conditions of air superiority.

The Bf 109 Staffeln coped somewhat better with the rigours of North African campaigning. This was due perhaps to I./SchlG 2 being created in part from the two original desert *Jabostaffeln* (of JGs 27 and 53). After combining to form the strengthened *Jabostaffel Afrika*, this unit had subsequently moved to Sicily, where it was redesignated as the *Jabogruppe OBS*. As its title implies, the *Gruppe* now came under the direct command of the *Oberbefehlshaber Süd* (Luftwaffe Commander-in-Chief South), Generalfeldmarschall Albert Kesselring, and was engaged in fighter-bomber attacks against Malta.

Late in October 1942, redesignated yet again to become I./SchlG 2, the *Gruppe* began transferring back to Africa. During the withdrawal across Libya's eastern province the *Gruppe* had lost some 12 Bf 109Fs and at least four pilots. The retreat into Tripolitania brought no respite. The Eighth Army kept up the pressure, driving the Afrika Korps and its Italian allies right out of Libya as it pushed through the Gabes Gap and up into southern Tunisia. The *Gruppe*, commanded now by a Major Fischer, did what it could to slow the enemy's advance, attacking not only his armour and supply columns, but also air bases, such as the RAF's fighter airfields around Medenine, with high explosive and anti-personnel bombs. Greatly outnumbered in the air and facing ever increasing AA fire from the ground, these operations proved costly. As it slowly fell back towards Tunis, I./SchlG 2 began to suffer a rising rate of attrition, and by the early spring of 1943 its serviceability returns were struggling to reach double figures.

The fall of Tunisia in May 1943 heralded a parting of the ways for SchlG 2's component units. The two anti-tank *Staffeln* were withdrawn from the Mediterranean theatre altogether. Staging via Berlin-Staaken, where their strength was increased to 16 Henschels apiece, they subsequently transferred to the Eastern Front to take part in the battle of Kursk.

Having survived its six-week foray into Tunisia relatively intact, II./SchlG 2 retired to central Italy, seemingly to await developments. I. Gruppe, meanwhile, was at Bari undergoing conversion to the Fw 190. Although no major ground operations were being fought in the Mediterranean theatre during this period, it could only be a matter of time before the Allies took their first steps towards a return to mainland Europe. Axis intelligence believed that an invasion of either Sardinia or Sicily would be their likeliest route.

Based in central and southern Italy, SchlG 2's two *Gruppen* were right in the front line of Europe's 'soft underbelly' – a fact forcibly driven home by the increasing ferocity of Allied bombing raids throughout the whole area. Unversed in bomber interception duties, SchlG 2 had to rely on their flak defences and neighbouring *Jagdgruppen* for protection. However, as an added precaution they dispersed their own aircraft as much as possible, with part of I. Gruppe deploying to Brindisi to complete its working-up on Fw 190s.

Towards the end of June, I./SchlG 2 transferred to Milis, in Sardinia. The move did not go unnoticed by the Allies, and the *Gruppe* was soon subjected to further bombing. A raid by waves of B-26s on 3 July resulted in the destruction of four of its new Fw 190s, plus damage to several others. Despite these depredations, the unit still had 20 serviceable Fw 190s on strength (four more than II. Gruppe) when Anglo-American troops landed on Sicily exactly one week later.

It appears, however, that only II./SchlG 2 joined the anti-invasion forces on Sicily – flying ground-attack operations out of both Gerbini and Castelvetrano – for Hauptmann Josef Berlage's I. Gruppe spent the ensuing month shuttling back and forth between Sardinia and Italy. During the latter half of July it was based at Aquino, near Monte Cassino, before returning briefly to Sardinia in early August. Then it was back to

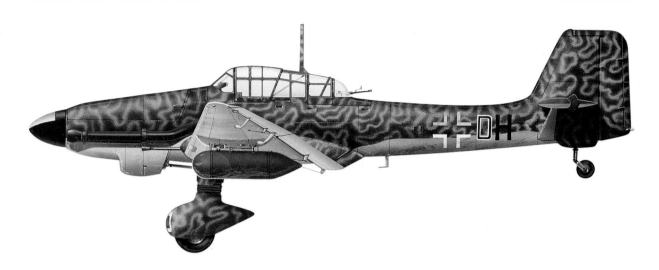

ABOVE: Ju 87D 'E8+DH' of 1./NSGr 9, Ravenna, Italy, July 1944. Originally just two *Staffeln* strong, and equipped with Italian machines (Fiat CR.42 biplanes and Caproni Ca.314 light twins), NSGr 9 converted to Ju 87s in the spring of 1944. Initially coming under the control of the Fliegerführer Italien, the *Gruppe*'s three *Staffeln* would operate independently of each other for much of the remainder of the war in Italy. The large underwing container shown here is the so-called Universal-Behälter, which could be used to carry both stores and supplies. (John Weal © Osprey Publishing)

Piacenza, in northern Italy, where orders were received directing I./SchlG 2 to Graz, in Austria, for further training.

It thus fell to II. Gruppe, under Hauptmann Dörnbrack, to carry out SchlG 2's final missions in the Mediterranean. These included attacks against the Salerno bridgehead to the south of Naples during the second week of September. The *Gruppe* would continue to participate in the stubborn defence of central Italy throughout the coming months, but after 18 October 1943 it would be under a new identity.

ABOVE: An Me 110 is fitted with a camera to perform aerial reconnaissance. While the Me 110 quickly showed up its deficiencies as a fighter, it was a proficient ground-attack platform, as it proved against British truck convoys in North Africa.

DOWNFALL OF THE *SCHLACHT* ARM

The creation of the new enlarged *Schlacht* arm on 18 October 1943 changed the underlying nature of the ground-attack force at a single stroke. Prior to this time, to be a *Schlacht* pilot was almost akin to gaining membership of a rather exclusive club – something along the lines of the pre-war Royal Air Force, where everyone knew, or knew of, everyone else.

BOTTOM LEFT: Stukas ranked up on an airfield in North Africa. One Stuka pilot, Hans-Ulrich Rudel, accounted for no fewer than 519 enemy tanks during his combat career, many of these killed using the cannon-armed Ju 87G.

However, the sudden five-fold expansion in strength, while undeniably elevating the ground-attack force to a position of much greater prominence within the ranks of the Luftwaffe, at the same time introduced the unavoidable veneer of impersonality which afflicts any large organization; and the *Schlacht* arm had just become a very large organization indeed, with units deployed from the Arctic Circle to the Mediterranean and from the English Channel to the Black Sea. As such, its many operations during the remaining months of the war can only be portrayed with the broadest of brush strokes.

The bulk of the new force had been brought into being by the simple expedient of redesignating all existing *Stukagruppen* as *Schlachtgruppen*. However, as this process was not entirely straightforward, and in order to be able to show how the four 'old guard' *Schlachtgruppen* (of SchlGs 1 and 2) were broken up and dispersed among the other units, the lineage of the new ground-attack formations is perhaps best, and most concisely, illustrated by the following table:

I.–III./SG 1	redesignated from	I.–III./StG 1
I./SG 2	redesignated from	I./StG 2
II./SG 2	previously	II./SchlG 1
III./SG 2	redesignated from	III./StG 2
10.(Pz)/SG 2	redesignated from	Pz.J.St./StG 2
I.–III./SG 3	redesignated from	I.–III/StG 3
I./SG 4	previously	II./SchlG 2
II./SG 4	previously	II./SKG 10
III./SG 4	previously	III./SKG 10
I./SG 5	redesignated from	I./StG 5
I./SG 10	previously	I./SchlG 2
II./SG 10	previously	IV./SKG 10
III./SG 10	previously	II./StG 77
I./SG 77	redesignated from	I./StG 77
II./SG 77	previously	I./SchlG 1
III./SG 77	redesignated from	III./StG 77
10.(Pz)/SG 77	redesignated from	Pz.J.St./StG 1

As may be seen from the above, II./StG 2 had not been included among the wholesale redesignations of October 1943. This unit remained operational as a specialized anti-tank *Gruppe* within Luftflotte 4 for the next five months as II./StG 2(Pz). Indeed, it was not until March 1944 that the unit was split up to create two new Ju 87G-equipped anti-tank *Staffeln* – 10.(Pz)/SG 3 and 10.(Pz)/SG 77. The latter then replaced the above-listed 10.(Pz)/SG 77, which in turn rejoined its original parent *Geschwader* as 10.(Pz)/SG 1.

The five Eastern Front Hs 129 anti-tank *Staffeln* were, however, part of the reorganization of 18 October 1943. They were united into a single *Gruppe* – IV.(Pz)/SG 9 – as follows:

10.(Pz)/SG 9	previously	4.(Pz)/SchlG 1
11.(Pz)/SG 9	previously	8.(Pz)/SchlG 1
12.(Pz)/SG 9	previously	4.(Pz)/SchlG 2
13.(Pz)/SG 9	previously	8.(Pz)/SchlG 2
14.(Pz)/SG 9	previously	Pz.J.St./JG 51

The intention to establish an entire anti-tank *Geschwader* never materialized, for the only other part of the planned SG 9 to see the light of day was its I. Gruppe. However, this was not activated until January 1945, when it comprised two *Staffeln* of Ju 87Gs – 10.(Pz)/SG 1 and 10.(Pz)/SG 3 – plus the erstwhile 12.(Pz)/SG 9 (since converted to rocket-firing Fw 190s).

The dissolution of the Stuka arm meant that all dive-bomber training establishments had likewise to be incorporated into the new ground-attack organization. This led to the creation of three new school *Geschwader*, SGs 101, 102 and 103 (a fourth would be added in December 1944), plus two advanced training units, SGs 151 and 152.

Several of these *Geschwader* subsequently set up so-called *Einsatz* (operational) formations of either *Staffel* or *Gruppe* strength. Crewed by instructors and selected pupils, they would see action on all fronts until the OKL ordered their disbandment on 13 February 1945.

The last of the units to be part of the major re-structuring of 18 October 1943 were the Eastern Front's night harassment squadrons. On the northern sector Luftflotte 1's four *Staffeln* were paired off into nocturnal *Nachtschlachtgruppen* (NSGrs) 1 and 3. The three central sector squadrons of Luftflotte 6 became NSGr 2, while in the south, Luftflotte 4 divided its six *Staffeln* into NSGrs 4, 5 and 6.

Two other *Gruppen* were activated at about the same time. NSGr 7 was formed from *Störkampfstaffel Südost* (South-east) and elements of the NASta *Kroatien* (Short-range Recce Squadron Croatia), primarily for day reconnaissance and nocturnal anti-partisan operations in the northern Balkans. NSGr 11 was manned by Estonian volunteers, who had previously been engaged on maritime patrol duties along their nation's Baltic coastline, for night ground-attack duties in the same region.

A further six *Nachtschlachtgruppen*, plus two autonomous *Staffeln*, would be set up during the closing months of the war. However, the final unit of all to be involved in the complex round of redesignations of October 1943 was blind-flying school BFS 11,

ABOVE: Hs 129B-2 'White M' of 10.(Pz)/SG 9, Byala-Zerkov, Southern Sector, February 1944. IV.(Pz)/SG 9 could lay better claim than most to being the eastern front's premier 'fire brigade' unit, for its five component *Staffeln* usually operated independently over wide areas of the southern and central sectors, their tank-busting Hs 129s being in constant demand as Red Army pressure intensified and armoured breakthroughs became ever more frequent. (John Weal © Osprey Publishing)

BELOW: Go 145A 'U9+HC' of 2./NSGr 3, Vecumi, Latvia, March 1944. Typical of the motley collection of elderly biplanes and light aircraft with which the Luftwaffe attempted to halt the enemy's advance through the Baltic States, NSGr 3's nocturnal 'Heinrich-Cäsar' sports a predominantly matt-black finish with toned-down national markings. Few details have survived of the unit's precise activities, as Luftflotte 1's official war diary simply summarized each night's events in only the most general of terms. (John Weal © Osprey Publishing)

ABOVE: Fw 190D-9 'Black 6' of II./SG 10, Kapfenberg, Austria, spring 1945. At least two *Schlachtgeschwader*, SGs 2 and 77, are known to have been operating the 'long-nose' Fw 190D-9 at the end of the war. 'Black 6' belonged to the latter's II. Gruppe which, from some half-dozen airfields in Austria, flew missions to the east and west against both Russian and American forces. Note that this aircraft still wears the yellow nose band from its recent service in Hungary (based at Tapolca and Lesvar). (John Weal © Osprey Publishing)

based at Stubendorf, in Upper Silesia, which as SG 111 became responsible for the training of all *Nachtschlacht* aircrew.

The changes set out above no doubt simplified the *Schlacht* arm. However, on the ground – where it really mattered – they initially had little noticeable effect. It was intended that every dive-bomber unit should ultimately convert to the Fw 190, but the

LEFT: Ju 87s are loaded up with 250kg bombs, which were hung beneath the centreline of the fuselage. While its bomb armament served it well in the ground-attack mode, it was the fitting of the 37mm cannon in the Ju 87G version that transformed the Stuka into an armour killer.

OVERLEAF: For many months, Hitler advocated that the Me 262 jet fighter was developed purely as a fast ground-attack fighter. This was actually a waste of the fighter's capabilities, and it eventually found its true purpose late in the war.

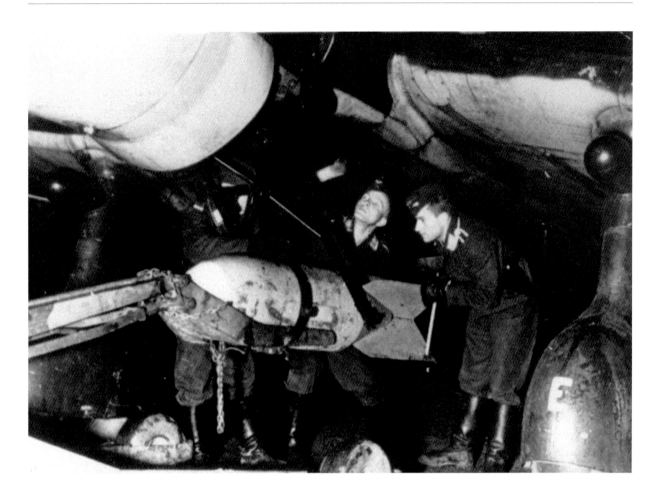

A ground crew bomb-up a Stuka for a night-time raid on England. The Stuka proved itself highly dangerous against Allied shipping and ground installations, but too vulnerable to British fighters to persist in unescorted daylight attacks.

first two *Gruppen* to re-equip, II. and III./SG 1, did not do so until the late spring/early summer of 1944. The majority of the ex-*Stukagruppen*, in fact, continued to operate their Ju 87s very much as before.

For the next eight months, therefore, it was still 'business as usual' for the quartet of original, pre-October 1943, *Schlachtgruppen* as they soldiered on under their new guises, under the collapse of the German defence on all fronts. However, after many long years in the wilderness, the *Schlacht* arm had finally been recognized and reorganized as a separate entity with a vital contribution to make to the Luftwaffe's fighting capabilities. It had replaced the once-vaunted Stukas as the primary tactical strike force, ex-Ju 87 units now returning to the front equipped with the more potent Fw 190. For the first time in its history the ground-attack arm was, at long last, in a position to mount large-scale operations.

Yet within just days of the first of the new Fw 190 *Gruppen*'s appearing on the frontline order of battle in late May 1944, and before they even had a chance to make their presence felt, the skies literally fell in for the Germans. The two Allies, eastern and western, each launched an offensive of unprecedented magnitude. In the north and south, too, the pressure was increasing, and Axis satellites were on the verge of toppling.

The largest and most powerful ground-attack force ever assembled by the Luftwaffe was immediately thrust on to the defensive, embarking upon a ten-month-long retreat that would only end in the ruins of a shattered and divided Reich. With time scarcely to draw breath in between, the end of the beginning had suddenly been transformed into the beginning of the end!

The price that the *Schlacht* arm inflicted on the Allies during the last months of the war was punishing, but there was no stemming the sense of crisis and the unsustainable rates of losses amongst all units. So deep was the crisis on the Eastern Front by this time that even the Heinkel He 177 – the Luftwaffe's only four-engined strategic heavy bomber – was also pressed into service in the anti-tank role! The specialized anti-tank units did what they could. On 25 September the Ju 87s of 10.(Pz)/SG 3 claimed their 300th enemy tank (*Staffelkapitän* Hauptmann Andreas Kuffner would take his personal score to 50 a month later). On the Vistula front a *Schwarm* of Hs 129s of 10.(Pz)/SG 9 brought a local Red Army thrust to a halt by knocking out 25 tanks. Eleven of them had been destroyed by *Schwarmführer* Feldwebel Otto Ritz alone, taking his personal tally of enemy tanks to 60 and earning him the Knight's Cross on 30 September.

However, such individual successes, however laudable, were by now almost meaningless when measured against the Soviets' overwhelming numerical superiority – still the casualty rates continued to rise, not least on the Western Front, where the US and British air forces exercised an enormous superiority in numbers. The *Schlacht* pilots fought until the last moments that Soviet forces poured into Berlin. Yet as one of their great pilots, Oberst Hans-Ulrich Rudel, stated, 'We were no more than a boulder, a small obstruction, but unable to stem the tide.'

SEA EAGLES — MARITIME OPERATIONS

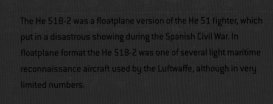

The He 51B-2 was a floatplane version of the He 51 fighter, which put in a disastrous showing during the Spanish Civil War. In floatplane format the He 51B-2 was one of several light maritime reconnaissance aircraft used by the Luftwaffe, although in very limited numbers.

As we have already noted throughout this book, the Luftwaffe was primarily tactical in its outlook. It was also largely focused on warfare over land rather than water, a natural perspective given Germany's landlocked location on the European continent. The result was that maritime air power was never convincingly embraced, despite its increasing importance as the war went on.

Until April 1939, the Luftwaffe's maritime arm consisted of the Seeluftstreitkräfte (Naval Air Arm), divided into 14 *Küstenfliegerstaffeln* (coastal aviation squadrons) and one *Bordfliegergruppe* (ship-based aviation group). Reorganization that spring, however, resulted in the formation of two *Fliegerdivisionen* – Flieger Division Luft West and Flieger Division Luft Ost, acting as aerial support to the Kriegsmarine's Marineoberkommando West and Ost respectively. One important point about this structure was that although naval in purpose it still rested under the authority of the Luftwaffe. Hermann Göring, being the possessive character that he was, never relinquished his grip over maritime aviation, depriving the German Navy itself of strategic control of this important asset.

This tension at the heart of maritime aviation would have important repercussions in later years. After the fall of France in June 1940, the Third Reich was faced with only two strategic military options to deal with its remaining enemy, Great Britain. It could mount a direct assault on the home islands or it could adopt a blockade strategy and attempt to cut off the British economy from its overseas sources of raw materials. Adolf Hitler was never confident about mounting an invasion of Great Britain, and even before the Luftwaffe made its bid to force the British to the negotiating table during the Battle of Britain he authorized the Luftwaffe and Kriegsmarine to mount intensive attacks on British trade to bring their war economy to a standstill. While the Kriegsmarine had prepared for an attack on British trade routes with its U-boat arm, the Luftwaffe had not seriously considered long-range attacks on enemy shipping prior to 1940. Ju 87s and various medium bombers were repurposed for anti-shipping duties, with some considerable effect in the *Kanalkampf*, but for longer-range operations a very different type of aircraft was required. In a remarkable display of ingenuity, and within a very short time, the Luftwaffe was able to adapt existing long-range Focke-Wulf Fw 200 Condor civil airliners to the anti-shipping mission and scored some impressive successes against Allied convoys that had little protection from air attack. Although not built for war, the Condor established such a combat reputation that Winston Churchill soon referred to it as 'the scourge of the Atlantic'.

In this chapter, we will look in depth at the role of the Condor in the battle of the Atlantic. As we shall see, this aircraft provides a useful starting point for understanding the Luftwaffe's limitations and opportunities when it came to maritime warfare. From the Condor, however, we will broaden our analysis to consider the many other aircraft co-opted into anti-shipping warfare, and the ultimately losing battle they fought over the world's seas and oceans.

The Blohm und Voss Bv 138 was a long-range maritime reconnaissance flying-boat. It had a maximum range of 4,300km, and had a distinctive three-engine stack above the wing. It could also be fitted with 500kg thrust-assisted take-off rockets.

THE CONDOR AND THE BATTLE FOR THE THE ATLANTIC

Once Hitler came to power in 1933, his regime was greatly interested in expanding the development of Germany's aviation industry and in conducting propaganda coups that would enhance the international prestige of the Third Reich. Whenever possible, these two policy goals were to be combined. The German national airline, Deutsche Lufthansa, offered excellent potential to develop such new dual-use technologies, both for future military applications and for shining a global spotlight on German technical prowess. The RLM, run by the former head of Lufthansa, Erhard Milch, was established to ensure close coordination between military and civil aviation.

Lufthansa was eager to carve out a dominant niche in the newly emerging commercial aviation market and in 1932 it had chosen the reliable Junkers-built Ju 52/3mce tri-motor as its standard passenger liner. By 1936, three-quarters of Lufthansa's 60-strong aircraft fleet were of this one type. Unfortunately, the Ju 52 could only compete economically on the medium-range routes to Spain, Italy and Scandinavia, and its lack of a pressurized cabin was hardly state-of-the-art in passenger comfort. When the American-built DC-2 appeared in 1934, followed by the even better DC-3 in 1935, Lufthansa's leadership knew that they needed a superior aircraft to the Ju 52 if they were going to compete for new long-haul routes to the Americas, Africa and the Far East. Developing a reliable means of transatlantic passenger service, which Lufthansa had been considering even before Hitler came to power, seemed a very attractive goal for German civil aviation. Initially, Lufthansa went with the 'lighter-than-air' approach, constructing the airships *Graf Zeppelin* and *Hindenburg*. These airships were used to validate long-range navigation techniques, but their inherent fragility and huge cost marked them more as test beds rather than the final solution.

Once the DC-3 appeared, Lufthansa wanted a new civil airliner with inter-continental range that would allow it to dominate the new routes. The RLM also favoured the development of long-range civilian airliners to compete with the new generation of American-built passenger planes, especially as Milch did not want the German aviation industry to fall behind foreign technological advances.

With the RLM's blessing, Lufthansa began to approach the major German aircraft designers, but the two logical choices, Junkers and Dornier, proved less than helpful. Both companies were focused on developing bombers and winning large contracts from the Luftwaffe, rather than diverting scarce resources towards a small-scale civilian project. Although Junkers did agree to rebuild the prototype of its cancelled Ju 89 heavy bomber into a transport version known as the Ju 90, it would not initially commit itself to full-scale development. As a fallback Dr Rolf Stüssel, Lufthansa's technical chief, approached Focke-Wulf Flugzeugbau GmbH in Bremen about the possibility of developing a long-range multi-engined passenger airliner. Compared to Junkers and Dornier, Focke-Wulf had negligible experience in building such large, all-metal aircraft.

Focke-Wulf had enjoyed a close relationship with Lufthansa since the late 1920s, providing it with the Fw A17, Fw A32, Fw A33 and Fw A38 single-engined passenger planes. Although Focke-Wulf lacked experience designing large, multi-engined aircraft, it made up for this deficiency with a high level of motivation and a 'can-do' attitude. In early July 1936, Stüssel and Lufthansa's director, Carl-August Freiherr von Gablenz, met with Kurt Tank to discuss Focke-Wulf's technical proposal for the new aircraft. Tank was an aeronautical engineer and test pilot who had been with Focke-Wulf for five years. As head of its technical department, he had recently designed the Fw 44 civilian biplane. Tank delivered an impressive presentation, convincing Stüssel and Gablenz that not only could Focke-Wulf design and build the new aircraft, but that a flying prototype could be ready within just one year. On 1 August 1936, Lufthansa signed an agreement with Focke-Wulf to develop an aircraft that could carry 25 passengers to a range of 1,500km, which the RLM designated as the Fw 200.

Tank was eager to make a name for himself as an aeronautical designer and he took to the new project with relish. The Focke-Wulf design team, led by Dr Wilhelm Bansemir, quickly sketched a layout for the all-metal aircraft and Tank began to procure off-the-shelf components such as American-built Pratt & Whitney S1E-G Hornet radial engines, although the production aircraft would actually use BMW 132 engines.

The Condor began its life as a civilian airliner, flying long-distance routes in competition with a new generation of American airliners. This Lufthansa Condor was used on the South Atlantic route.

D-ASBK

Amazingly, Tank accomplished this feat on schedule, with the V1 prototype being designed and assembled within 12 months. Even before Tank took the V1 on its inaugural flight on 6 September 1937, Lufthansa's leadership was so impressed that they pledged to order two more prototypes as well as three production aircraft. The airline kept its options open, however, and also showed interest in the larger Ju 90 passenger plane that made its first flight soon after the V1.

Although Tank was keen to show off the prototype, which was named 'Condor', it took another year of further refinements before it was ready for long-distance flights. By the summer of 1938, Focke-Wulf and the RLM agreed to use the V1 prototype on a propaganda tour that would highlight the range and speed of the new aircraft. In June 1938, Kurt Tank flew the prototype from Berlin to Cairo with 21 passengers on board. On 10 August 1938, a selected crew flew the prototype non-stop from Berlin to New York, a distance of 6,371km in just under 25 hours. Few of the reporters who witnessed this historic event noticed that the Condor's faulty brake system caused damage to its landing gear. Having set the transatlantic record, the prototype was sent on a round-the-world flight via Basra, Karachi, Hanoi and Tokyo, in November 1938. Emperor Hirohito of Japan personally met the crew and the Japanese were very impressed by the V1. However, when continuing on to Manila, the crew made a mistake with the fuel pumping

An Fw 200 Condor revs up its engines, while the groundcrew look on. In order to achieve the Condor's remarkable 2,400km combat radius, Kurt Tank had six 300-litre fuel tanks installed in the former passenger compartment.

system that caused the aircraft to ditch offshore. Despite the loss of the prototype and indications that this finicky aircraft was quite fragile, Tank had impressed the world with his Condor.

Converting this technological marvel into a profitable airliner proved to be more difficult than Lufthansa had realized. Since an Fw 200 cost almost three times as much as a Ju 52, the airline decided to order only three of them in 1938 and four more in 1939. The Condors were used on trial flights to Brazil and West Africa in 1939, further demonstrating the long-range capabilities of the aircraft, but these flights served more as a propaganda stunt than as a demonstration of the viability of a commercial passenger service. In order to keep the production line open and hopefully recoup its development costs, Focke-Wulf sought to export the Condor and sold two planes each to Denmark, Finland and Brazil. Two more were sold to the Luftwaffe to provide VIP transport for Hitler and other high-ranking Nazis, and in early 1939, the Japanese airline Dai Nippon Kabushiki Kaisha ordered a further five. The Imperial Japanese Navy was also interested in using the Condor as a maritime patrol bomber and asked Focke-Wulf to develop a military version. In March 1939, Focke-Wulf introduced the Fw 200 B as the standard production version and Tank selected the Fw 200 V10 (named 'Hessen') – which was the prototype for the new B-series model – as the basis for a militarized version of the Condor to meet the Japanese requirement. The V10 was equipped with cameras and five light machine guns but had no provision for carrying bombs. However, before the V10 was even ready, World War II broke out in September 1939. Lufthansa was forced to suspend most of its long-distance international flights, but kept a few civilian Condors serving the routes to Rome, Madrid and Stockholm. Six of the existing Condors were handed over to the Luftwaffe's 4. Staffel of KG z.b.V. 105 for use as transports.

Although British Intelligence was convinced that the Luftwaffe was using Lufthansa as a test bed to covertly develop long-range bombers, the Luftwaffe leadership had no interest in the Fw 200 as a military aircraft prior to World War II. The Luftwaffe had begun developing the Do 19 and Ju 89 four-engined heavy bombers in 1936, but as they proved to be too expensive, both these projects were cancelled after just a few prototypes had been built. Subsequently the Luftwaffe leadership saw the Ju 86B passenger airliner as having potential use as a bomber and encouraged Lufthansa to order five of them. The Fw 200, however, was considered to be more a propaganda device than a potential weapon. Not expecting an imminent outbreak of war, the RLM had placed an order with Heinkel in early 1938 for the He 177, believing this would provide a long-range bomber for the Luftwaffe. The He 177 could carry 1,000kg of bombs over a distance of 6,695km, which far exceeded the capabilities of militarized versions of civilian airliners. Yet the aircraft would not make its first flight until November 1939 and would not be ready for operational use until 1941–42 at best.

German propaganda photo of a Condor crew receiving a pre-mission brief in 1941. During the winter of 1940–41, KG 40's exploits against British shipping helped to restore some of the Luftwaffe's lustre after its failure to defeat the RAF in the Battle of Britain.

Just before war broke out, the Luftwaffe realized that it needed some kind of offensive anti-shipping capability in case of hostilities with Great Britain, and Generalleutnant Hans Geisler, a former officer in the Imperial Navy, was ordered to begin forming the cadre of a new special-purpose unit. Once war began, Geisler's embryonic unit was organized as the X. Fliegerkorps and it was tasked with attacking British warships and merchant ships in the North Sea.

At first, Geisler had three bomber groups with medium-range He 111s and Ju 88s, but he had no long-range aircraft. Since the He 177 bomber would not be ready for some time, Geisler ordered one of his staff officers, Hauptmann Edgar Petersen, to examine existing civilian airliners and determine if any would be suitable for use as auxiliary maritime patrol aircraft. Petersen initially looked at the Ju 90 passenger airliner, but only two had been completed before Junkers suspended the programme. On 5 September 1939, Petersen went to the Focke-Wulf plant and met with Kurt Tank. Once again energetic in promoting his design, Tank convinced Petersen that the six nearly completed

Fw 200 C3/U4 Condor

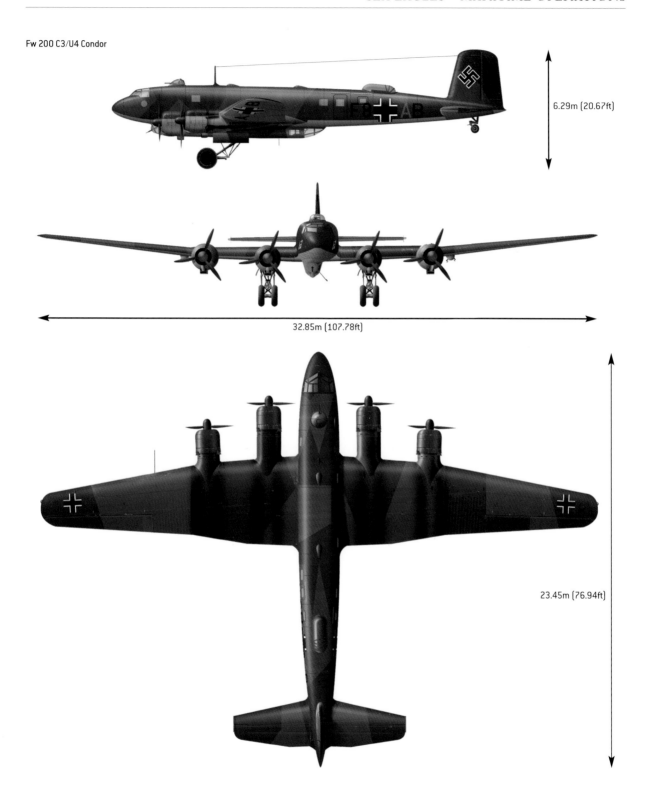

6.29m (20.67ft)

32.85m (107.78ft)

23.45m (76.94ft)

An Arado Ar 196 is prepared for launch from the rails of a Kriegsmarine warship. In naval service, the Ar 196 provided an over-the-horizon reconnaissance capability, gaining visual access of enemy ships well before closing to gun range.

Fw 200 Bs intended for Japan could be converted into armed maritime patrol aircraft in just eight weeks and that more could be built in a matter of months.

Petersen wrote a memorandum after his visit to Focke-Wulf, recommending that X. Fliegerkorps use armed Condors for both maritime reconnaissance and attacks on lone vessels. Generalmajor Hans Jeschonnek, Chief of the Luftwaffe's Generalstab, was reluctant to waste scarce resources on fielding an experimental unit with jury-rigged bombers, but General der Flieger Albert Kesselring, commander of Luftflotte 1, thought the concept was interesting and passed it on to Hitler. Petersen then found himself invited to Obersalzberg, where Hitler heard his briefing on the Fw 200 and gave approval to set up the new unit. With the Führer's blessing, the Luftwaffe High Command sanctioned Petersen's plan on 18 September 1939, and agreed to purchase the six nearly completed Fw 200 Bs intended for Japan, along with the two earmarked for Finland, and convert them into armed Fw 200 C-0 models. Even though the civilian version of the Fw 200 was priced at more than 300,000 Reichsmarks, Kurt Tank was so desperate to land a contract with the Luftwaffe that he sold these first aircraft to the RLM for only about 280,000RM each. Indeed, in 1939 Focke-Wulf only sold these eight Condors and six Fw 189 reconnaissance planes to the Luftwaffe, compared to the hundreds of aircraft sold by Dornier, Junkers and Heinkel. Jeschonnek also remained ambivalent about how the Fw 200 C should be used and Petersen was initially authorized to form them into a *Fernaufklärungsstaffel* (long-range reconnaissance squadron), not an anti-shipping unit.

Although some sources identify the V10 prototype as the genesis of the armed Condor, it was only equipped with defensive armament. In order to meet the X. Fliegerkorps' requirement for a reconnaissance bomber, Tank had to provide the Condor with the ability to both carry and accurately deliver bombs. This was no easy task since, in contrast to purpose-built bombers, the Condor did not have either a bomb bay or a glazed nose for the bombardier. Starting with a standard Fw 200 B, which was redesignated V11, Tank added a ventral gondola beneath the fuselage, which could carry a simple bombsight and two light machine guns. Rather than try to fit bombs internally, Tank installed hardpoints under the wings and outboard engine nacelles to carry a total of four 250kg bombs. He also added a small dorsal turret (A-stand) behind the cockpit and another dorsal MG15 position (B-stand) further aft. By removing all the seats from the passenger area and replacing them with internal fuel tanks, he increased fuel capacity by 60 per cent, which resulted in a combat radius of about 1,500km. Overall weight of the aircraft was increased by about 2 tonnes, but Tank was in such a hurry to deliver the Fw 200 C-0 to the Luftwaffe that he failed to strengthen the structure or examine the impact of carrying bombs and a heavy fuel load. The Fw 200 C-0 was also significantly slower than the civilian passenger version. Once completed in December 1939, the V11 was standardized as the Fw 200 C-1, which the Luftwaffe initially designated as the '*Kurier*' to differentiate it from Condor civilian models.

On 10 October 1939, Hauptmann Petersen took command of the *Fernaufklärungsstaffel* at Bremen. This *Staffel*, which was redesignated as 1./KG 40 in November, trained on unarmed Condor transports until the first Fw 200 C models began to arrive in February 1940. The RLM waited until 4 March 1940, to sign a series production contract with Focke-Wulf, which specified the construction of 38 Fw 200 C-1 and C-2 models for a fixed price of 273,500RM each, minus weapons. At that point, Focke-Wulf began serial production of the Fw 200 at the rate of four aircraft per month, a situation which remained in effect until 1942.

By the start of the invasion of Norway in April 1940, Petersen had a handful of operational Fw 200 C-0 and C-1s, which he used to conduct long-range reconnaissance missions around Narvik and to harass British shipping. Although Petersen's unit was able to sink only one British merchant ship during the Norwegian campaign, some of the limitations of the Fw 200 were now realized and valuable experience was gained. Most of the pre-production Fw 200 C-0s that Tank had built so quickly suffered from cracks in their fuselage and wings, caused by the problems of overloading and a landing gear that could not handle rough airstrips. Furthermore, the defensive armament was quite weak and the lack of armour plate and self-sealing fuel tanks made the Fw 200 extremely vulnerable to even light damage. On 25 May 1940, a British Gloster Gladiator pilot intercepted one of KG 40's Fw 200 C-1s over Norway and was amazed to see the aircraft crash after a brief burst of .303in. machine-gun fire. Petersen remained convinced as to the potential of the Fw 200, but recommended that Focke-Wulf quickly develop more robust and better-armed Condors in order to carry the fight to the British at sea. Kurt Tank spent the next three years trying to upgrade the Condor, increasing its range, armament and protection, but was never able to escape the fact that the basic design was poorly suited for a demanding combat environment.

STRATEGIC SITUATION

The maritime strategic situation turned drastically against Great Britain with the German occupation of Norway by 8 June 1940, and the capitulation of France on 22 June. British pre-war planning by the Admiralty for trade protection had not expected the Luftwaffe to pose a significant threat in the Atlantic. Instead, the sudden German victories in Norway and France gave the predatory Luftwaffe and Kriegsmarine unprecedented access to Britain's transatlantic trade routes. Operating from French bases, even medium-range German aircraft could now attack British shipping in the South-west Approaches, the Irish Sea and on the convoy routes to Gibraltar. Just as enemy attack against convoys stepped up in August 1940, the Royal Navy was forced to keep a significant portion of its strength – including destroyers – in home waters to deter a possible German invasion.

Hitler's main strategic objective after the fall of France was to force Britain to the negotiating table in order to gain an armistice, so that Germany could then throw its full weight against the Soviet Union. Never sanguine about conducting an amphibious invasion across the English Channel (despite the overt preparations for Unternehmen *Seelöwe*), Hitler preferred to exert pressure on Britain's sea lines of communications to bring about the country's submission. He was receptive both to Grossadmiral Erich Raeder's recommendations to step up the war against Britain's merchant convoys with his U-boats and surface raiders, and to Reichsmarschall Hermann Göring's claims that his Luftwaffe could smash the RAF and then close Britain's ports by bombing and mining them. This strategy appeared to offer the Third Reich a low-cost way to drive Britain out

A German bomber defiantly displays its grim tally of Allied shipping, destroyed around the coasts of Norway and Britain. Strengthened Allied fighter escorts made coastal shipping a much harder target from 1941 onwards.

of the war, without risking a potential bloodbath in the English Channel. Accordingly, Hitler declared a total blockade of the British Isles on August 17, 1940, and authorized the Kriegsmarine and Luftwaffe to sever Britain's economic lifelines. Consequently, the role of the Fw 200 Condor anti-shipping operations should be considered in the context of the German strategic dynamic in 1940–41, which consisted of five concurrent but uncoordinated campaigns: air raids on ports, mining of coastal ports, and air, U-boat and surface warship attacks on convoys. If these campaigns had been properly coordinated, Germany had the means to strangle the British war economy. Yet the OKW failed to efficiently synchronize these five campaigns against British shipping and allowed the Luftwaffe and Kriegsmarine to conduct independent operations.

Generalfeldmarschall Hugo Sperrle's Luftflotte 3 began attacks against British convoys in the Irish Sea with He 111 and Ju 88 bombers, but these aircraft only had an effective anti-shipping radius of operations of about 805km. Given this range restriction, the medium bombers had little time to search for maritime targets at sea and had to operate within range of British land-based fighters. The Fw 200 C, with an effective range that was triple that of other bombers, was the only aircraft that could conduct maritime air reconnaissance and anti-shipping operations beyond the range of British land-based fighters. Among the new tenants moving into French air bases soon after the 1940 armistice was a detachment of KG 40. It first operated from Brest in July, but then on 2 August 1940 began deploying to Bordeaux-Merignac, the same airbase from which Charles de Gaulle

A British merchant vessel is attacked by a German bomber in 1940. Luftwaffe anti-shipping attacks accounted for the loss of dozens of vessels around the British coastline, and for a time the Royal Navy cancelled all naval traffic through the Channel straits.

had fled on 17 June. By mid-August, Major Petersen had nine Fw 200s on hand, but operational readiness for the early C-1 model Condors rarely exceeded 30 per cent. The first batch of Fw 200 C-1s had been rushed into service and after just moderate use in the Norwegian campaign, many were sidelined by cracks in their fuselage and faulty brakes. Although the RLM placed orders for more and improved Fw 200s after the fall of France, Focke-Wulf was only able to deliver another 20 aircraft to I./KG 40 in the last six months of 1940. Amazingly, Focke-Wulf continued deliveries of civilian Fw 200 models to Lufthansa.

The Arado Ar 196 twin-float seaplane was a popular aircraft amongst its crews, being easy to fly and with good all-round visibility for the pilot and observer. It began the war in shipboard service, but then entered service with Luftwaffe coastal units in 1940.

Initially, the Luftwaffe did not know how to use the Fw 200 to best advantage. In July 1940, I./KG 40 fell under the 9. Flieger Division of Sperrle's Luftflotte 3, which decided to employ the Condors in the aerial minelaying campaign. I./KG 40 conducted 12 night minelaying missions in British and Irish waters between July 15 and 27, which resulted in the loss of two Condors. Petersen complained about this costly misuse of his aircraft and at the end of July, I./KG 40 was switched back to maritime reconnaissance. Nevertheless, Petersen continued to argue for using the Fw 200s in an anti-shipping role and after Hitler's blockade order, Sperrle decided to unleash Petersen's Condors against the relatively unprotected British shipping west of Ireland. Even though Petersen

FW 200 CONDOR C-3 COCKPIT

1. Undercarriage de-icing cock
2. Suction-air throw-over switch (starboard)
3. Suction-air throw-over switch (port)
4. Instrument panel lighting switch (port)
5. Pilot's oxygen pressure gauge
6. NACA cowling floodlight switch
7. Pilot's control column
8. Intercom switch
9. Clock
10. Illumination buttons
11. Pilot's repeater compass
12. Airspeed indicator
13. Gyro-compass course indicator
14. Turn-and-bank indicator
15. Course-fine altimeter
16. External temperature gauge
17. Rate-of-climb indicator
18. Artificial horizon
19. Coarse altimeter
20. Fuselage flap control lamp
21. Fuselage flap release handle
22. Radio beacon visual indicator
23. Gyro-compass
24. Gyro-compass heating indicator
25. Gyro-compass heating switch
26. Pilot's rudder pedal
27. Pilot's rudder pedal
28. Pilot's seat pan (seat-back removed for clarity)
29. Compass installation
30. RPM indicator (port outer)
31. RPM indicator (port inner)
32. RPM indicator (starboard inner)
33. RPM indicator (starboard outer)
34. Double manifold pressure gauges (port engines)
35. Oil and fuel pressure gauges (port engines)
36. Oil and fuel pressure gauges (starboard engines)
37. Double manifold pressure gauges (starboard engines)
38. Pitch indicator (port outer)
39. Emergency bomb release
40. Pitch indicator (port inner)
41. Bomb-arming lever
42. Pitch indicator (starboard inner)
43. Pitch indicator (starboard outer)
44. Oil temperature gauge (port outer)
45. Oil temperature gauge (port inner)
46. Oil temperature gauge (starboard inner)
47. Oil temperature gauge (starboard outer)
48. Instrument panel dimmer switch
49. Undercarriage and landing flap indicators
50. Starter selector switch
51. Master battery cut-off switch
52. Ignition switches (port)
53. Ignition switches (starboard)
54. Landing light switch
55. Servo unit emergency button
56. UV-lighting switch
57. Longitudinal trim emergency switch
58. Directional trim emergency switch
59. Longitudinal trim indicator
60. Throttles
61. Supercharger levers
62. Fuel tank selectors
63. Throttle locks
64. Directional trim indicator
65. Directional trim switch
66. Undercarriage retraction lever
67. Airscrew pitch control levers (port)
68. Airscrew pitch control levers (starboard)
69. Wing flap lever
70. Parking switch activating handle
71. Fuel safety cock levers (port tanks)
72. Servo unit emergency pull-out knob
73. Fire extinguisher pressure gauge
74. Fuel safety cock levers (starboard tanks)
75. Fire extinguishers (port engines)
76. Fire extinguishers (starboard engines)
77. RPM Synchronization selector switch
78. Remote compass course indicator
79. Pitot head heating indicator
80. Airspeed indicator
81. Turn-and-bank indicator

rarely had more than four operational aircraft in 1940, his group began to steadily sink and damage enemy freighters around Ireland, and it was soon clear that the Condor had found its niche in the war.

When the Condor attacks began, Great Britain had four main convoy routes that were vulnerable to long-range air strikes: the HX and SC convoys on the Halifax-to-Liverpool run; the OA and OB convoys on the route between the southern British ports and Halifax; the HG and OG convoys running between Gibraltar and

82. Rate-of-climb indicator
83. Control surface temperature gauge
84. Course-fine altimeter
85. Artificial horizon
86. Cylinder temperature gauge
87. Cylinder temperature throw-over switch
88. Starting fuel contents gauge
89. Cruise fuel contents gauge
90. Cruise fuel transfer switch
91. Clock
92. Starting fuel transfer switch
93. Oil contents gauge
94. Starter switches
95. Suction and pressure gauges for undercarriage de-icing and gyro devices
96. Injection valve press buttons
97. Hydraulic systems pressure gauge
98. Windscreen heating
99. Control surfaces temperature switch
100. Fuel pump switches (port tanks)
101. Fuel pump switches (starboard tanks)
102. Controllable-gill adjustment
103. Airscrew de-icing levers (starboard engines)
104. Co-pilot's seat pan (seat-back removed for clarity)
105. Co-pilot's rudder pedal
106. Co-pilot's rudder pedal
107. Co-pilot's control column

Liverpool; and the SL convoys from Sierra Leone to Liverpool. A snapshot of shipping on August 17, 1940, for example, would have shown 13 convoys at sea on these routes, made up of 531 merchant vessels and 22 escort warships. Most convoys received a strong escort three days out from Liverpool, but they crossed the Atlantic with minimal protection. The greatest danger of Condor attack therefore occurred when poorly escorted convoys were still about 965km out from Liverpool or Gibraltar and were beyond the range of effective land-based air cover.

Despite the Condor's early successes against weakly defended British shipping, the Luftwaffe failed miserably to use KG 40 to best advantage in supporting U-boat attacks on convoys. With a limited number of operational aircraft available, KG 40 could only shadow a convoy for three to four hours and lacked sufficient aircraft to maintain contact for an extended period. In essence, KG 40 was only capable of sporadic maritime reconnaissance, not the consistent surveillance that the U-boats needed. Both Raeder and his U-boat chief, Vizeadmiral Karl Dönitz, were incensed that their small number of U-boats at sea had to waste valuable time searching for British convoys while the Luftwaffe failed to provide adequate maritime reconnaissance. Prior to the war, Raeder had lost the argument with Göring about creating an independent naval air arm to support the fleet and now the Luftwaffe High Command was unwilling to commit major resources to support maritime operations.

In November 1940, Britain's only real offensive tool was RAF Bomber Command, and Churchill redirected it squarely at the Fw 200 threat by ordering raids against Bordeaux-Merignac airfield and the Focke-Wulf plant in Bremen. The first raid on Bordeaux-Merignac took place on the night of 22–23 November 1940, and saw 32 bombers destroy four hangars and two Fw 200s on the ground. Three follow-up raids were unsuccessful and it was not until the raid on April 13, 1941, that three more Condors were destroyed at the base. Bomber Command continued to raid the airfield on occasion, but Luftwaffe AA defences improved to the point that no more Condors were destroyed on the ground. Given that Bomber Command's aircraft had little ability to hit point targets at night and were generally missing their aim points by about 3km or more in 1940–41, the fact that 191 sorties on Bordeaux-Merignac destroyed five Condors on the ground is remarkable. The first major raid against the Focke-Wulf plant did not occur until 1 January 1941 and, although it caused some minor disruption in Condor production, it only encouraged the company to shift much of the Fw 200 production inland to Cottbus.

Despite the inability of the British to intercept Fw 200s over water or destroy their bases and factories, the duel between the Condors and the British Atlantic convoys was ultimately shaped by each side's different approach to inter-service cooperation.

In order to make Hitler's blockade work, the Luftwaffe and the Kriegsmarine had to work together, which included using the Fw 200s to support anti-convoy operations in conjunction with the ongoing U-boat campaign. However, both services constantly squabbled over the best way to use KG 40's Condors. Göring was more concerned about maintaining control over his air units than in helping the U-boats deliver a knockout blow against Britain's convoys. Raeder temporarily gained Kriegsmarine control over KG 40 (while Göring was on Christmas holiday) when he sent Dönitz to brief the OKW on how the Condors could support the U-boat campaign. Dönitz claimed:

'Just let me have a minimum of 20 Fw 200s solely for reconnaissance purposes and the U-boat successes will shoot up!' Hitler obliged Dönitz by ordering I./KG 40 to be subordinated to the Kriegsmarine on 6 January 1941, but as soon as Göring returned from holiday he pressed Hitler to reverse his decision. Two months later, Hitler gave in and returned I./KG 40 to Luftwaffe control, but authorized the creation of the Fliegerführer Atlantik in Lorient to better synchronize Luftwaffe support for maritime operations. Generalmajor Martin Harlinghausen from IX. Fliegerkorps was appointed to this post and he made every effort to increase cooperation between KG 40 and the U-boats. Nevertheless, the Luftwaffe continued to divert KG 40's planes and aircrew away from maritime operations to support special projects.

COMBAT CAPABILITIES

The Condor's combat prowess rested on three primary capabilities: its ability to find targets, to hit targets and then to evade enemy defences. In 1940 the Condor had only a rudimentary capability of finding convoys and other suitable merchant targets. On a typical mission, an Fw 200 would fly about 1,500km from Bordeaux to look for targets west of Ireland, which would give the aircraft about three hours to conduct its search. Normally, Condors flew quite low (about 500–600m off the water), which made it easier to spot ships outlined against the horizon and avoided giving the enemy too much early warning. From this low altitude, the Condor could search an area of approximately 320km x 120km, with several of its crew scanning the horizon with binoculars. In decent weather, which was rare in the Atlantic, the observers might be able to spot a convoy up to 15–20km away, but cloud cover could reduce this by half. In 1941, improved Condors with longer range had four hours on-station time, increasing the search area by about 25 per cent. When the Condors gained a search-radar capability with the FuG 200 Hohentwiel radar in December 1942 and their on-station endurance doubled, their search area increased to nearly four times the size it had been in 1940. The Hohentwiel radar could detect surface targets up to 80km distant and its beam was 41km wide at that range. Nevertheless, the perennial problem remained for the Condors that due to limited numbers, KG 40 had difficulty maintaining a consistent presence along known convoy routes. With one sortie sent every day or so for three to eight hours, there was no guarantee that they would be operational at the very time a convoy was passing through the area. Thus the Condor's actual ability to find targets was rather sporadic until late in the war, which accounts for the fact that KG 40 missed more convoys than it found.

As a converted civilian aircraft, the Fw 200's ability to hit targets was severely limited by the lack of a proper bombsight and poor forward visibility. From the beginning, it was

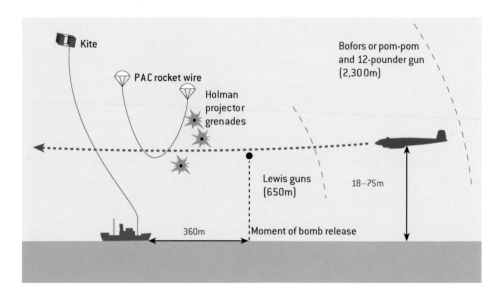

ABOVE: From a German diagram showing the variety of Allied responses to low-level attack, ranging from AA guns to rocket-launched cables. Note that this diagram shows a bows-on attack, when most attacks occurred either from astern or abeam. (© Osprey Publishing)

obvious that the Fw 200 could not attack in the way a normal bomber did, but had to rely on low-level attack (*Tiefangriff*) tactics. Approaching as low as 45m off the water at 290km/h, a Condor would release one or two bombs at a distance of about 240m from the target. This method ensured a high probability that the bomb would either strike the ship directly or detonate in the water alongside, causing damage. Although the early Condors only carried a load of four 250kg bombs, the low-level method made it highly likely that at least one ship would be sunk or damaged on each sortie that found a target. Since most civilian freighters were unarmoured and lacked robust damage control, even moderate damage inflicted would often prove fatal.

KG 40 became so adept at low-level tactics in early 1941 that some attacks scored three out of four hits. However, many of the bombs that struck the target failed to explode due to improper fusing – a nagging problem for the low-level method. Once the Condors shifted to attacks from 3,000m with the Lotfe 7D bombsight, which had a circular error probability of 91m with a single bomb against a stationary target, about one bomb in three landed close enough to inflict at least some damage. The Condors were also capable of low-level machine gun strafing. In 1940, a Condor using the low-level attack profile only had time to fire a single 75-round drum of ball ammunition from the MG15 machine gun in the gondola during each eight-second pass on a ship. This type of strafing inflicted little damage. Oberleutnant Bernhard Jope made three

The He 115 was an excellent seaplane, used for minelaying and torpedo-bombing in addition to reconnaissance duties. During the 1930s, the He 115 established eight world speed records for its class of aircraft.

An Fw 200C-3 in flight. The C-3 model received a strengthened fuselage, a heavier bomb and fuel load, armour plating over key areas, an upgraded powerplant and a crew increase to seven members. Total strike radius was 1,750km.

strafing runs on the *Empress of Britain* and wounded only one person on the vessel (his 250kg bombs, however, did far more damage). When improved Condors mounted larger 13mm and 20mm weapons in the gondola, firing AP-T and HEI-T ammunition, their strafing became far deadlier and the superstructures of merchant ships proved highly vulnerable to this type of fire. However, once Allied defences made low-level attacks too costly, the strafing capability of Condors was effectively neutralized.

The Condor's ability to manoeuvre, absorb damage and evade enemy interception was always problematic. The Fw 200 B was built to fly in thin air at medium altitudes, with no sharp manoeuvring. Tank made the aircraft's remarkable long range possible by designing a very lightweight airframe. Early military versions lacked armour plate, self-sealing fuel tanks or structural strengthening and the Condor was at least 2–4 tonnes lighter than other four-engined bombers in this class. Unlike purpose-built bombers that had some armour plate and redundant flight controls, the Condor was always exceedingly vulnerable to damage. When moderately damaged by a hit, chunks of the fuselage or tail often fell off, and the underpowered aircraft had difficulty staying in the air if it lost one of its engines. Even worse, there were six large unarmoured fuel tanks inside the cabin, which could turn the Condor into a blazing torch if hit by tracer ammunition. When Condors tried to manoeuvre sharply to avoid enemy flak or fighters, their weak structure could be damaged, leading to metal fatigue, cracks and loss of the aircraft. Defensive armament was initially weak but had improved greatly by the C-4 variant, causing enemy fighters to avoid lengthy gun duels with Fw 200s. Since the Condors were usually operating close to the water, they did not normally have to worry about fighter attacks from below, but this also severely limited their options. At these low altitudes, they were unable to dive and they could not out-turn or outrun an opponent. This limited them to 'jinking' to upset an opponent's aim, hoping that the A- and B-stand gunners would score a lucky hit on the pursuing fighter. Thus

THE FW 200 CREW

During the course of the war, the size of the Fw 200 crew increased from five members to six, and finally to seven. Each aircraft had a *Flugzeugführer* and co-pilot/bombardier, as well as a *Bordfunker*, a *Bordmechaniker* and a *Bordschütz*. As defensive armament increased, another *Bordschütz* was needed and in 1943, another *Bordfunker* was added to operate the radar. The airmen on Condors required a great deal of training and experience to function as a well-knit team on this complicated multi-engined aircraft. Small mistakes, such as failing to properly monitor fuel flow to the engines in a shallow dive, would lead to aircraft losses. Also, the Fw 200 crews often had to operate alone, almost always over water and at great distances from any friendly assistance. Crews had to learn to be efficient and self-reliant to avoid ending up at the bottom of the Atlantic.

In the beginning, KG 40 benefited from a cadre of Lufthansa aircrew with some experience on the Fw 200, although commercial passenger missions were considerably different from low-level anti-shipping attacks. Even experienced pilots like Edgar Petersen had to learn through experience the difficult art of finding convoys at sea. In August 1940, with only a handful of aircrew having any experience in low-level anti-shipping strikes, KG 40 had to gradually familiarize its personnel with their unique mission, and develop a set of effective tactical procedures as the

best means to attack enemy shipping. Petersen was sparing of his crews and precious aircraft and he wisely refused to commit crews to long-range Atlantic missions until he judged they were ready, which limited the group to a low sortie rate in the autumn of 1940. Under these circumstances, I./KG 40 was not a fully trained or combat-ready group until spring 1941.

Like all Luftwaffe bomber pilots, the men who flew Fw 200s required about two years of flight training before they reached KG 40. After completing their initial flight training in the first year, they progressed to multi-engined aircraft, blind-flying school and advanced navigation. Once they had gone through the standard Luftwaffe pilot schooling, they were transferred to KG 40's conversion unit, IV.(Erg)/KG 40, which was stationed in Germany until January 1942. This unit trained pilots and other aircrew on over-water operations using half-a-dozen of the original unarmed Fw 200s and some He 111s and Do 217s. In 1942, Condor conversion training was shifted to central France. The following year, the conversion group also began to conduct He 177 training, as the Fw 200 began to be replaced.

In 1940, all Condor pilots were officers, usually *Oberleutnante*, with the rest of the crew consisting of *Feldwebel* or *Unteroffiziere*, apart from the gunners, who were *Obergefreite*. By 1942, KG 40 was finding it difficult to keep up with high officer losses so more aircraft were flown by NCOs.

An He 115 seaplane of KG 54 is readied for action. Some of the type's earliest combat operations in World War II involved minelaying sorties off the British coastline, and it was later used heavily in missions against the Arctic convoy, flying from bases in northern Norway.

the Condor essentially had poor evasion capabilities, which ultimately was a major contributor to its operational failure.

ATTACK PROFILE

A typical KG 40 Condor sortie from Bordeaux-Merignac would see the crew rising around midnight, eating breakfast and then heading to a target briefing. Usually sorties were directed towards known convoy routes where either U-boats or the Kriegsmarine's B-Dienst (Intelligence Service) had detected recent traffic, although the information could be 12–24 hours old by the time the crew received it. Unlike a standard bomber mission against a fixed target, the Condor was assigned a search area where either moving convoys or independently steaming ships were expected to pass through. While the

CONVOY HG 53

Convoy HG 53 left Gibraltar on the afternoon of 6 February 1941, bound for Liverpool with 19 merchant ships escorted by the destroyer HMS *Velox* and the sloop HMS *Deptford*. U-37 spotted the convoy and attacked at 0440hrs on 9 February, sinking two ships. The U-boat captain reported the sighting, which was relayed to KG 40 in Bordeaux. Rather than sending one or two Condors as usual, KG 40 launched its first mass attack against a convoy with five Condors, led by Hauptmann Fritz Fliegel. They found the convoy 640km south-west of Lisbon around 1600hrs. One Condor quickly scored hits on the steamer *Britannic,* which sank in minutes. As the Condors began another run, the convoy opened fire with every available gun and HMS *Deptford* was able to damage the wing of Oberleutnant Erich Adam's Condor. Adam managed to complete his bombing run but had to land in Spain due to the loss of fuel. Nevertheless, the four remaining Condors sank four more steamers. Here, Schlosser has just turned away after hitting the *Britannic,* while Adam is beginning his bomb run on the steamer *Jura*. (Howard Gerrard © Osprey Publishing)

navigator plotted the appropriate course, the ground crews finished fuelling and arming the plane. If more than one Fw 200 was involved in the mission, they would coordinate their search zones to cover the maximum amount of area near the suspected convoy. Between 0100 and 0200hrs, the aircraft would take off and head west towards the

The tail of this Fw 200 Condor is adorned with the record of its maritime kills. The figures also include the tonnage of each vessel sunk. Although the Condor became a leading Luftwaffe anti-shipping aircraft, ultimately it was specially adapted medium bombers that shouldered much of the burden of the maritime war.

convoy routes. Usually, the Condor would reach its search zone in about six hours, after a long boring flight over the Atlantic. In 1940–42 there was little or no risk of enemy interception on the outbound leg, but by 1943 aircrews had to be alert for enemy air activity over the Bay of Biscay. During the outbound leg, Condors flew in radio silence, even if operating with several aircraft.

Finding convoys or independent ships proved to be far more difficult than Petersen expected. The combination of stale intelligence and poor long-range navigation skills

over water led to many of the early Condor missions failing in their task. Convoys were usually difficult to spot, particularly in overcast winter weather over the Atlantic, when visibility was often reduced to only a few kilometres. Once a Condor arrived in its target area, as many of the crew as possible would use binoculars to scan the sea for shipping while the pilot flew several search legs through the zone. If multiple aircraft were involved in the mission, they would split up at this point to cover their individual areas. Typical endurance in the search area was initially about three to four hours, but this was extended as improved Fw 200 models arrived in 1941–42.

If a convoy or other significant target was spotted by the observers, the pilot would usually manoeuvre in closer, using clouds for concealment as much as possible, and observe the target for a while. The *Bordfunker* would break radio silence to vector in other Condors if they were nearby, so as to mount a coordinated attack. During this observation phase, which could last up to an hour, the crew would try to identify the escorts, if any, as well as the best targets to attack. Ideally, the Fw 200 sought its victims from stragglers or 'tail-end Charlies', minimizing the risk of defensive fire. Since the early Condors lacked an effective bombsight, strikes were only possible at low level. Martin Harlinghausen had developed the 'Swedish turnip' attack method with X. Fliegerkorps, which entailed approaching the target from abeam at a height of 45–50m and then releasing the bombs about 300–400m short of the target. Ideally, the bombs would glide into the target, striking at the waterline. This method offered a high probability of a hit, but also exposed the attacking aircraft to the vessel's AA guns (if it was equipped with any).

KG 40 used the 'Swedish turnip' extensively in 1940–41 but many pilots preferred the safer approach of attacking from dead astern. From that angle the chances of a hit were reduced, but it was safer for the Condor as the DEMS ships normally carried their AA guns towards the bow. Just in case, most Fw 200s would use their ventral machine guns or 20mm cannon to strafe the decks, in order to suppress any flak gunners.

Normally, a Condor would make several passes on a target, dropping only one or two bombs each time. As it overflew, hopefully not taking too much AA fire, the pilot would pull up sharply and turn around for another pass, or if the first attack was successful, shift to another target. Once all bombs were expended, the Condor would depart, heading back either to Bordeaux, or to Værnes in Norway. From Værnes, it would return to Bordeaux via Bremen, giving Focke-Wulf the chance to repair any damage or mechanical defects. With an individual aircraft usually taking anything from a few days to a week to do the entire return cycle, this system further reduced the operational sortie rate, but helped keep the available Condors in satisfactory shape.

THE HAPPY TIME, AUGUST 1940– JUNE 1941

Flying-boat crews stand to attention for a visit by Grossadmiral Erich Raeder, the commander-in-chief of the German Navy. The Kriegsmarine also operated its own maritime aircraft, although the Luftwaffe retained control of much of the aerial anti-shipping campaign.

Condor operations from Bordeaux-Merignac began sporadically in mid-August 1940 and continued from that location until July 1943. The first operations were tentative and designated as armed reconnaissance sorties rather than as anti-shipping strikes. Three days after Hitler announced his blockade of the British Isles, the Condor's participation in events began inauspiciously when an Fw 200 C-1, sent to check for Allied shipping west of Ireland, developed mechanical difficulties and was forced to conduct a belly-landing near Mount Brandon on the south-west coast. Petersen was able to mount a few sorties with his remaining two operational Condors and they succeeded in sinking the SS *Goathland*, a 3,821-tonne merchant ship sailing alone, on 25 August. Five more

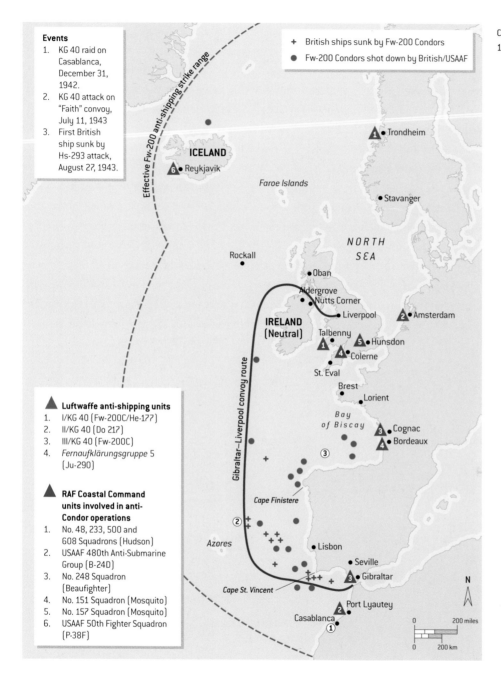

Events

1. KG 40 raid on Casablanca, December 31, 1942.
2. KG 40 attack on "Faith" convoy, July 11, 1943
3. First British ship sunk by Hs-293 attack, August 27, 1943.

+ British ships sunk by Fw-200 Condors
● Fw-200 Condors shot down by British/USAAF

Condor attacks on British shipping, 1943. (© Osprey Publishing)

Luftwaffe anti-shipping units
1. I/KG 40 (Fw-200C/He-177)
2. II/KG 40 (Do 217)
3. III/KG 40 (Fw-200C)
4. *Fernaufklärungsgruppe* 5 (Ju-290)

RAF Coastal Command units involved in anti-Condor operations
1. No. 48, 233, 500 and 608 Squadrons (Hudson)
2. USAAF 480th Anti-Submarine Group (B-24D)
3. No. 248 Squadron (Beaufighter)
4. No. 151 Squadron (Mosquito)
5. No. 157 Squadron (Mosquito)
6. USAAF 50th Fighter Squadron (P-38F)

Effective Fw-200 anti-shipping strike range

ICELAND • Reykjavik

Faroe Islands

• Trondheim

• Stavanger

NORTH SEA

Rockall

• Oban
Aldergrove
• Nutts Corner
• Liverpool

IRELAND (Neutral)

Talbenny • Hunsdon
• Colerne

St. Eval

• Amsterdam

Brest
• Lorient

Bay of Biscay

• Cognac
• Bordeaux

Gibraltar–Liverpool convoy route

Cape Finistere

Azores

• Lisbon

• Seville

• Gibraltar

Cape St. Vincent

• Port Lyautey

Casablanca

N

0   200 miles
0   200 km

ships were damaged west of Ireland by the end of August. The situation did not improve much in September, when KG 40 sank just one Greek freighter and damaged nine other ships. A further small freighter was sunk on 2 October and the 20,000-tonne troop transport *Oronsay* was damaged on 8 October. After eight weeks of limited operations,

KG 40 had sunk only three ships totalling 11,000 tonnes and damaged 21 ships totalling about 90,000 tonnes. Bombing accuracy was poor, with most damage inflicted by near-misses. In reality the Condor appeared to have difficulty inflicting enough damage to actually sink ships and seemed to be more of a nuisance than a lethal threat. Given that U-boats sank more than 500,000 tonnes of shipping in the same period, the British Admiralty was not unduly disturbed at the Fw 200's combat debut.

However, this attitude was forever altered when Oberleutnant Bernhard Jope crippled the 42,348-tonne ocean liner *Empress of Britain* on the morning of 26 October (U-32 finished the liner off on 28 October). The *Empress of Britain* was the largest British vessel sunk to date and her vulnerability to air attack shocked the Admiralty. Jope's attack also convinced the Luftwaffe leadership that the Fw 200 was capable of more than just armed reconnaissance. On 27 October, a lone Fw 200 attacked convoy OB 234 west of Ireland. Despite the presence of nine escort vessels, a Condor succeeded in damaging the 5,013-ton vessel *Alfred Jones*. An RAF Hudson from No. 224 Sqn based at Aldergrove in Northern Ireland arrived on the scene but when it attempted to interfere with the Condor attack, the Fw 200's gunners riddled it with 7.92mm fire. This attack was the first time that a Condor deliberately targeted a convoy.

An Fw 200 Condor at its airbase in France. The fall of France in 1940 meant that the Luftwaffe was able to project its reach deep out into the Atlantic, using the long-range Condor in anti-shipping and reconnaissance capacities.

In November, Petersen began to ramp up KG 40's operational tempo against lucrative targets off the north-west coast of Ireland. By Christmas, KG 40 had sunk 19 ships of 100,000 tonnes and damaged 37 ships of 180,000 tonnes, while British convoy defences had failed to destroy a single Condor. The first round in this duel had clearly gone to the Luftwaffe. KG 40 now had enough trained crews and new aircraft to form two complete operational *Staffeln* of six Condors each. It was also over New Year that the Kriegsmarine temporarily gained tactical control over KG 40.

Rested over the holidays with home leave in Germany, KG 40's crews returned with a vengeance on 8 January 1941, when they attacked the 6,278-tonne cargo ship *Clytoneus* near Rockall and scored a direct hit that split the unfortunate vessel wide open. Again and again over the next weeks, KG 40 exploited the feebleness of the Royal Navy's low-level air defences and RAF Coastal Command's failure to provide effective air cover, enabling it to savage one convoy after another. By the end of January, the surge in Condor attacks had sunk 17 ships of 65,000 tonnes and damaged five others. Yet if January was bad for the British, February 1941 was worse. KG 40 continued to pick off individual merchant ships west of Ireland with single-plane sorties but on 9 February Peterson shifted tactics and area of operations. He sent five Fw 200s, flown by the best pilots in the group, against convoy HG 53, which had been detected by U-boats south-west of Portugal. Aside from a few two-plane sorties, KG 40 had not previously launched multi-plane strikes against a single convoy and this attack caught the British by surprise. The Condors only sank five small ships, but they caused the convoy to scatter so badly that U-37 was able to slip in and sink three more. This was the classic joint attack that Dönitz had envisioned when he lobbied for the Fw 200 and it proved devastating in practice. The Kriegsmarine was quite pleased with the success of KG 40's Condors in February; they had not only managed to sink 21 ships of 84,301 tons, but had also improved the lethal nature of wolfpack tactics by introducing a new combat dynamic – daylight air attacks to scatter the convoy, followed up by massed U-boat night attacks. Despite the promise these tactics held for winning the Battle of the Atlantic, the Condors had in fact already reached their high-water mark.

In March, the Luftwaffe regained control over KG 40 and put it under Martin Harlinghausen as Fliegerführer Atlantik. Yet problems for the Condors were mounting. Losses of aircraft were increasing significantly from more effective British AA fire and the predations of RAF Coastal Command aircraft. Better convoy tactics meant that

OVERLEAF: A British Martlet fighter flying from the auxiliary aircraft carrier, HMS *Audacity*, destroys an Fw 200 C-3/U4 flown by Oberleutnant Karl Krüger on 8 November 1941. Both Krüger and his co-pilot were killed as the windscreen shattered under the fusillade. (Howard Gerrard © Osprey Publishing)

the Condors often struggled to find enemy ships in the first place, and when they did the attacks were frequently ineffective. Thus in July 1941, KG 40 shifted entirely to the maritime reconnaissance role and only authorized anti-shipping attacks against lone vessels. Condors therefore succeeded in locating four convoys for the U-boats in July, but they sank no ships themselves.

The last six months of 1941 confirmed the operational decline of KG 40. Only four ships of 10,298 tonnes had been sunk in anti-shipping operations with two more damaged, whereas 16 Condors had been lost, including seven shot down by convoy defences. Although the Condors had enjoyed some success in guiding U-boats towards convoys, it was clear that the days of easy low-level air attacks were over and that the duel for supremacy over Britain's lifelines had turned against the Germans.

THE WIDER MARITIME WAR

In March 1942, it was decided to send Major Edmund Daser's I./KG 40 to Værnes airfield near Trondheim to provide long-range reconnaissance for Luftflotte 5 against the Arctic convoys. Major Robert Kowalewski's III./KG 40, which was still converting from He 111s to Fw 200s, would remain at Bordeaux and continue to operate against the Gibraltar convoys. Fliegerführer Atlantik was stripped to the bone to provide anti-shipping units for Norway, which effectively brought the aerial blockade of Great Britain to an abrupt end.

The Luftwaffe's operations in the far north illustrate the fact that Fw 200s were far from the only aircraft type employed in maritime missions. In fact, compared with other aircraft involved in such operations, such as the He 111H, Ju 88 and Do 217E, the Fw 200 had a very low operational readiness rate – often as low as 25 per cent. It also suffered from a very high level of non-combat losses, at 52 per cent, compared to 35–38 per cent for all aircraft losses typically suffered by the seven other bomber *Gruppen* supporting Fliegerführer Atlantik. Based upon the results of operations to date, Fliegerführer Atlantik reported on 3 December 1942, that 'because of inadequate armament, the Fw 200 is unfit for use in areas that are within range of land-based fighter planes. Confrontations between the Fw 200 and such fighters in medium cloud cover almost always lead to the destruction of the Fw 200. Further development of the Fw 200 cannot be recommended because its development has reached its limits and the aircraft should be replaced by the He 177.'

Fliegerführer Atlantik, and indeed all the Luftwaffe formations with an anti-shipping or maritime reconnaissance purpose, had numerous specialist aircraft to draw upon. At the smaller end of the scale were a range of single-engined floatplanes, such as the Heinkel He 60 (a biplane removed from service in 1943), Heinkel He 114 and Arado

Ar 196. The latter, for example, was initially a Kriegsmarine aircraft, embarked aboard great battleships such as *Deutschland*, *Admiral Graf Spee*, *Scharnhorst* and *Gneisenau*, plus a variety of heavy and light cruisers. In mid-1940, with French ports now in German hands, the Ar 196 was taken widely into Luftwaffe service, to perform coastal reconnaissance and light maritime attack duties, particularly against Allied submarines operating in the Bay of Biscay. The aircraft did not offer overwhelming performance. Powered by a single 723kW BMW 132K radial engine, the aircraft had a maximum speed of just 310km/h, a range of 1,070km and an armament of two forward-firing 20mm cannon, a forward-firing 7.92mm machine gun, two backwards-facing trainable 7.92mm machine guns in the rear cockpit, and a maximum bomb load of 100kg (one 50kg bomb under each wing). Thus armed, it was capable of giving a merchant vessel or surfaced submarine more than enough cause for concern, although if 'bounced' by enemy monoplane fighters it would find itself at a severe disadvantage.

In addition to light floatplanes, the Luftwaffe also deployed a remarkable range of more substantial two-engined aircraft. The ageing but robust He 59 was put to a myriad of uses. It acted as a minelayer (it could deploy two 500kg magnetic mines), a reconnaissance

Only a single example of the Bv 238 was produced in World War II, and it constituted one of the largest aircraft of the war. It had a crew of 12, a wingspan of over 60m and a length of 43m.

aircraft and an air–sea rescue aircraft – in this latter role it rescued 400 German aircrew from British waters during the Battle of Britain. It was even used as an assault transport aircraft, flying German assault units into Norwegian fjords in April 1940, and landing on the River Maas the following May during actions to seize Dutch bridges. Similar versatility was also offered by the He 115, which like the He 59 was also capable of carrying a single torpedo for anti-shipping duties.

The true workhorses of Germany's anti-shipping campaign, however, were actually variants of its medium bomber fleet, particularly the He 111 and the Ju 88. The He 111, in its initial guise as a land bomber, was not particularly suited to maritime work, as its level-bombing tactic gave poor accuracy against a ship far below taking evasive manoeuvres. Yet its availability, range and serviceability meant that aircraft designers soon looked for ways in which it could be converted to anti-shipping duties. The solution was found in the He 111H torpedo-bomber, which mounted two 765kg LT F5b torpedoes under its wing roots. This type of aircraft began operations against the Allied Arctic

The Bv 222 was another hefty flying-boat in the Luftwaffe inventory. Only 13 examples of the six-engine aircraft were produced, operating principally around Mediterranean and northern European waters. As a transporter, the Bv 222 could carry around 90 fully armed troops.

An Fw 200 Condor undergoes engine maintenance. The Condor was powered by four 1,000hp Brahmo 323 R-2 supercharged radial engines, and had a cruising speed of 335km/h.

convoys in mid-1942 with some success. In an operation against convoy PQ18 in September 1942, 42 He 111s accounted for eight out of 13 ships sunk. (They were supported by 35 Ju 88s, which confused the Allied response by delivering dive-attacks mixed in with the He 111's level attacks.)

The He 111H forces in the far north were, in late 1942, redeployed for service in the Mediterranean. This move was prompted by the Allies' increasingly heavy use of fighter escorts to protect its convoys, plus the deteriorating weather of the far north. In sunnier climes it continued to perform its duties well, albeit under the undeniable loss of air superiority. There it also fought alongside another of the Luftwaffe's great anti-shipping aircraft, the Ju 88. The Ju 88, through its dive-bombing capability, was always well-suited to maritime operations. Even its earliest variants, therefore, were used against naval targets during the battles of 1940–41. It was during the Greek campaign, however, that the

OVERLEAF: As well as delivering anti-shipping and reconnaissance duties, large seaplanes were also extremely useful for coastal resupply missions. Here we see a Bv 222 offloading supplies in a North African port; the aircraft could carry up to 20,000kg of supplies.

An He 115 is bombed-up. The aircraft could take up to 1,250kg of bombs and/or mines, or it could carry a single 500kg torpedo on the centreline.

Ju 88 demonstrated just how effective that could be in this role. The Junkers' first success of the campaign was a devastating raid on Piraeus harbour. Serving as the destination for the vast majority of the supply convoys that had been bringing men and materials from Egypt since early February, Piraeus was packed with shipping on the evening of 6 April when 20 Ju 88s of III./KG 30 lifted off from Catania.

Most of the bombers were armed with just two aerial mines apiece, the intention being to block the narrow entrance to the harbour. However, Hauptmann Hajo Herrmann had ordered that his 7. Staffel machines should each be loaded with two 250kg bombs as well. At the end of the 748km flight to the target area, he did not want to see his mines drift down on their parachutes and simply disappear into the water. After all that effort, he was determined to attack the merchantmen berthed in the harbour – it was to prove a momentous decision.

The more heavily loaded aircraft of 7./KG 30 were flying the low position in the loose formation as the Ju 88s swooped down on Piraeus from the direction of Corinth at 2100hrs. After releasing their mines as directed, Herrmann's crews made for the ships. At least three of the *Staffel's* bombs – Herrmann's among them – struck the 7,529-tonne *Clan Fraser*, a recently arrived ammunition ship packed with 350 tonnes of TNT, only 100 tonnes of which had been unloaded when the attack came in.

As well as the three direct hits, it was surrounded by near misses, which destroyed buildings and stores on the quayside. The initial blast lifted the vessel out of the water and snapped its mooring lines. The shockwave from the explosion was felt by Herrmann and his crew as their aircraft was thrown about 'like a leaf in a squall' 1,000m above the harbour.

However, worse was to follow. As the *Clan Fraser* drifted, its plates glowing from the fires raging inside her, the flames spread to other vessels in the harbour, including the 7,100-tonne *City of Roubaix*, which was also carrying munitions. Despite the danger, desperate efforts were made to get the situation under control. But the blazing ships could not be towed away for fear that they would hit a mine and block the harbour approach channel. Suddenly, in the early hours of 7 April, the *Clan Fraser* erupted in a giant fireball. Minutes later the *City of Roubaix* went up as well. The resultant series of explosions, which destroyed nine other merchantmen and devastated the port of Piraeus, shattered windows in Athens 11km away, and were reportedly heard over a distance of up to 241km.

In all, close on 100 vessels were lost, including some 60 small lighters and barges. Grievous as this was, the damage to the port of Piraeus itself was far more serious. In the explosions, described by one historian as 'of near nuclear proportions', it had been razed almost from end to end. Admiral Sir Andrew Cunningham, Commander-in-Chief of the Mediterranean Fleet, called the raid on Piraeus a 'devastating blow'. At a single stroke it had destroyed the one port sufficiently and adequately equipped to serve as a base through which the British Army could be supplied.

ABOVE: Ju 88A-4/Torp '1T+ET' of 9./KG 26, Villacidro, Sardinia, April 1943. The history of III./KG 26 between 1940 and 1942 was particularly complex, even by Luftwaffe standards. Suffice it to say that during this period no fewer than three different *Gruppen* bearing designation III./KG 26 were formed. (John Weal © Osprey Publishing)

Piraeus would be closed to all shipping for the next ten days. During this time incoming vessels had to be diverted to other ports such as nearby Salamis, or Volos far up on Greece's Aegean coast. Even after it had been partially reopened, such was the damage that it was no longer able to operate properly. The master of one vessel that put in to Salamis on 9 April and visited Piraeus two days later described the place as being 'in a state of chaos caused by the explosion of the *Clan Fraser*, which had been hit while discharging ammunition. The ship had disappeared and blown up the rest of the docks, and pieces of her were littered about the streets.'

The man responsible for much of this chaos and mayhem, Hauptmann Hajo Herrmann, had not escaped totally unscathed. At some stage during the raid the port engine of his Ju 88 had been damaged by AA fire. And for safety's sake, rather than risk the long flight back to Catania, he headed eastwards and landed on Rhodes – only to run his aircraft off the end of the runway!

In addition to port raids, Ju 88s were used extensively in anti-convoy duties, accounting for the loss of thousands of tons of Allied shipping sailing across the Mediterranean, despite no major anti-shipping modifications to its structure. However, recognizing that the Ju 88 had some talent in this area, the Luftwaffe did adapt the Ju 188 (a high-performance version of the Ju 88) to a more direct anti-shipping format. Ju 188E-2 was a torpedo-bomber, and could carry two 800kg torpedoes under wing hardpoints. It was also equipped with the FuG sea-search radar, to scan for enemy vessels. Although the Ju 188 did see anti-shipping service, its effect was limited by its numbers – only just over a thousand were built, and many of those were used in tactical bombing and reconnaissance duties rather than naval attacks.

The target. Convoy PQ 17, sailing in June–July 1942, was a terrible example of how efficient German anti-shipping tactics could be. A combination of constant aerial and U-boat attacks sank 24 of the 35 merchant vessels.

The Luftwaffe was one of the most technologically innovative arms of service in the Wehrmacht (sometimes at its strategic expense), and this was no less true in its pursuit of decisive air-launched anti-shipping weapons. Paving the way for the future of guided weaponry were the Ruhrstahl/Kramer X-1 (Fritz X) and the Henschel Hs 293. Developed during 1942, the Fritz X was essentially a freefall bomb fitted with electromagnetically operated spoilers that could give the bomb directional guidance following its release at an altitude of around 6,000m. The flight of the bomb was controlled via radio signal from the deployment aircraft, the bombardier maintaining visual contact with the weapon via a Lotfe 7 bombsight.

The Fritz X was a signal leap forward in aerial weaponry, but it was surpassed in sophistication by the Hs 293. This consisted of a rocket-powered glide bomb which could be deployed against ship targets potentially up to 3km away, giving the weapon a genuine stand-off range. Once it was dropped from a bomber, the Hs 293's rocket motor would ignite, pushing it to a maximum speed of 900km/h. A red flare on the rear of the bomb enabled the bombardier to maintain visual contact, and again the flight was radio controlled, via a small joystick.

The aircraft mainly responsible for using these weapons was the Dornier Do 217, a four-seat bomber that went into service with KG 40 and II./KG 2 in the summer of 1941. The Do 217 offered decent speed (515km/h) and a useful maximum range of 2,200km. When fitted with an anti-shipping conversion kit, the Do 217 was a formidable prospect for Allied shipping, and particularly so when III./KG 100 began to deploy the guided weapons in the Mediterranean in August 1943. On 27 August, Do 217s sank the destroyer HMCS *Athabaskan* and the corvette HMS *Egret* in the Bay of Biscay. Two weeks late, on 9 September, the Fritz X/Do 217 combination scored even greater successes by sinking the Italian battleship *Roma* and damaging its sister ship, *Italia*. The British battleship *Warspite* was also put out of action by a Fritz X on 16 September. Other victims of the Fritz X were the US light cruiser *Savannah* and the light cruiser HMS *Uganda*. Numerous other ships were either damaged or sunk by the Hs 293, although the crew deploying this weapon struggled against the fact that the aircraft had to fly straight and level during the bomb's flight to the target, a period that naturally caused problems in attracting AA fire or evading enemy fighters.

The guided weapons were impressive and groundbreaking, but they were no universal solution to Germany's anti-shipping war. In the late summer of 1943, for example, several of the late-model Fw 200 C-6s in III./KG 40 were also being converted to launch this new weapon. Until they were ready, the He 177 was used in their stead. Fliegerführer Atlantik decided to send 25 He 177s from II./KG 40 against convoy MKS 30 on 21 November, hoping to achieve a major success with a massed attack. The He 177s launched a total of 40 Hs 293s against the convoy, but only sank one

CONDOR ATTACK

On 11 July 1943, a group of Allied ships heading south was detected about 480km off the Portuguese coast. This was a special convoy known as 'Faith', consisting of three large troopships escorted by two destroyers and a frigate. Three Condors attacked from medium altitude and this time achieved spectacular results with the Lotfe 7D bombsight. Both the 16,792-tonne SS *California* and the 20,021-tonne *Duchess of York* were hit and set on fire and were soon abandoned. The attack killed more than 100 personnel aboard these two ships but 1,500 survivors were taken on board the remaining troopship, SS *Port Fairy*, which set off towards Gibraltar escorted by a single frigate. Two Condors spotted the *Port Fairy* and succeeded in hitting this ship as well before being driven off by two US Navy PBY Catalinas from Gibraltar. The attack on 'Faith' was a shock to the British since the Condor threat was no longer regarded as significant by mid-1943. Furthermore, the success of medium-altitude bombing with the Lotfe 7D emboldened KG 40 to renew attacks on larger convoys.

freighter and damaged another at the cost of three He 177s lost. On 26 November, II./KG 40 tried another mission against a convoy sighted off Algeria and succeeded in hitting the troopship *Rohna* with an Hs 293. *Rohna* sank with the loss of 1,138 lives – mostly US Army troops. Although this attack demonstrated the potential of the Hs 293 in standoff attacks, the He 177 proved vulnerable to interception and II./KG 40 lost 12 of its 47 He 177s in November 1943.

LOST ADVANTAGE

As with the U-boat war, by the end of 1943 the Luftwaffe's anti-shipping efforts were starting to become more a matter of survival rather than a strategically significant offensive, even with the introduction of the precision-guided bombs. The destruction visited upon the Allies had certainly been significant. During the period June 1940 to September 1943, for example, the Fw 200s of KG 40 alone sank a total of 93 ships of 433,447 tonnes and damaged a further 70 ships of 353,752 tonnes, and these figures were less than one-quarter of all Allied merchant tonnage sunk by German air attacks. While the actual physical damage accomplished by the Fw 200s was fairly minor, the psychological impact of successful air attacks in areas where the British did not expect them – west of Ireland and off the Portuguese coast – was such as to cause the Admiralty great anxiety. The vulnerability of convoys to the low-level attacks of the Fw 200 in 1940 was particularly unnerving to the British, and following the sinking of the *Empress of Britain*, Churchill became actively involved. German propaganda, which greatly

The pilot and observer of a German floatplane stare forward across the engine cowling of their aircraft. The Luftwaffe's various biplane maritime reconnaissance aircraft were invaluable eyes and ears over contested waters, but production of the aircraft tended to be sidelined by combat aircraft.

exaggerated the success of the Condor attacks, further pushed the British prime minister to demand immediate action to counteract the threat posed by KG 40. Churchill, given the feebleness of Britain's overall military position in the winter of 1940–41 and his inclination to strike back whenever possible, pushed both the Admiralty and the RAF to devote disproportionate resources to deal with the Condor threat, despite the fact that it was the shorter-range Ju 88s and He 111s that were doing the most damage to Allied shipping, if we look across all the theatres.

The maritime Luftwaffe began to run up against a formidable strengthening of Allied defences as the war went on, resulting in an escalating attrition from 1942 onwards. Again, the experience of the Condor formations is instructive. By way of comparison, British defences against the Condor in the period 1940–43 saw 45 Condors destroyed in the air and on the ground, although AA and fighter damage probably contributed to the loss of a number of other Fw 200s over water. Surprisingly, the biggest eliminator of Condors was AA fire from the ubiquitous Defensively Equipped Merchant Ships (DEMS), which destroyed nine Fw 200s. In comparison, AA fire from Allied warships escorting the convoys only shot down four Condors with any certainty. Fleet Air Arm (FAA) fighters from escort carriers claimed five Condors in 1941–43 and RAF fighters from Catapult Aircraft Merchantmen (CAM) ships claimed another three. Land-based

A side view of the enormous Bv 138 flying-boat. The bow and stern turrets each held a 20mm MG151 cannon, and the aircraft had two other machine guns as defensive armament.

aircraft succeeded in intercepting at least 15 Condors, including eight by RAF Coastal Command and seven by the USAAF. In 1940, British convoy defences were unable to shoot down any Condors, but by 1941 about half the convoys that were attacked were able to damage or shoot down at least one Fw 200. Attrition came from other causes. In addition to a significant number of crashes during take-off and landing, many Condors and other aircraft simply disappeared over hostile seas, the fate of their crews unknown.

By mid-1944, German aircraft production had largely switched away from maritime aircraft, in favour of fighter and ground-attack aircraft. Furthermore, once the Allies had taken much of the French coastline following the D-Day landings, and had gained undoubted air superiority over Western Europe and the Mediterranean, the anti-shipping formations lost much of their rationale. Operations still continued over the Baltic against the Soviet forces. (The maritime formation covering the Black Sea – Seefliegerführer Schwarzes Meer – was disbanded in September 1944.) Yet with so few aircraft, and such mighty enemies, the Luftwaffe's maritime force could do little to change the war's outcome.

This view of the Bv 222 shows the power needed to haul the huge aircraft and its load into the air. It was fitted with no fewer than six Jumo 207C inline diesel engines, each generating 1,000hp.

CONCLUSION

April 1945. The wreckage of German night-fighters litters an airfield in Germany. The aircraft were probably the victims of Allied ground-attack missions, which had virtually free run over much of Germany by this stage of the war.

Behind a book such as this, tens of thousand of stories remain untold. While it is appropriate and historically interesting to focus on the strategies, tactics and actions of this fascinating organization, there is the need to remind ourselves of the extraordinary lives the young aviators lived, and the terrifying ends that many of them met. From times of relative peace, it is hard to imagine a generation of very young men climbing into cockpits, gun turrets or other aircraft positions, and then taking off to meet other young men in mass aerial battle. Needless to say, the extraordinary sights, sounds and sensations of those days live with veterans to this day.

Some of those memories are gripping in the retelling. Take, for example, this memory of the great Walter Nowotny, the Austrian pilot who achieved 258 confirmed kills on the Eastern Front:

This area, dotted with several Soviet landing strips, has always been a good hunting ground in the past. We don't have to wait long today either. Ahead to the left, a few tiny specks emerge from the mist in the far distance. They quickly get bigger and reveal themselves as a gaggle of 20 Soviet ground-attack aircraft. A few moments later we spot six more machines, American fighters, flying escort.

We are flying at about 1,000m, the Soviets are some 200m below us – their escort at about 1,200m. I immediately climb to get above them. The sun is in the south-west. The 'Americans', now below me, haven't noticed anything. I get one in my sights and open fire – he immediately dives away on fire, hitting the ground in a burst of flame. Startled, the remaining five curve away to the right. I have achieved my object. The fighters are now some 500 to 600m away from the ground-attackers, and my men have a clear field.

Meanwhile, as I try for another fighter, they are attempting to get on my tail. They end up in a circle, with me in the middle trying to get into position for a good shot. We are all gradually losing height. I hardly fire a shot, while behind me one or two of the opposition loose off wildly at me – at much too great a range and far wide of the mark. Then, at about 50m off the ground, I get the second one in my sights. He too immediately goes into the ground in a ball of flame.

I look over my shoulder. The fight has taken a nasty turn. Eight Soviet fighters have arrived on the scene and join in the proceedings! I am sitting on the tail of one of the 'Americans'. Behind me is one of the Soviets. A few quick glances convince me he is getting closer. To my right a line of bullet holes suddenly appears in my wing. The Soviet is letting fly with everything he has got. His firing hardly stops. A cannon shell smashes into my wing, tearing open the surface. Ivan is getting closer and closer. He's almost within ramming distance. Whenever I glance behind me, the huge Soviet star seems to fill my vision. Bullets continue to hit my wing. They are getting closer to my cockpit.

RIGHT: An artistic representation of one of Walter Nowotny's many victories on the Eastern Front. A Soviet Ilyushin Il-2 ground-attack aircraft starts to trail smoke after being hit by a burst of fire from Nowotny's Fw 190. (Iain Wyllie © Osprey Publishing)

Iain Wyllie

The moment of decision has come. I take one last chance and dump as much speed as I dare. I use all the skill and expertise I have gained in my many previous dogfights to hold her steady as my speed sinks suddenly and dangerously low.

Fifty metres ahead of me is the 'American'. Little more than ten metres behind me the Russian. Throughout the chase I have been slipping to the right in an attempt to dodge my pursuer's shots. I try the same manoeuvre one last time. And this time Ivan falls for it. For a split-second, as I wallow once more to the right at little more than a stall, he loses concentration. I take two more cannon hits before I complete the manoeuvre, but then he has overshot me, flashing past beneath my wings.

He appears ahead of me. I clearly see the pilot in his cockpit, the Soviet star. I ram home the throttle – full power! I hope the good old Focke-Wulf, hurt though she is, can take it! Within a trice I am on top of the Russian. He goes down under my first burst of fire. The duel is over. The whole fight has lasted exactly 45 minutes.

Such an incident would be the dominating event in many people's lives, but for the Luftwaffe aviators such drama could be played out on an almost daily basis. Furthermore, the tales of the aces are generally those of the survivors. Arriving at accurate casualty figures for the Luftwaffe during World War II is almost impossible, given the often over-enthusiastic recording of kills by Allied pilots, and the loss of wartime documentation. Informed estimates place the total loss of Luftwaffe aircraft, from all causes, in the region of 116,500 aircraft. Even allowing for mechanical damage, the human cost hidden in these figures must be immense.

Since the war, the Luftwaffe has maintained an enduring fascination for historians and aviation enthusiasts. It is not difficult to see why. The Luftwaffe, for all its failings, was at the cutting edge of aviation technology and tactics. It was consistently professional, even as the Reich was collapsing around it, and kept up the fight until the bitter end. Regardless of the side it fought on, it was an extraordinary organization in extraordinary times.

FURTHER READING

Ailsby, Chris, *Sky Warriors: German Paratroopers in Action 1939–45* (Spellmount, 2000)

Baumbach, Werner, *The Life and Death of the Luftwaffe* (Noontide Press, 1991)

Blandford, Edmund, *Target England* (Airlife, 1997)

Buckley, John, *Air Power in the Age of Total War* (UCL Press, 1999)

Bungay, S., *The Most Dangerous Enemy* (Aurum, 2000)

Caldwell, Donald, *The JG 26 War Diary Volume One 1939–1942* (Grub Street, 1996)

Caldwell, Donald and Richard Muller, *The Luftwaffe over Germany: Defense of the Reich* (London, Greenhill, 2007)

Campbell, Jerry L., *Focke-Wulf Fw 190 in Action* (Squadron/Signal Publications, 1975)

Davis, Brian L., *German Parachute Forces 1935–45* (Arms & Armour Press, 1974)

Deighton, L., *Fighter* (Book Club Associates, 1978)

Forsyth, Robert, *Jagdwaffe: Defending the Reich 1943–1944* (Classic Publications, 2004)

Forsyth, Robert, *Jagdwaffe: Defending the Reich 1944–1945* (Classic Publications, 2005)

Galland, Adolf, *The First and the Last* (Ballantine Books Inc., 1954)

Goss, Chris, *The Luftwaffe Fighters' Battle of Britain* (Crécy, 2000)

Goss, Chris, *Sea Eagles: Luftwaffe Anti-Shipping Units*, Vols 1 & 2 (Ian Allan Publishing, 2005–6)

Gould, Winston A., *Luftwaffe Maritime Operations in World War II: Thought, Organization and Technology* (USAF Air Command and Staff College, 2005)

Green, W., *Warplanes of the Third Reich* (Doubleday, 1972)

Gregory, Barry and John Batchelor, *Airborne Warfare 1918–1945* (Phoebus, 1979)

Hannig, Norbert, *Luftwaffe Fighter Ace* (Grub Street, 2004)

Heilmann, Wilhelm, *Alert in the West* (Cerberus Publishing Ltd, 2003)

Hetherington, John, *Airborne Invasion: The Story of the Battle of Crete* (Angus & Robertson, 1944)

Knocke, Heinz, *I Flew for the Führer* (Evans Brothers Ltd, 1953)

Lucas, James, *Screaming Eagles: German Airborne Forces in World War Two* (Arms & Armour Press, 1988)

McFarland, Stephen L. and Wesley Newton Phillips, *To Command the Sky: The Battle for Air Superiority over Germany, 1942–1944* (Smithsonian Institution Press, 1991)

Murray, Williamson, *Strategy for Defeat: The* Luftwaffe *1933–1945* (Eagle Editions, 2000)

Price, Dr A., *Luftwaffe Handbook 1939–1945* (Ian Allan, 1976)

Spick, Mike, *Luftwaffe Bomber Aces* (Greenhill Books, 2001)

Spoden, Peter, *Enemy in the Dark* (Mönch Medien & Print, 2008)

Stahl, Peter, *The Diving Eagle* (Motorbuch Verlag, 1978)

Van Ishoven, Armand, *Messerschmitt Bf 109 at War* (Ian Allan, 1977)

Van Ishoven, Armand, *The* Luftwaffe *in the Battle of Britain* (Ian Allan, 1980)

OSPREY TITLES USED IN THE PRODUCTION OF THIS BOOK

Antill, Peter, *Crete 1941* (Osprey, 2005)

Bowman, Martin, *P-51 Mustange vs Fw 190: Europe 1943–45* (Osprey, 2007)

Bowman, Martin, *P-47 Thunderbolt vs Bf 109G: Europe 1943–45* (Osprey, 2008)

Davis, Brian L., *The German Home Front 1939–45* (Osprey, 2007)

Forczyk, Robert and Tim Brown, *Fw-200 Condor vs Atlantic Convoys: 1941–43* (Osprey, 2010)

Forsyth, Robert, *Fw 190 Sturmböcke vs B-17 Flying Fortress: Europe 1944–45* (Osprey, 2009)

Forsyth, Robert, *Jagdgeschwader 7 'Nowotny'* (Osprey, 2008)

Forsyth, Robert, *Jagdverband 44: Squadron of Experten* (Osprey, 2008)

Holmes, Tony, *Spitfire vs Bf 109: Battle of Britain* (Osprey, 2007)

Holmes, Tony, *Hurricane vs Bf 110: 1940* (Osprey, 2010)

Morgan, H., *German Jet Aces of World War 2* (Osprey, 1998)

Quarrie, Bruce, *German Airborne Divisions: Blitzkrieg 1940–41* (Osprey, 2004)

Quarrie, Bruce, *German Airborne Divisions: Mediterranean Theatre 1942–45* (Osprey, 2005)

Ransom, S. and Hans-Hermann Cammann, *Jagdgeschwader 400: Germany's Elite Rocket Fighters* (Osprey, 2010)

Rottman, Gordon, *WWII Airborne Warfare Tactics* (Osprey, 2006)

Scutts, Jerry, *Bf 109 Aces of North Africa and the Mediterranean* (Osprey, 1994)

Scutts, Jerry, *German Night Fighter Aces of World War II* (Osprey, 1998)

Stedman, Robert, *Luftwaffe Air and Ground Crew 1939–45* (Osprey, 2002)

Stedman, Robert, *Kampfflieger: Bomber Crewman of the Luftwaffe 1939–45* (Osprey, 2005)

Stedman, Robert, *Jagdflieger: Luftwaffe Fighter Pilot 1939–45* (Osprey, 2008)

Weal, John, *Bf 109D/E Aces 1939–41* (Osprey, 1996)

Weal, John, *Bf 109 F/G/K Aces of the Western Front* (Osprey, 1999)

Weal, John, *Bf 109 Aces of the Russian Front* (Osprey, 2001)

Weal, John, *Bf 109 Defence of the Reich Aces* (Osprey, 2006)

Weal, John, *More Bf 109 Aces of the Russian Front* (Osprey, 2007)

Weal, John, *Focke-Wulf Fw 190 Aces of the Russian Front* (Osprey, 1995)

Weal, John, *Focke-Wulf Fw 190 Aces of the Western Front* (Osprey, 1996)

Weal, John, *Fw 190 Defence of the Reich Aces* (Osprey, 2011)

Weal, John, *Jagdgeschwader 2 'Richthofen'* (Osprey, 2000)

Weal, John, *Jagdgeschwader 54 'Grünherz'* (Osprey, 2001)

Weal, John, *Jagdgeschwader 27 'Afrika'* (Osprey, 2003)

Weal, John, *Jagdgeschwader 52: The Experten* (Osprey, 2004)

Weal, John, *Jagdgeschwader 51 'Mölders'* (Osprey, 2006)

Weal, John, *Jagdgeschwader 53 'Pik-As'* (Osprey, 2007)

Weal, John, *Junkers Ju 87 Stukageschwader 1937–41* (Osprey, 1997)

Weal, John, *Junkers Ju 87 Stukageschwader of North Africa and the Mediterranean* (Osprey, 1998)

Weal, John, *Junkers Ju 87 Stukageschwader on the Russian Front* (Osprey, 2008)

Weal, John, *Ju 88 Kampfgeschwader on the Western Front* (Osprey, 2000)

Weal, John, *Ju 88 Kampfgeschwader in North Africa and the Mediterranean* (Osprey, 2009)

Weal, John, *Ju 88 Kampfgeschwader on the Russian Front* (Osprey, 2010)

Weal, John, *Luftwaffe Schlachtgruppen* (Osprey, 2003)

Weal, John, *Luftwaffe Sturmgruppen* (Osprey, 2005)

Weal, John, *Messerschmitt Bf 110 Zerstörer Aces of World War II* (Osprey, 1999)

Windrow, Martin, *Luftwaffe Airborne and Field Units* (Osprey, 1972)

Williamson, Gordon, *German Commanders of WWII (2): Waffen-SS,* Luftwaffe *and Navy* (Osprey, 2006)

Williamson, Gordon, *Knight's Cross, Oak Leaves and Swords Recipients 1941–45* (Osprey, 2005)

Williamson, Gordon, *Knight's Cross with Diamonds Recipients 1941–45* (Osprey, 2006)

INDEX

References to illustrations are shown
in **bold**.